The Sodomy Cases

LANDMARK LAW CASES

AMERICAN SOCIETY

Peter Charles Hoffer
N. E. H. Hull
Series Editors

For a complete list of titles in the series go to www.kansaspress.ku.edu

DAVID A. J. RICHARDS

The Sodomy Cases

Bowers v. Hardwick and *Lawrence v. Texas*

UNIVERSITY PRESS OF KANSAS

Published by the University Press of Kansas (Lawrence, Kansas 66045), which was
organized by the Kansas Board of Regents and is operated and funded by Emporia
State University, Fort Hays State University, Kansas State University, Pittsburg State
University, the University of Kansas, and Wichita State University

Library of Congress Cataloging-in-Publication Data

Richards, David A. J.

The sodomy cases : Bowers v. Hardwick and Lawrence v. Texas /

David A. J. Richards.

p. cm. — (Landmark law cases & American society)

Includes bibliographical references and index.

ISBN 978-0-7006-1636-7 (cloth : alk. paper)

ISBN 978-0-7006-1637-4 (pbk. : alk. paper)

1. Sodomy—United States—Cases. 2. Privacy, Right of—United States—Cases.

I. Title.

KF9328.S6A52 2009

342.7308'58—dc22

2008044516

British Library Cataloguing-in-Publication Data is available.

Printed in the United States of America

10 9 8 7 6 5 4 3 2 1

The paper used in this publication is recycled and contains 30 percent postconsumer
waste. It is acid free and meets the minimum requirements of the American National
Standard for Permanence of Paper for Printed Library Materials Z39.48-1992.

For my life partner, Donald Levy, with love

"Had those who drew and ratified the Due Process Clauses of the Fifth Amendment or the Fourteenth Amendment known the components of liberty in its manifold possibilities, they might have been more specific. They did not presume to have this insight. They knew times can blind us to certain truths and later generations can see that laws once thought necessary and proper in fact serve only to oppress. As the Constitution endures, persons in every generation can invoke its principles in their own search for greater freedom."

Justice Anthony Kennedy, Lawrence v. Texas

CONTENTS

EDITORS' PREFACE

Sometimes a story is too personal for us to tell it. Such stories invade our privacy. All of us understand what privacy is and how important it can be to our personal lives. From the preteen who wants her own room to the mature scholar who resists the intrusion of the university into her electronic correspondence, privacy is a right we claim against the world. Privacy is our personal liberty to be ourselves, without fear of pressures to conform.

An old ideal, surely this is, but one whose legal embodiment is quite recent. It was little more than a century ago that Louis Brandeis insisted that a domestic rite as central to our lives as marriage ought to be protected against the prying eyes of newspaper cameras. Only a half century ago, our highest court extended this right to what a married couple did, or did not do, in the privacy of their bedroom. That decision, *Griswold v. Connecticut* (1965), found the right to privacy in the penumbras of the Bill of Rights and in the Ninth Amendment itself. But that right need not have been anywhere in the text or the context of the Constitution, for as the justices then and later hinted, the Constitution enfolded and protected some rights that preceded the drafting of the document itself.

Privacy rights were again explored in the most controversial U.S. Supreme Court decision of our times, *Roe v. Wade* (1973). Then a pregnant woman's right to determine the course of her reproductive career was found in the Due Process Clause of the Fourteenth Amendment. The woman's choice to end a pregnancy should be private in a clinical procedure involving doctors, nurses, and hospital administrators. Where and when the pregnancy was terminated might be the subject of myriad regulations to protect the health of the woman and the potential for future human life. But *Roe* rested squarely upon the right to privacy.

Roe also raised Equal Protection Clause questions, for only a woman can become pregnant, with all the tribulations and joys that condition entails. Law to require a woman to carry a pregnancy to term was law that discriminated against women on the basis of their sex. Discrimination of this type was barred by the Civil Rights Act of 1964 and by a series of High Court decisions. Such discrimination was hardly private, for it reached into the workplace, the school, and public life as well as the home.

The two concepts of privacy and discrimination against a group because of the characteristics of the group came together in state sodomy laws. By the 1980s, many states had repealed these archaic criminal ordinances against gay sexual intercourse, and those states such as Georgia with such statutes still on the books rarely enforced them — though some states did enforce them. They stood as a statement of moral outrage at gay lifestyles even when they went unenforced. Gays were deviant in the eyes of the law, and such deviance greatly troubled moral conservatives.

But in the 1960s, 1970s, and 1980s, the civil rights revolution, the legal elaboration of concepts of privacy, and the revelation to all but the most morally hidebound that gays were as moral — loving, caring, productive, considerate — members of society as any other cultural community might well have led to sweeping reform of state laws. The spread of Acquired Immune Deficiency Syndrome (AIDS), although confirming for some that gay sexual habits were unacceptable, gave insight to the majority of Americans into the strengths of gay partnerships and the courage of gay men faced with almost insuperable tribulation.

Still, the Court in the troubled and troubling decision of *Bowers v. Hardwick* (1986) allowed Georgia to keep its sodomy statute on the books. Then, in 2003, the Court reversed itself, finding that a comparable Texas statute violated the constitutional right to privacy of gays and lesbians. How had this remarkable turnabout occurred? What did it mean for our laws and our culture? How did it bring us into accord with European laws?

David A. J. Richards's account in the following pages is personal in the best sense of the word. Not only does he care about the outcome of these cases, he has been a major advocate for tolerance and liberality for many decades. The resulting book is deeply thoughtful, genuinely moving, and powerfully persuasive. Shifting gracefully from the law to literature and from the courts to the wider culture, Richards offers readers a brilliant intellectual tour of the origin and context of the arguments in *Bowers v. Hardwick* and *Lawrence v. Texas*. His analysis of these arguments is equally valuable, going beneath their surface to link them to the emotional and moral foundations of the controversy.

Most often, the books in the Landmark Law Cases and American Society series are found in the classroom. This book will surely be adopted for classroom use as well. But the editors believe that this book will also edify every American interested in gay rights. That will make this book personal in the best sense of the word.

ACKNOWLEDGMENTS

This historical study was conceived and written at the suggestion of Editor in Chief Michael J. Briggs of the University Press of Kansas, who wisely guided the process of research, writing, and revision. It differs from my earlier book, a personal memoir of my own resistance, *The Case for Gay Rights: From* Bowers *to* Lawrence *and Beyond* (University Press of Kansas, 2005), in its more historical examination of the background and arguments in each case (in the genre of the series for which it was written). I am especially grateful for the advice of the two anonymous readers of the manuscript, for the help of the series editors, Peter Charles Hoffer and N. E. H. Hull, and for the excellent copyediting of the manuscript by Melanie Stafford.

All my work was also illuminated by conversations with my life partner, Donald Levy, and with the two good and loving friends, Carol Gilligan and Nicholas Bamforth, with whom I have now coauthored *The Deepening Darkness: Patriarchy, Resistance, and Democracy's Future* (Cambridge University Press, 2009) (with Carol Gilligan) and *Patriarchal Religion, Sexuality, and Gender: A Critique of New Natural Law* (Cambridge University Press, 2008) (with Nicholas Bamforth).

Work on the book profited from research grants from the New York University School of Law Filomen D'Agostino and Max E. Greenberg Faculty Research Fund as well as the School of Law's payment of the costs of professional indexing, from the able research assistance of Molly Wallace (while she was a first-year student at the School of Law), from the invaluable library support of Liz Evans, and from the help of my assistant, Lavinia Barbu.

New York, N.Y.
May 2008

The Sodomy Cases

Introduction

Lawrence v. Texas, decided in 2003, was the second case in which the Supreme Court of the United States addressed the issue of whether, consistent with the constitutional right to privacy recognized in earlier cases, the state could criminalize gay/lesbian sex acts among consenting adults. The earlier case, *Bowers v. Hardwick*, decided in 1986 by a five-to-four vote, had declined to apply the constitutional right to privacy to a Georgia criminal statute that, although criminalizing all forms of sodomy (including heterosexual anal intercourse, fellatio, and cunnilingus), was brought against a gay couple for having sex in one of the men's homes. *Lawrence* dealt with the constitutionality of a Texas law that by its terms criminalized only homosexual forms of sex, also applied against a gay couple for having sex in one of the men's homes. One justice, Sandra Day O'Connor, although she did not join the majority of five justices in overruling *Bowers*, addressed the equal protection issue raised by the Texas statute limiting criminal sanctions to homosexual as opposed to heterosexual forms of fellatio, cunnilingus, and anal intercourse. The majority, however, in an opinion written by Justice Anthony Kennedy, struck down not only the Texas statute but all such statutes, including the Georgia statute, and thereby overruled *Bowers*.

This book is a historical study of *Lawrence v. Texas*, which thus must include not only *Bowers v. Hardwick* but the entire development and elaboration of the constitutional right to privacy in U.S. law. This development is one of the most controversial interpretive issues in constitutional law. There are two forms this controversy takes in the United States. The first controversy is over how and why the Supreme Court inferred the constitutional right to privacy at all. The second controversy is over its application, in particular, to the criminalization of abortion services in *Roe v. Wade* by married and unmarried women (an application reaffirmed by the Supreme Court in 1992 in *Planned Parenthood of Southeastern Pennsylvania v. Casey*). Thus a work of this sort must address such controversies over constitutional interpretation, for they are at the heart of the history of both *Bowers v. Hardwick* and *Lawrence v. Texas*.

There is a further historical dimension to the discussion of these opinions of the U.S. Supreme Court. Both opinions show a Supreme Court now ready to take seriously and indeed discuss critically not only the idea that gay/lesbian people have human rights but that these human rights are the basis of judicially enforceable constitutional rights. Another important historical question is how and why these normative ideas arose and why some of them are now acceptable as the bases of arguments about constitutional principle. There are two aspects of this historical question that require investigation, one normative, the other culturally developmental.

First, there is the development within liberal political theory by John Stuart Mill and others in the nineteenth century of growing worry about majoritarian democracy, including a specific concern with the criminalization of consensual adult activities that failed to meet the standards of what Mill called in *On Liberty* (1859) the harm principle (that is, only acts that harmed others could be criminalized). That powerful political theory had led in Great Britain to the path-breaking 1957 Wolfenden Committee recommendation that consensual homosexuality be decriminalized (Parliament enacted the substance of the recommendation ten years later in 1967). Such arguments in Britain were directed to Parliament, not the judiciary, which did not have the powers of U.S.-style judicial review. But the United States and Britain historically share an Anglo-American legal tradition, and thus the British debates leading to decriminalization had an impact in the United States not limited to appeals for decriminalization through legislation. For example, Justice Kennedy in *Lawrence v. Texas* cited the British developments as reasonably relevant to the question of judicial review before the Court in *Lawrence*.

Although Mill's argument undoubtedly had an influence on liberal thought in Britain, the United States, and elsewhere, the impact of his argument on democratic politics (leading to decriminalization through parliamentary repeal) is a different matter than its effect on American-style judicial review as a basis for the interpretation of judicially enforceable constitutional principles against democratic majorities. A history of *Lawrence v. Texas*, overruling *Bowers v. Hardwick*, must address this question, namely, how an argument of liberal political theory became, in light of the text and history of U.S. constitutionalism, the basis for the interpretive development of a free-standing constitutional right. Mill's argument is quite general, certainly not by its terms limited to sexual matters; it might apply as well to the criminalization of certain decisions to die or the use of certain drugs. But this constitutional development has been based largely on sexual matters. Why have sexual matters played such a central role in the interpretive development and elaboration of the constitutional right to privacy? I will explore this question in this volume.

Second, one of the distinctive features of the cultural history of homosexuality in the United States was given classic legal expression for Americans at the founding of the republic by William Blackstone's hesitation to even discuss something "the very mention of which is a disgrace to human nature . . . a crime not fit to be named: *'peccatum illud horrible, inter christianos non nominandum.'*" Historical arguments played a notably different role in *Bowers v. Hardwick* than in *Lawrence v. Texas*, and much of the difference turns pivotally on the different ways the opinions for the Court of Justice Byron White in *Bowers* and Justice Kennedy in *Lawrence* read the history of U.S. legal treatment of sexual offenses in general and homosexual sexual offenses in particular. It is against the benchmark of this cultural history that we can see how far the country had come by the time of *Bowers v. Hardwick* and *Lawrence v. Texas* when its highest court of law would not only break the cultural silencing of homosexuality but give resonance to the voices of gays and lesbians who argued not only that such silencing was unjust but that it had abridged their constitutionally protected basic rights. The history of that cultural change must, accordingly, be part of our examination of these cases, for without it we cannot appreciate the forces that made it happen.

However, the judicial protection of the constitutional right to privacy (on which the interpretive arguments in both *Bowers v. Hardwick* and *Lawrence v. Texas* turn) is itself highly controversial. Many Americans who would have accepted the decriminalization of abortion if it had been democratically achieved (as it largely was in Europe) did not accept such decriminalization through the judicial interpretation of a right of constitutional privacy in *Roe v. Wade.* Indeed, a powerful political movement of religious fundamentalists has emerged to oppose such decisions, voting for presidential candidates and others because they will appoint justices who will reverse such decisions. Such a reaction, and its expression in constitutional interpretation (originalism), must also be part of the story.

We begin with the history of this cultural change in the United States (chapter 2). In light of these arguments, we then examine the development of the right of constitutional privacy in the area of contraception (chapter 3) and then abortion (chapter 4). The work then examines the background, arguments, and opinions in *Bowers v. Hardwick* (chapters 5–6), the period between *Bowers* and *Lawrence* (chapter 7), and the arguments and opinions in *Lawrence v. Texas* (chapters 8–9). The book ends with a discussion of several constitutional matters *Lawrence* has opened up for further discussion and debate, namely, decriminalization in other areas and the question of same-sex marriage (chapter 10). The argument reflects legal developments as of May 2008.

This book is one in a series of other historical studies of landmark cases of U.S. constitutional law, including two illuminating studies of the role the judicial protection of a free-standing right of constitutional privacy played in these developments (on contraception, see John W. Johnson's 2005 book Griswold v. Connecticut: *Birth Control and the Constitutional Right to Privacy*; on abortion, see N. E. H. Hull and Peter Charles Hoffer's 2001 book Roe v. Wade: *The Abortion Rights Controversy in American History*). In chapter 11, I review the argument of this book, which regards the decision on behalf of gay and lesbian rights in *Lawrence v. Texas* as a landmark case in U.S. constitutional law for the gay rights movement in the same way *Brown v. Board of Education* and *Reynolds v. Sims* were for the civil rights movement. Just as such cases challenged long-held assumptions and led to more just politics and law, no one, after such cases, can think of constitutional law in quite the same way. Such cases challenge both the practice and theory of constitutional law.

Breaking the Silence

We begin with a closer examination of the history of the treatment of homosexuality in Western culture, and then turn to the relatively late development in the United States (after World War II) of resistance to such treatment. The cultural shift in U.S. attitudes is discussed in the post–World War II period as an outgrowth of the civil rights movement and second-wave feminism. This shift expressed itself in new forms of gay/lesbian personal and political life, including public advocacy of gay rights that, as we see in later chapters, had an impact on constitutional developments.

Homosexuality in Western Culture

Homosexuality, as I will use the term, describes a dominant erotic preference for persons of one's own gender, a structure of sexual fantasies and vulnerabilities that has existed in all human cultures. How cultures deal with this erotic preference, including the cultural role, if any, they offer homosexuals differs greatly. Ancient Greek culture not only tolerated but idealized pederastic male homosexual relations as central elements in Greek pedagogy and artistic and political culture. Peter Brown observes that Christian moral teaching, sharply critical of Greek sexual morality, went well beyond the traditional pagan distaste for a man taking the passive (female) role in being penetrated by another man (the active role was quite a different matter) to a remarkably cruel reprobation of homosexual relations:

> For the first time in history, in 390 [c.e.], the Roman people witnessed the public burning of male prostitutes, dragged from the homosexual brothels of Rome. The Emperor Theodosius' edict

(preserved in full, significantly by a writer anxious to prove the agreement of the Mosaic with the Roman laws) shows clearly, in the very incoherence of its moral indignation, the slow turning of the tide. For a male to play a female role, by allowing himself to become the passive partner in a sexual act, had long been repugnant. . . . But it was now assumed to be equally shocking that a soul allotted in perpetuity to the "sacrosanct dwelling-place" of a recognizably male body should have tried to force that body into female poses.

Christian moral thought on sexuality and gender had implicit within it a valuation of asexuality (or the renunciation of sexuality) that made possible a moral space for a theory and practice treating women as persons and as equals. Such suspension of gender differences might reasonably have been interpreted to justify gender equality and even more humane treatment of homosexual love as a variation on the theme of gender equality. Certainly, abolitionist feminist women in the antebellum period interpreted their Christian convictions as mandating gender equality, and some gay Christians today not unreasonably interpret their tradition as requiring recognition of the dignity of homosexual love. But the idea of gender equality in early Christianity was increasingly interpreted in otherworldly terms without relevance to gender roles in this world, indeed hardening the impermeability of gender roles in Western society (as the edict of Theodosius clearly does). Although there were periods of relative tolerance of homosexuals, the dominant religious and political culture of Christian Europe, perhaps because it misidentified homosexuality with either pederastic pedophilia or with the sexual exploitation of slaves, was given classic legal expression for Americans at the founding of the republic by William Blackstone's aforementioned hesitation to even discuss something "the very mention of which is a disgrace to human nature." Citing with approval Constantine's sanguinary edict, Blackstone grounded capital punishment for the offense not only in "the voice of nature and of reason" but "the express law of God" in the biblical "destruction of two cities by fire from heaven," a punishment imitated by "our antienct [sic] law . . . by commanding such miscreants to be burnt to death." By Blackstone's time, however, the standard capital punishment applied to this crime as it did to other capital offenses, namely, hanging.

6

During this long period of lethally punitive reprobation, homo-sexual activity existed outside the law as a kind of ultimate heresy against religion or treason against law. Retribution took the form, as it did in renaissance Venice, of sometimes barbarously punished active partners (burned alive, or after decapitation) and much less severely punished passive (often younger) partners (sometimes including women who had been sodomized). Homosexual activity was thus interpreted as an atavistic vestige of animalistic sexual barbarism at war with civilization. Its presence in the berdache as a tolerated cul-tural form of homosexuality among the Amerindians of the New World was thus one of the aspects of those cultures that, like canni-balism or the powerful leadership roles of women, simply outraged European colonialists. Such unexamined prejudice led them to inter-pret Amerindian cultures as barbarous and thus rationalized the nor-mative judgment that the Amerindians were, in Aristotle's terms, natural slaves who might justly be enslaved. From this pejorative per-spective, Amerindian sodomy was conflated as a form of diabolic evil in the Amerindians with cannibalism. This view notably rationalized the Spanish conquest of the Americas in particular (and no doubt echoed Spain's powerfully irrational inquisitorial anti-Semitism and expulsion of the Jews in 1492, the year of Columbus's discovery of America for the Spanish monarchy). Such an approach included judg-ing the Amerindians as women (the "weaker sex"), as diabolic heretics like the Jews (thus, also subject to inquisitions), and, prophetically for the later history of U.S. slavery and racism, as descendants of compa-rably degraded African cultures. Similarly, in British North America, the Amerindians were analogized to the Jews (as well as to the Irish). Such reinforcing prejudices (homophobia, sexism, anti-Semitism, racism) naturally laid the foundation, in turn, for developing forms of Spanish and British racism and their later enslavement of Africans. The African cultures were interpreted also as involving comparably degraded forms of intimate life (for example, there were allegations of Africans selling children and of their sexual promiscuity) that rationalized their natural slavery. Indeed, the largely successful rebut-tal of the argument of natural slavery of the Amerindians by Las Casas was accompanied by the quite uncritical application of such arguments to Africans. Such attitudes of reprobation rested, at least in part, on European rejection of any cultural legitimation of the homosexual role (largely understood in terms of men having sex with boys) as animalistic barbarism.

However, the cultural role of the homosexual in European cultures in the eighteenth and nineteenth centuries underwent a significant change associated with the development of urban anonymity and a new ethics of gender relations. This shift could be characterized as from men who had sex with boys to men in subcultures who "are effeminate members of a third or intermediate gender, who surrender their rights to be treated as dominant males and are exposed instead to a merited contempt as a species of male whore." Homosexual activity was, if anything, even more persecuted throughout Europe, as it was in Britain, because it now took more publicly organized subcultural forms. But persecution now had a different focus. The sodomite was labeled a "he-whore," a transvestite, and no longer seen as a promiscuous rake (a role sometimes glamorized in patriarchal culture) "but a species of outcast woman of the lowest standing." Randolph Trumbach has eloquently explained this development in terms of rising anxieties about gender associated with "the rise of the egalitarian family":

> The degree of equality between men and women, along with parents and children, that resulted from companionate marriage and closer attachment to one's children raised profound anxiety in both men and women. The anxiety resulted in a compromise with full equality that historians have called domesticity. Men and women were equal, but they were supposed to live in separate spheres, he dominant in the economy, she in the home. Women were no longer supposed to have bodies which were inferior copies of men's; instead, as Thomas Laqueur has shown, their bodies were now seen to be biologically different; and of course, on these differences could be founded supposed inescapable differences in gender role, despite the morality of equality.

The cultural transformation of the homosexual role was a form of symbolic scapegoating to rigidify the new pattern of patriarchal gender roles:

> The transvestite was a wall that guaranteed the permanent, lifelong separation of the majority of men and women, in societies where

their relative equality must have been a perpetual danger tᴏ ̠ archy. A minority of adult males was allowed to be passive, but ι̖ overwhelming majority of males can never have had the experience of being sexually submissive in their boyhood. The transvestite was the dike that held back the flood of true equality between men and women, where both genders would experience power and submission in equal degrees. All women in societies with transvestites experienced sexual domination all their lives, but only the transvestite minority of males ever did so.

This cultural construction of the homosexual role guaranteed that men lived "in a sphere completely separated by biological nature from women": only women desired men in the appropriately subordinated mode. A man who ostensibly violated this norm was simply not a man but a woman. By the late nineteenth century, women too were drawn into this normative world: a woman desiring a woman must be a man.

As George Chauncey had made clear about the later development of this perceived cultural role in the United States, male homosexuals and prostitutes were culturally assimilated: indeed, the word *gay*, which applied originally to prostitutes, was transferred to homosexuals. The U.S. cultural construction of the male homosexual as a female prostitute powerfully reinforced the embattled normative theory of radically different spheres of gender. To immunize women's traditional normative sphere from the rights-based skepticism of abolitionist feminism, a reactionary moral and political epistemology of gender roles was defended and aggressively used against dissenting views, including those of advocates of free love. Women's normative sphere was, from this perspective, religiously idealized as the source of a superior maternal morality. Such a sectarian (that is, internal to a moral tradition not based on reasons available and accessible to all) gender orthodoxy made its idealization of intimately domestic maternal purity the measure of who could count as women and degraded dissenters to this conception as fallen nonwomen; thus prostitutes were scapegoated as outside the reasonable scope of what women could do or be. Male homosexuals, traditionally even more culturally marginalized than women, were the dissidents to male gender that the female prostitutes were to their gender. Male homosexuals' love for other men not only challenged the male gender norm of aggressive competition with other object (love between men) unspeakably affirmed what ...cates of heterosexual love anxiously did not want even ...lone debate (real equality in love). Such sectarian anx... ...onto the most symbolically marginal form of dissent... ...ble (male homosexuality) and mythologically erased ...ove. In light of the sectarian image of patriarchal gender ... the essence of anything that could even count as romantic love, the very idea of homosexual love was a conceptual absurdity, an unnatural act, which made such a man loving another man doubly disgraced and stigmatized, not a man, and, as a woman, a fallen woman. The greater dehumanization of the homosexual over the prostitute was in this double disgrace, so disgraceful, indeed, that its disgrace could not even be spoken.

An ideology of gender roles embattled by rights-based abolitionist feminism enforced its sectarian orthodoxy by remaking reality in its own image. The measure of its mythologizing character was its frenzied reinterpretation of the traditional unspeakability of the homosexual role (its role as never to have voice) in terms of the image of the most degraded of women, dehumanized as a sexual animal owed nothing by the community of civil discourse. In a constitutional community otherwise committed to human rights, it was easy enough not to extend such rights to women if an appropriate idealization could ostensibly invest them, in exchange, with a higher moral value. It was quite another matter not to extend such rights to men (and often white men at that). That could be rationalized only by ascribing to such men, already traditionally voiceless as heretics and traitors to the moral and religious community, a more radical dehumanization that would legitimate their exile from the realm of the publicly speakable and thus of the thinkable or the imaginable. The homosexual thus was the placeholder for the most threatening doubts of the embattled hierarchy of gender at the intimate heart of self-consciously egalitarian Americans. Such creatures must at all costs keep their degraded and silenced place in the hierarchical order of things if that order was to remain so unconscious of itself as in normative contradiction to equal liberty in the United States.

{ *Chapter 1* }

Civil Rights Movements, U.S. Constitutional Law, and the Case for Gay Rights

In contrast to Britain and Western Europe, serious claims for gay rights came quite late in the United States, after World War II, and then only in the wake of the impact on U.S. culture and constitutional law of the civil rights and related movements for justice under the law.

There was certainly a time when gay Europeans looked to the United States as a beacon in the recognition of their rights, notably, in the response of late nineteenth-century Europeans such as Oscar Wilde, Edward Carpenter, and John Addington Symonds to the poetry and prose of nineteenth-century U.S. writer Walt Whitman. Both Wilde and Carpenter made what can only be called pilgrimages to visit Whitman, a man they regarded as a prophet of gay rights in a larger ethical conception of democracy. Whitman, however, wrote his great poem, *Leaves of Grass*, before the Civil War, a period in many ways remarkable for its openness to radical ideas and ways of life. After the Civil War, however, Americans' openness narrowed sharply, as demonstrated in the aggressive use of obscenity prosecutions against publication of Whitman's works. This backlash led to Whitman's own panic in responding to the homophobic wall of U.S. repression by denying his work had anything to do with endorsing gay sex. Early in the twentieth century, obscenity prosecutions were also used against Margaret Sanger's and Emma Goldman's arguments for legal recognition of a right to contraception among other women's human rights. Any serious argument for gay rights in the United States during the period at least up to World War II would have met aggressive obscenity prosecutions. To the extent U.S. cities such as New York were famous as congenial places for living a gay life, that life took place underground and did not raise its voice to publicly demand legal recognition of basic rights on fair terms.

The repressiveness of U.S. political culture during this period was framed by a development I have explored and criticized at some length elsewhere, the compromises of rights-based principles central to the alliance of suffrage feminism with the temperance and the purity movements. Obscenity prosecutions of advocates of free love and contraception were successfully brought in the United States under the

Comstock Act, and the purity movement enjoyed remarkable success in the repression of prostitution. In the gender symbolism current in the period, advocacy of homosexuality was certainly regarded as obscene, and homosexual activity construed as prostitution. After their success in repressing female prostitution, the purity leagues turned their focus on gay activity and were as generally uncontradicted in their sectarian political moralism as they had been in regard to prostitution.

Ironically, whatever self-conscious political organization there was around the issue of gay rights in the United States before World War II (for example, the short-lived homosexual rights group, the Society for Human Rights, organized by the writer Henry Gerber in Chicago in 1924) was inspired by developments in Europe — in particular, Carpenter's books and the work of the German homosexual emancipationist Magnus Hirschfeld. Gerber's group was promptly suppressed by the Chicago police. In 1932 Gerber denounced U.S. repression in contrast to European (in particular, French and German) toleration. He noted that many "homosexuals live in happy, blissful unions, especially in Europe, where homosexuals are unmolested as long as they mind their own business, and are not, as in England and in the United States, driven to the underworld of perversions and crime for satisfaction of their very real craving for love."

If Whitman was not during this period self-consciously invoked in the United States (as he was in Europe) as the democratic prophet of homosexual love, he was notably cited as a source of inspiration for the development of a more inclusively democratic U.S. culture by leading figures in the Harlem renaissance and associated movements of black and socialist emancipation. Both black gay critic Alain Locke and black gay poet Langston Hughes interpreted Whitman as making possible a distinctive form of black protest and art, one that, in Locke's case, self-consciously included a revolt against U.S. puritanism. Even if covertly, Whitman thus was interpreted by leading gay figures in the ongoing U.S. antiracist struggle as making possible a distinctive procedure and substance of critical voice and protest.

In contrast, although Oscar Wilde was famously criminally prosecuted and convicted in Britain in 1898 for having gay sex, serious arguments for recognition of gay rights were at least made and published in Europe, including, among others, the various books of

Edward Carpenter in Britain and works of Magnus Hirschfeld in Weimar Germany. The situation for gays and lesbians was by no means idyllic; in Britain, for example, it was a matter of public intolerance and private excess, at least in the upper classes. It was no accident, but practical good sense, that led some of the most creative writers from the United States, including lesbian Gertrude Stein and gay black novelist James Baldwin to find their voices as writers largely while living in Europe. One could live a gay or lesbian life in the United States, but not as an out gay or lesbian, let alone someone writing as a gay or lesbian (either in one's forms and/or one's subject matter) in a way arising from one's life and experience. Life for gays and lesbians was much freer and tolerated in Europe with the devastating exception of Nazi persecutions, which, though largely directed against Jews, included gays as well. The Nazi campaign against homosexuality included, for example, the criminalization of "a kiss, an embrace, even homosexual fantasies."

A central feature of such dehumanization in the modern era was its abuse by science in terms of reinterpretation of race or gender or sexuality. As Bram Dijkstra, an astute historian of this period, observed: "To combat the already diminishing influence of the orthodox religious conceptions which had formed a solid basis for antidiscriminatory activity in the fields of sex and race at midcentury, evolutionary theory had arrived in the nick of time, a resplendent white knight in the service of discrimination." No argument was more abusive in this way than the translation of what had traditionally been a sectarian argument of moral condemnation (for example, of Jews as heretics) into the pseudoscientific discourse of degeneration or madness. The rights-denying character of such claims is as transparent as when madness was adduced as the discrediting explanation for Jewish claims of basic rights or when medical claims of disease or insanity were used in response to women's claims of human rights. The effect was, of course, exactly the same as traditional sectarian ideological views: reducing the scope of legitimate public discussion to the dominant patriarchal heterosexual white culture.

The same indignity was inflicted on homosexuals in the United States during much of the twentieth century. Advocacy on behalf of gay and lesbian rights was quashed by obscenity prosecutions and related police crackdowns. No fair discussion by homosexuals in their own voices was tolerated during a period when such arguments by African Americans and women were increasingly allowed fuller critical scope. The deepest damage to the normative possibility of such gay and lesbian conscientious voice was inflicted, however, by establishment U.S. psychiatrists. Freud and his early followers had offered a surprisingly subtle and compassionate view of homosexuality as one of a wide variety of healthy outcomes of psychosexual development; but in the United States, psychoanalysis morphed from an open-minded and humane study to an increasingly insular and sectarian view of sexual preference as a mental disease, which reflected more moral orthodoxy than it did careful empirical study. The Supreme Court itself in 1967, in a six-to-three decision in *Boutelier v. Immigration and Naturalization Service*, uncritically endorsed this psychiatric view when it held that homosexuality reflected a "psychopathic personality" and constituted a ground for deportation. After some internal struggle, only in 1973 did the Board of Trustees of the American Psychiatric Association decide to remove homosexuality from the *Diagnostic and Statistical Manual of Psychiatric Disorders* (DSM-I). This development was an outgrowth of a new struggle in the United States to understand and elaborate the human and civil rights of African Americans and women and the impact of that struggle on gay and lesbian persons forging claims of human and constitutional rights.

In the wake of World War II, despite massive police repression in Great Britain during the 1950s and the post–World War II German government's denial of any compensation to gays for their incarceration in concentration camps and keeping in place the infamous anti-homosexual section of the German Penal Code, European tolerance of gays slowly reasserted itself. The constitutional institutions throughout Europe were eventually responsive to claims for recognition of gay rights.

It was only *well* after World War II that U.S. constitutional institutions became more responsive even to hearing arguments for gay rights. The United States with its allies had defeated a fascist power, Nazi Germany, which perpetrated militaristic and genocidal racism. Both the allies' defeat of Hitler and the resulting U.S. international position in a new world order committed to values of human rights (including its role in establishing and supporting the United Nations) put critical pressure on U.S. institutions to question their own long-standing cultural racism and related evils. Among such institutions, the judiciary, under the leadership of the U.S. Supreme Court, played a pivotal role: vindicating arguments of African Americans against the unconstitutionality of state-sponsored racial apartheid including antimiscegenation laws, and, correlatively, expanding the U.S. constitutional principles of protection of free speech to include not only arguments of the civil rights movement of Martin Luther King, Jr., but other arguments and claimants as well.

The judicially enforced protection of free speech included, for the first time in U.S. constitutional history, not only the civil rights movement's criticism of and resistance to long-standing patterns of cultural racism but also the antiwar movement's ultimately successful criticism of the U.S. misadventure in Vietnam along with second-wave feminist criticism of long-standing patterns of cultural sexism. Such expansive protection of dissenting public conscience legitimated the important role in U.S. constitutional democracy of a range of resistance movements and their growing impact not only on U.S. politics but on the interpretation of legal principles. For example, the constitutional guarantee of equal protection under the Fourteenth Amendment increasingly condemned as constitutionally suspect not only the political expression of extreme religious intolerance and racial/ethnic prejudice but of misogyny as well.

Long-standing cultural evils like extreme religious intolerance (anti-Semitism), racism, and sexism are made possible by patterns of subordination of whole groups of persons that abridge their basic human rights, including the rights of conscience and free speech, intimate life, and work, and are unjustly rationalized by popular cultural stereotypes. This circularity can be exposed for the injustice it is by an expansive protection of free speech that allows a subordinated group to break the silence imposed upon them and reasonably challenge the cultural stereotypes often enforced through violence and intimidation. The nonviolent resistance movement led, until his assassination, by Martin Luther King, Jr., had the constitutional and political impact it did because it brilliantly dramatized through the exercise of free speech how and why U.S. cultural racism had developed and been supported, namely, through violence directed against the reasonable and nonviolent exercise by people of color of their basic human rights, including their rights of conscience and speech in protesting and resisting the injustice. Because the popular force of ethnic stereotypes was increasingly shown to rest on such irrational injustice (creating differences where none exist), ethnic discrimination was increasingly condemned as an unconstitutional basis for laws or policies. The growing constitutional suspectness of gender as a basis for discrimination reflects a similar dynamic, as second-wave feminism gave voice to forms of resistance that traditional gender stereotypes had unjustly silenced.

The resistance movements both of people of color and second-wave feminists exposed the crucial role that the unjust abridgment of basic rights to intimate sexual life played in supporting popular stereotypes that effectively dehumanized them — antimiscegenation laws in the case of people of color and laws infringing reproductive autonomy in the case of women. Both forms of resistance reasonably challenged such laws as not only suspect but also resting on the unjust infringement of the basic right to intimate life. One form of this latter challenge was the development and elaboration of the constitutional right to privacy, to be discussed in later chapters at length. For present purposes, it is important to see the close normative relationship between the growing suspectness of race/ethnicity and gender categories and the fuller constitutional protection of basic human rights, including not only free speech but the right to intimate life. Alfred Kinsey's rather dry and academic study of the sex lives of U.S. men (1948), including an incidence of male homosexuality that surprised and shocked Americans, had prepared the way for a freer discussion of sexual matters, and the Supreme Court played an important role in further protecting such discussion, which included not only Kinsey's later studies but those of Masters and Johnson and others.

For gays and lesbians, the most important such development of the interpretation of U.S. principles of free speech was the Supreme Court's narrowing of what could count as obscene speech in 1957 in *Roth v. United States* and later cases. As unprotected speech, it had not been subjected to close scrutiny under otherwise applicable principles of free speech. *Roth* effectively limited obscenity prosecutions to hardcore pornographic depictions of certain sorts, thus pushing anything else into the domain of free speech protection. But that remainder included all of the speech protesting conventionally repressive U.S. laws that had previously defined some sexuality and gender-based behavior as unnatural and therefore obscene. Such repression had been aggressively directed against feminists such as Sanger and Goldman who extended arguments for women's rights beyond suffrage to include use of contraceptives and much else. It is no accident that the serious development of substantive constitutional privacy claims to contraception and abortion, previously subject to prosecution as obscene, were made possible by broadening of free speech protection to advocacy of such claims. Such broadening began in 1936 in the Second Circuit opinion in *U.S. v. One Package*, which held that the Comstock Act could not deny physicians articles (including contraceptives) mailed for purposes of public health. Sanger regarded the opinion as an important step forward in her struggle to secure legal recognition of women's right to contraceptives.

But the most liberating consequence of the narrowing of obscenity law was its empowering of public arguments for gay rights. Sanger had at least been able to publish books calling for the liberalization of contraception laws in 1920 and 1922, well prior to World War II. People of color, including W. E. B. Du Bois, had published brilliant critical studies of the unjust construction of U.S. racism well prior to World War II. But U.S. gays and lesbians had been able to publish nothing comparable, because any such advocacy was supposedly so obscene as to be properly censored without implicating constitutional principles of free speech. Indeed, the discussion of homosexuality was out of the question except in the pathologizing forms of U.S. psychiatry (which confirmed and, unlike Freud himself, never reasonably contested, homophobic stereotypes). The constitutional narrowing of obscenity definitions changed all that. As Vito Russo has shown, movies—always an important expression of shifts in U.S. popular culture—began at least to represent, however covertly, tentatively, and sometimes quite unfairly, homosexuals. The first novels dealing with gay men by important U.S. gay artists (Gore Vidal's *The City and the Pillar*, 1949, and James Baldwin's *Giovanni's Room*, 1956) were also published (albeit ending with dead or raped protagonists), and at least one great play by a famous playwright and gay man, Tennessee Williams's *A Streetcar Named Desire* (1947) touched sympathetically on gay issues and brilliantly showed, in Blanche DuBois, the plight of a highly sexual straight woman whose life challenged dominant stereotypes of women's sexuality in the same way the lives of gay men challenged stereotypes of male sexuality. More importantly, for the first time in U.S. history, arguments for gay rights could be made without censorship by the state, and this new freedom undoubtedly energized, in the wake of the successes of the feminist movement with contraception and abortion, gay voices arguing for a comparable recognition of their rights. The movement for gay rights in the United States thus started, in comparison to Europe, quite late, and then only in the wake of the transformative impact on U.S. politics and constitutional law of the civil rights movement and related movements.

It cannot be emphasized strongly enough how uncontested and uncontestable U.S. cultural homophobia was—in contrast to religious intolerance, racism, and sexism—before World War II, and how important such radical silencing is both to understanding how historically remarkable the emergence of the voice of gay rights was and how vulnerable it has been to reactionary forces, including the closet. In his *Persecution and the Art of Writing* (1952), Leo Strauss observed "that the truth of a statement which is constantly repeated by the head of the government and never contradicted is absolutely certain." But this was exactly the situation in the United States for homosexuals (in contrast to racism or sexism) until the developments during and after World War II. It was this implacably intolerant cultural tradition (in contrast to the forms of resistance in Britain and Europe) that explains just how entrenched and "absolutely certain" of itself U.S. cultural homophobia both has been and still is. Without any cultural or political support (until quite recently) for the view that such homophobia was inconsistent with U.S. constitutional values, it flourished even in U.S. religions, which were never under critical constitutional pressure to examine (as they have been in the cases of anti-Semitism, racism, and sexism) just how inconsistent homophobia is with their own religious traditions. It is this background of deeply entrenched cultural homophobia that may explain why the reaction to gay rights has been driven by U.S. religious fundamentalists and why such reaction has in some areas enjoyed the level of broad support that it has (for example, opposition to same-sex marriage).

World War II was important both in advancing U.S. public opinion toward recognizing stronger antiracist principles and in unsettling gender roles (women entering the job markets) as a preliminary to second-wave feminism. World War II also set the stage for gay rights. Many gay and lesbian Americans experienced during their military service away from their homes and in the context of serving with wider ranges of persons of the same gender and sexual preference transformative opportunities for a new dissenting practice of gay life, including protests on grounds of justice about the treatment of homosexuals in the military. These new forms of experience and associations outside their communities and families of origin were, if anything, greatly extended after World War II as the United States entered a period of unprecedented prosperity. There was a sense of confidence in a market economy in which gays and lesbians, like other Americans, could achieve new levels and kinds of economic prosperity and use their economic independence as a basis for personal independence and mobility, resources that made possible as well the growing value Americans placed on privacy, a value particularly important to gays and lesbians. Because most gays and lesbians in this period lived closeted lives, this growing valuation of privacy enabled them to avoid at least many of the sanctions and disadvantages that would otherwise have been inflicted on them. Although gays and lesbians profited personally from these general developments in U.S. economic and social life, which made possible a growing sense of confidence as a basis for later resistance, they faced as well in the U.S. public an implacable wall of rhetorically frenzied opposition, sponsored by a war hero elected president, Dwight Eisenhower, who banned homosexuals from the civil service, as gays were regarded during this period of the Cold War as subversive as communists.

In 1951 Donald Webster Cory (a pseudonym for Edward Sagarin) gave pathbreaking expression to emerging dissent to such homophobic laws and policies, explicitly using the discourse of civil rights that was gathering force in resistance to U.S. racism and anti-Semitism. Cory argued in his *The Homosexual in America* that there were convincing analogies between such protests on behalf of justice for homosexuals and the claims of civil rights of other minority groups (blacks and Jews). Although Cory noted some other differences (the involuntary character of sexual preference, lack of an associated philosophy of life, not being rooted in the family), he pointed to the crucial difference that separates the homosexual minority from all others, and that is its lack of recognition, its lack of respectability in the eyes of the public. . . . As a minority, we homosexuals are therefore caught in a particularly vicious circle. . . . Until the world is able to accept us on an equal basis as human beings entitled to the full rights of life, we are unlikely to have any great numbers willing to become martyrs by carrying the burden of the cross. But until we are willing to speak out openly and frankly in defense of our activities, we are unlikely to find the attitudes of the world undergoing any significant change.

Cory thus identified an unjust culture that immunized itself from criticism of the vicious circularity of its degrading stereotypes (drawing an express analogy to Du Bois on race). U.S. homosexuals needed, Cory argued, cultural heroes who would break the silence, along the lines of a Carpenter or an even more forthright Whitman. They also simply needed a public culture in which they could find themselves represented as persons, one that fairly explored relevant history (for example, the Amerindians), wrote truer fictional narratives (citing Gore Vidal), and offered better speculative models for the proper place of homosexuality in nature and culture (citing Gide's *Corydon*).

Against the background of the greater judicial protection of freedom of speech (including, eventually, the constitutional narrowing of antiobscenity laws), some homosexual Americans were politically ready as early as 1950 to organize for gay rights. In that year the founding of the Mattachine Society in Los Angeles marked the beginning of what would grow into a nationwide effort. Harry Hay, an ex-communist, brought his organizational skills to bear on the new organization and sought to develop an appropriate theory of the movement as a dissenting cultural minority. Importantly, Hay explicitly built upon Edward Carpenter's earlier work on the Amerindian homosexual role. The Daughters of Bilitis followed, founded in 1955 in San Francisco by Phyllis Lyon and Del Martin. By the new millennium, there would be a wide range of such groups, some of them specifically concerned with gay issues relating to the AIDS health crisis.

Neither the antiracist civil rights movement nor second-wave feminism were initially hospitable to the claims made by such groups. As we have seen, women in the civil rights movement had raised trou-

{ *Chapter 1* }

bling questions about its sexism that were among the motivating sources of second-wave feminism. It is not surprising, in light of this, that James Baldwin, a gay black man and influential antiracist advocate, should have been subject to homophobic attacks from heterosexual male black leaders. Betty Friedan notoriously stereotyped gay men in *The Feminine Mystique* (1963), and as a leader of NOW, warned against the "lavender menace" and failed to support Kate Millett when her lesbianism was publicized. Even the American Civil Liberties Union (ACLU) refused early pleas from gay and lesbian advocates in the early 1960s. Views, of course, later changed, but only in response to growing challenges on grounds of rights-based principles by increasingly vocal gays and lesbians and their allies in the antiracist and antisexist movements.

The defining moment for the dramatic entrance of gay and lesbian resistance in U.S. politics and law came in New York City in the Stonewall riots of 1969. Gay men and lesbians had long settled in parts of New York City but on terms that did not publicly challenge the laws criminalizing gay/lesbian sex or the other laws and policies that subjected them to discrimination and even violence, sometimes including police violence directed at gay bars. It was at the end of a remarkable decade of activism and successes of the civil rights movement that not long-term New Yorkers but Puerto Rican gays who were newcomers — some of them quite flamboyantly effeminate in ways that challenged gay male norms of the period — publicly resisted a police action directed against Stonewall, a gay bar, rioting over several nights, capturing media attention for their uncharacteristic resistance. Those who resisted at Stonewall were doubly resisters: they resisted the culture of unspeakability around them, but they also resisted the norms of the closet, which most New York City gay men and lesbians had come to accept as in the nature of things. It is striking that many of these resisters challenged gender norms (men who identified with and were in mourning for Judy Garland, who had just died) in ways that disturbed and enraged both straight and gay people in this historical period. The history of gay rights has a distinctively feminist edge here as elsewhere (as we shall see). The first gay rights march followed in 1970 in New York City.

If the case for gay rights was to be understood and acknowledged, it evidently would have to be made by gay people in their own voices and on their own terms, originating claims to their basic human rights to conscience, speech, workplace equality, and intimate life against the dominant moral orthodoxy that traditionally silenced and stigmatized them. By 1971, when Dennis Altman published his *Homosexual Oppression and Liberation*, the central rights-based point was construed as a search for identity, and analogies were drawn to the comparable identity-transformative struggles of women (including consciousness-raising) and blacks. Such a rights-based investigation required skepticism about the unjustly self-fulfilling stereotypes so fundamental to homophobia as well as racism. For historical models of dissent, gays looked to Allen Ginsberg's retelling in contemporary terms of Whitman's defense of homosexual love, or to Jean Genet, who wrote, unlike Proust and Gide, conspicuously as and from the experience of a gay man. By 1982, Altman would be struck, following Susan Sontag, by analogies (first suggested by Proust) between developments of gay and Jewish identity grounded in similar styles of critical moral independence.

It was the public emergence of such gay voices, both at Stonewall and in published works by Altman and others, that for the first time in U.S. history raised serious questions about the pseudoscientific complicity of U.S. psychiatrists with homophobia, setting the stage for the 1973 removal of homosexuality from the list of psychiatric disorders. The condemnation of homosexuality was increasingly seen — like the analogous condemnation of contraception, abortion, masturbation, and the like — to rest not on any scientific ground but on long-standing normative judgments. These prejudices appeared in contemporary circumstances increasingly anachronistic, indeed, religiously sectarian, in ways that flouted constitutional guarantees of the separation of church and state. Scientific research increasingly understood sexual orientation as having at least some probable genetic connections and certainly as a dominant and deep sexual propensity settled early in a child's development. As gays and lesbians increasingly went public about the psychic costs imposed on them by living in the closet, the question became what, if anything, could justify in a secular society the use of criminal sanctions against the sexual expression of such propensities in loving relationships?

Unfortunately, activism on behalf of gay and lesbian rights became prominent in the United States during a period of political backlash against the successes of the civil rights movements of the 1960s, including the constitutional and legal recognition of the rights of people of color and straight women. Presidents such as Ronald Reagan forged a populist and reactionary politics that declared war on the legitimacy of *Roe v. Wade* and on affirmative action and notably turned away from the leadership on matters of human rights in the presidencies of Truman, Kennedy, Johnson, and Carter. Such reactionary politics soon turned as well on the gay and lesbian social justice movement, legitimating public hostility to gay rights that made progress difficult. Even the constitutional successes of the civil rights and feminist movements were turned against the recognition of gay/lesbian rights, as conservatives argued that equal protection must be limited to discrimination on the basis of immutable factors such as race and gender. Reactionary leaders failed to see that the oldest form of constitutionally condemned discrimination under U.S. law was religious discrimination, which never turned on immutability but rather on forcing or encouraging people not to express or to change their conscientious convictions. Prejudice against gay/lesbian rights was precisely of this forbidden sort.

But the reactionary politicians of this period increasingly drew their power from their appeal to such sectarian religious prejudices, which they lacked the moral vision and constitutional leadership to question. Religious conservatives, encouraged by such politicians, successfully opposed advances of gay rights at the local level (for example, Anita Bryant in Dade County, Florida) and used the easy amendment process of many state constitutions to repeal advances in gay rights. For example, legal prohibitions on discrimination on grounds of sexual orientation were repealed by constitutional amendment in Colorado in a campaign that approximated a "reverse discrimination" campaign against affirmative action, claiming that gays and lesbians were asking for "special rights." The Supreme Court struck down this amendment in *Romer v. Evans*, as we shall see, but other such reactionary campaigns succeeded. In Canada, in contrast, the moral leadership of President Trudeau in advocating a new charter of human rights that would bind Canadians (including Quebec) into an enduring union, would prove much more hospitable to gay/lesbian rights. Moral leadership by politicians on issues of human rights clearly matters, which the United States has lacked for some time.

Such prejudice was so powerful because gay/lesbian sex acts remained criminal in the United States, whereas in nations such as Britain and Canada they were decriminalized as of the late 1960s, as many European nations had done or shortly would do. Because criminal law in the United States remains largely a state matter, decriminalization could not take place, as it had done in Britain and Canada, by a change in national law reflecting an advance in human rights. Decriminalization in the states occurred at a much slower pace than in Europe (culminating in *Lawrence v. Texas* invalidating the relatively few state laws remaining). Meanwhile, the history of such judicially legitimated prejudice in the United States remained conspicuous in the U.S. public response after *Lawrence v. Texas* to same-sex marriage. In nations that enjoyed much longer historical periods of decriminalization, there was no comparable reaction. *Bowers v. Hardwick* had made matters much worse when it announced such criminalization was not unconstitutional. As the Supreme Court acknowledged in *Lawrence v. Texas, Bowers* was so constitutionally problematic because it legitimated irrational hatred of gays and lesbians in the same way *Plessy v. Ferguson* (1896) had legitimated racism.

It was in this environment in 1980–1981 that the AIDS health crisis emerged in the form of a lethal infection that in the United States was transmitted largely by unprotected sex between gay men, a disease that afflicted and killed many sexually active gay men. AIDS was a grievous tragedy for the men it killed and for those who loved and nursed them, who, in some cases, themselves died from the disease. It would have been better for everyone if this fatal disease had never appeared, but, paradoxically, although it took individual gay lives, it was not fatal to the gay rights movement though it may have brought to a halt, at least for a while, advances in the legal recognition of gay rights. By 1979, Stonewall's tenth anniversary, twenty-one states had invalidated their sodomy laws, but sodomy reform stalled in the period from 1984 to 1991, during which *Bowers* was decided. Not a single state, however, recriminalized sodomy in response to *Bowers*, and the movement to decriminalize sodomy soon gathered momentum again at the state level. Why was AIDS not fatal to this movement?

For one thing, the depth of the health crisis made homosexuality more a subject of responsible public discussion than it had ever been, and in some highly visible cases dragged into public light the homosexuality of leading icons of U.S. public life, including actor Rock Hudson and right-wing politician Roy Cohn. The nature of the transmission of AIDS compelled widespread public discussion of gay sex acts, which had never before even been regarded as worthy of any discussion at all. More open discussion of gay sex opened minds to issues never even thought of before.

The health crisis exposed to public attention the lives and relationships of gay men generally, including the people who loved them, who nursed them, and who grieved for them. Loss and grief and loving care are universal experiences, and these stories touched Americans, humanizing the lives and loves of gay people. In many cases, gay people otherwise uninterested in gay rights were now mobilized into public forms of activism (such as the AIDS Coalition to Unleash Power [ACT-UP]) to get the attention of politicians such as Ronald Reagan and others who refused to address the issues responsibly as health issues.

Gay people themselves began to organize around prudent steps of prophylaxis, changing their sexual lives responsibly to deal with the health risks. The losses suffered by gay people were sobering, as the crisis made the survivors think prematurely of something relatively young people think of rarely, the life expectancy in a world of AIDS and modern health care and how their relationships might better sustain a healthy, fulfilling, loving, and desirably long life.

Finally, as the 1980s became the 1990s and Americans observed the more heterosexual spread of AIDS in Africa and Asia, AIDS began to lose much of its connotation of homosexual threat, becoming both medically and legally normalized. Medically the disease was much better understood as one that threatened straights as well as gays not only through sexual transmission but through drug use. New drug "cocktail" treatments made the disease no longer a death sentence. Congress passed a number of laws forbidding discrimination against those with disabilities, specifying HIV as a condition included within the definition of disabilities.

The AIDS crisis was also part of a larger shift in the understanding of the public/private distinction, a development that led to public discussion of many sexual issues (such as incest and priest sexual abuse of parishioners) that would not previously have been regarded as matters of public debate. Sexuality in general and homosexuality in particular — especially in public officials and figures — were now a matter of public discussion: think, in this context, of the public fascination with the details of Monica Lewinsky's sexual relations with then-president William Clinton. To the extent homophobia had flourished by rendering homosexuality unspeakable, its cultural force was now subject to reasonable discussion and debate in a way it had never been before in U.S. history.

This growing speakability expressed itself through various organizations. Following Stonewall, a number of gay liberation groups were founded in the United States. The Gay Liberation Front (GLF) in New York and other radicalized homophile groups made common cause with the antiwar movement and with black nationalists such as the Black Panthers. In part in reaction to debates over alliances with other groups and different issues, the GLF splintered and the Gay Activists Alliance (GAA) was established in order to focus solely on the achievement of gay civil rights. The radical direction of gay liberation, as exemplified by the GLF and the GAA, was tempered somewhat as the GAA became more focused on state-based lobbying and was reconstituted as the National Gay Task Force in 1973 (now known as the National Gay and Lesbian Task Force [NGLTF]). Interestingly, the Task Force (as it's known for short), is now well-known for its antiracism work in the context of gay rights. The Gay Rights National Lobby was founded in 1978 and renamed itself the Human Rights Campaign Fund (now known simply as Human Rights Campaign [HRC]) in 1980.

The U.S. movement focused on the main goals of enacting antidiscrimination measures to protect lesbians and gays in areas such as housing and employment and overturning the state sodomy laws. A number of organizations took on the sodomy laws. One of the most important of these was Lambda Legal Defense and Education Fund (hereinafter Lambda), established in 1973. Together with the ACLU, the organization took on lesbian and gay rights cases and played an important role in the *Lawrence* litigation. Even when such organizations lost in court or failed to persuade legislatures (as they more often did than not), the very fact of their litigating or arguing for gay/lesbian rights crucially broke the silencing of resisting voices that had sustained U.S. cultural homophobia for so long.

All of these themes became the subject of art, including gay artist Tony Kushner's representation of the interlinked personal and public issues (dealing, for example, with the closeted homosexuality of Roy Cohn) in his remarkable play *Angels in America* (1992), later made into an important movie (2003). Kushner's play and movie followed the emergence of important earlier movies dealing with the complexity of gay passion in transcending the barriers of class (James Ivory's *Maurice*, 1987, based on the novel of E. M. Forster) and ethnicity (Stephen Frears and Henif Kureishi's *My Beautiful Launderette*, 1985), and paved the way for Ang Lee's sensitive and moving depiction of the tormented love of two closeted cowboys in *Brokeback Mountain* (2005).

Many of the gay men and lesbians who lived through this period came to experience their relationships and lives in ways quite discontinuous with the stigma of gay life in the period before World War II. In contrast to people of color and women, U.S. gays and lesbians in the pre–World War II period could avoid the penalties traditionally inflicted on homosexuals by withdrawing to the closet — understandably leading a public life that accommodated itself to dominant heterosexual norms, but privately pursuing sexual intimacies with persons of the same gender.

The resisting voices of gays and lesbians to their unjust treatment persuaded many gays and lesbians that the closet, once regarded as a refuge from injustice, was itself a prison, confining their public and private lives to the terms of dehumanizing stereotypes that stripped them of much that made life worth living, including recognized loving relationships and the ethical values such relationships sustain. The most important consequence of this coming out was not gay activism, although many increasingly publicly supported and identified themselves with such activism. The deepest shift was intrapsychic — living the experience of one's sexual passion and loving relationships as a great human good, rooted in the universal good of intimate life to which all persons have a basic right.

It is difficult to explain adequately to people always comfortable with their sexual lives and loves what such a shift could mean. A thought experiment might be in order. Suppose you had been brought up in and lived in a hegemonic culture that told you, from the earliest years of your nascent erotic feelings, that they were unspeakable and could not reasonably connect to one's ethical intelligence, let alone to a way of life centered in passionate erotic love and all that makes creatively possible in a human life, personally and ethically. Suppose also you were subjected to continual lies about your sexuality (that it was always violent or exploitative and never pleasurable or fulfilling), and also to every kind of pressure (including coercion by law and unremitting social pressure) to live a lie, tearing one apart from the only loving sexual relationships that made life worth living.

It would be psychologically difficult in such an environment to see clearly and feel precisely sexual love for another person, if one has the grace to experience love, and to understand and value its place in what makes a life human. For one thing, the lies one uncritically accepted as truths would make it difficult to see and experience one's same-sex beloved as an individual as opposed to an objectified sexist trope. For another, unremitting legal and social pressures silence one's own sexual voice, let alone one's sensitivity to the sexual voice of the person one desires. Gay sex might flourish under such circumstances, but often in traumatic disassociation from one's relational intelligence and voice.

Arguments for gay rights in their nature resisted the unjust stereotypes imposed on gay sexuality, expressing the free ethical voices of persons who reasonably contest such stereotypes. Such resistance in its nature challenged the lies and pressures that supported homophobia and made psychologically possible or much easier the experience of reciprocal sexual love between individuals as individuals. Resistance became for this reason the condition of loving relationship, and such resistance had a much broader resonance as others found in it the route to some measure of personal fulfillment.

New forms of loving gay and lesbian relationships, some quite long-term, became for these reasons both more common and certainly much more visible. Like all such loving relationships, the relationship was not just between the partners but with their networks, including families of origin, many of whom increasingly came to understand the lives and support the loves of their sons and daughters, sisters and brothers, nephews and nieces.

There was a backlash to such visibility in the early 1990s when the recently elected President Clinton tried to deliver on a campaign promise that he would end the exclusion of gays and lesbians from military service. The response of Congress and the military was to require of Clinton a compromise — Don't Ask, Don't Tell — that drew the line at any public identification of oneself as gay or lesbian. The compromise bespeaks, on the one hand, a public shift to some meas-

ure of toleration, but only on terms that institutionalized, as a quali-
fication for military service, staying in the closet. What had once been
the only option for gays and lesbians to avoid sanctions now became
the canonical measure of public acceptability.

Although the closet was no longer the unquestioned and unquestionable condition of any legitimate gay life at all, it retained its force
not only in the dominant culture but among those gays and lesbians
who prefer the limited measure of tolerance now available to them on
these terms to anything more public. The consequence was that
activism for gay rights was much more politically fragmented than the
leadership and coordination of other resistance movements. There
was no public figure in the struggle for gay rights analogous to the
role of Martin Luther King, Jr., in the civil rights movements, or Betty
Friedan and Gloria Steinem in the feminist movement, figures who
combined quite remarkable intellectual as well as strategic leadership
and coordination abilities in the movements they mobilized and led.
Gay people were divided from each other as well as from the larger
culture around them by the closet. Many gays and lesbians stayed
there rather than admitted to having a gay/lesbian sex life.

It was evidently one thing for the U.S. public to accept Don't Ask,
Don't Tell, but it was quite another to take seriously a gay or lesbian
couple, who both ask and tell, and who live increasingly visible lives
together much like those of increasing numbers of heterosexual couples. Such lives include not only shared economic contributions to the
household and convergent styles of nonprocreational sex and elaboration of erotic play as an end in itself, but the interest in sex as an
expressive bond in companionate relationships of friendship and love
as ends in themselves; several partners over a lifetime; when there is
interest in children, only in few of them; and the insistence on the
romantic love of tender and equal companions as the democratized
core of sharing intimate daily life. More children lived in families with
same-sex parents, whether through adoption or through the use of
new reproductive technologies; and as more opposite-sex partners and
single women undertook reproduction using new technologies rather
than traditional biological means, the idea of discriminating against
such children on the basis of their adopted status or their biological
origin became increasingly problematic. For many lesbian couples and
some gay couples, such relationships increasingly included responsi-

bly caring for and bringing up the children of one or the other partner or an adopted child, and/or caring for aging parents and/or other members of their families of origin.

It is striking that the codification of the closet in Don't Ask, Don't Tell includes, as a ground for disqualification from military service, not only public identification of one's identity as a gay or lesbian, but one's marriage to a person of the same gender. Of course, at the time of the compromise, gay marriage was legal nowhere in the United States. The way in which the compromise was drafted, however, and overwhelmingly accepted by Congress bespeaks the state of U.S. public culture at the time: no gays or lesbians could be qualified for military service who believed and acted on the belief that their relationships were of a status that required public acknowledgment as a marriage. We are confronted with two discordant developments: on the one hand, the development of long-term gay and lesbian relationships that are empirically indistinguishable from many heterosexual relationships; and on the other hand, a political and legal demand that such relationships must be regarded, in law, as absolutely distinguishable from heterosexual relationships in general and marriage in particular.

Many gays and lesbians—in particular, those who had lived through the period after World War II—now regarded resistance to the homophobic unspeakability of their lives as more reasonable than it had ever been, and began to live more openly in relationship to those they loved. It was more commonly believed that gay/lesbian sex must be decriminalized, and a number of states—whether politically or judicially—had moved in that direction (the federal constitutional argument to decriminalize failed in *Bowers v. Hardwick* and succeeded in *Lawrence v. Texas*, to be discussed in later chapters).

The growing reality of gay and lesbian relationships in the population—reflected in census data (the 2000 U.S. Census identified more than 600,000 households of same-sex partners)—gave rise to concern as well for legal protections from discrimination akin to the constitutional protections now accorded religion, ethnicity/race, and gender by the courts. The complex lives of gays and lesbians in long-term relationships, including the care of children and others, gave rise as well to calls for legalization of those relationships akin to the protections long accorded heterosexual couples, including questions of forming and dissolving such relationships, economic and other obligations and rights arising from the relationships (including in matters of health and upon death), and matters of custody and related rights and duties relating to the care, support, and education of children. New practices along these lines were already being developed contractually and in other ways, as gays and lesbians had learned to live loving lives in relationships without, to say the least, the support of the state and society. But, to the extent such practices would be improved by appropriate legal and constitutional developments, gays and lesbians increasingly worked for such rights and were sometimes successful. The issue of same-sex marriage, which had not been publicly debated at the time of *Bowers*, was now increasingly a subject of national discussion, reflecting a growing public consciousness of the new forms of gay/lesbian family life that were increasingly visible and audible.

Such arguments were met, however, by opposing groups of religious fundamentalists who had organized politically to oppose the successes of second-wave feminism (in particular, *Roe v. Wade*) and now organized to oppose the agenda of gay rights, in particular, antidiscrimination laws and claims to equal treatment of gay/lesbian relationships (including marriage rights). Some fundamentalists were willing to accept, like increasing numbers of Americans, that gay/lesbian sex should not be criminal, which was consistent with Don't Ask, Don't Tell. But they drew the line at any more legal protection or recognition of gay/lesbian relationships. Thus, such groups had in some cases secured repeal of antidiscrimination protections, and, as earlier noted, indeed in Colorado passed a constitutional amendment that forbade such protections. Religious groups have been particularly effective in mobilizing forms of political resistance to same-sex marriage (to be discussed later), a success that would not have been possible unless many Americans regarded Don't Ask, Don't Tell as the measure of acceptability of gays and lesbians.

Second-Wave Feminism and Gay Rights

Gays and lesbians who lived through the post–World War II period became for the first time in U.S. history moral and political agents in its cultural development. What made their agency possible were the flourishing voices of resistance (to racism and sexism) that achieved a remarkable level of impact on U.S. political and constitutional culture during this period. People of color and women as well as traditionally oppressed religious minorities such as Jews had found their voices in resistance to the injustices that afflicted them and achieved a resonance for their issues both in U.S. politics and constitutional law. Such resisting groups were joined as well by those, including soldiers who served in Vietnam, who protested the Vietnam War and over time shifted national policy. All of these groups not only brilliantly used constitutional principles of free speech and religious liberty to find and use their moral voices in resistance but challenged the judiciary to expand its protection of dissent. Under the pressure of such activism, the judiciary expanded its protection of free speech and religious liberty to accord them a constitutionally guaranteed platform from which they might more reasonably challenge entrenched injustices. To this extent, the judiciary itself gave resonance to such resisting voices, to which it responded by reasonably taking into account such voices in its interpretation of other substantive constitutional guarantees, including, among others, both equal protection and the right to privacy.

Gays and lesbians had lived through a period in which previously stigmatized and marginalized groups had broken the silence that supported their subordination. The unspeakability of homosexuality was, if anything, even more radically entrenched. For this reason the much more muscular judicial protection of free speech and religious liberty — forged by people of color, religious minorities, and feminists — struck such a responsive chord among U.S. gays and lesbians, who found their resisting voices on a similar basis. My historical work here discusses the part of this narrative that bears on U.S. constitutional law. For this purpose, it is important to underscore the particular relevance to the emergence and impact of gay and lesbian resistance of second-wave feminism. The development of the constitutional right to privacy and its application to contraception coincided with the birth of second-wave feminism. Its leading proponents on the Supreme Court (Justice William O. Douglas and Justice John Marshall Harlan) did not embrace such feminism, however, but grounded their arguments in the legitimacy of inferring and protecting an unenumerated right of marital intimacy. But even before this period the leading national proponent of such a right, Margaret Sanger, based

{ *Chapter 1* }

her argument clearly on feminist grounds. Second-wave feminism, when it emerged into national politics, supported the further elaboration of the constitutional right to privacy beyond contraception to abortion, and gay/lesbian arguments about the unconstitutionality of the criminalization of gay/lesbian sex arose from the interpretation of these judicial precedents, as we shall see. There appears to be a particularly close normative connection between second-wave feminism and the case for gay rights. Indeed, the case for gay rights may be regarded as an elaboration, on grounds of principle, of second-wave feminism, which some activists characterize as the rights to bodily integrity and self-determination.

It is striking, in this connection, that the early case for gay rights in the post–World War II period was made in terms of rights-based feminism, bringing to the interpretation of such feminism the insights forged by the struggles for the ethical identity of women in general and lesbian women in particular. The poet and essayist Adrienne Rich powerfully explored, citing Sarah and Angelina Grimke (sisters who were nineteenth-century abolitionists and suffragists), the centrality to women's emancipation of independent moral agency and the ways in which a still largely mythologically idealized conception of maternal gender roles (both mother-son and mother-daughter) subordinated that status to the claims of male supremacy. Rich carefully analyzed, on the basis of her own experience as a wife and mother, both the profound sexuality of mothering as an interest many women legitimately have and the moral degradation inflicted on women by the sectarian orthodoxy of "compulsory" motherhood (including when, how, and on what terms they would have children), including the burdens of an idealized duty of maternal self-sacrifice. Only critical rethinking of the injustice of such maternal gender roles would ensure women sufficient scope for their rational and reasonable moral powers, in personal and public life, so that children need no longer "live under the burden of their mother's unlived lives."

Rich generalized her argument about the need to reexamine women's gender roles (so that motherhood is no longer a forced identity for women) in two ways. First, U.S. feminists must rediscover the roots of their criticism of gender roles in the antiracism struggle (not only in terms of the first-wave feminists who discovered their moral voice in the abolitionist movement but the second-wave feminists who became aware of their oppression while working in the civil rights movement of the 1960s). Second, a rights-based feminism should call for the legitimacy of lesbianism as an option for women, precisely because it so fundamentally challenged unjust gender roles.

If the rights-based feminist struggle is one for moral identity in terms of respect for basic human rights against an unjustly enforceable orthodoxy of gender roles, lesbianism must be regarded as a legitimate option for women both because it is grounded in such rights and because it represents so fundamental a criticism of the sectarian orthodoxy. For Rich, this right of association included not only the right to intimate life but the right to moral independence central to the feminist struggle. In particular, such a struggle encompassed the right to identify with other women in what Rich calls a "lesbian continuum" and to live a "lesbian existence" centering on such moral identification, which may or may not include sexual relations or having and raising children.

Nothing in Rich's argument requires that it be limited to lesbians as opposed to gay men. Certainly, relationships of love between gay men and between lesbians directly challenge the conception central to traditional gender hierarchy of masculine and feminine identity—that love in its intimate nature cannot be between equals and that relationships between men or between women must be fraught with competition and hostility. On the contrary, such relationships embody a normative model for intimate life that apparently more fully develops features of egalitarian sharing that are more often the theory than the practice of heterosexual relations. Gay men, precisely because they do not sexualize women but nonetheless often form profound moral identifications with them not based on or distorted by sexual objectification, may indeed contribute something unique to rights-based feminism.

Increasingly, such claims as Rich's shaped arguments of basic constitutional rights in the United States, Canada, and Europe. I focus in the next chapter on the U.S. history of these constitutional developments, starting with the inference and elaboration of the constitutional right to privacy in the areas of contraception and abortion as interpreted by rights-based feminism, and then turning to the struggles over the extension of this right to decriminalization of gay/lesbian sex.

The Constitutional Right to Privacy
Contraception

The judicial inference and elaboration of a free-standing constitutional right to privacy must be understood against the background of rights-based feminism, as the constitutional right expresses one of the distinctive demands of such feminism in the pivotal arguments of Margaret Sanger and others for legal recognition of women's basic human right to intimate life. Sanger argued that this basic human right was the ground for women's right to access to contraceptives and contraception information, thus changing the history of women's subjugation to male control of their bodies and destinies. The question is how and why this argument, which Sanger had been making since the first decades of the twentieth century, was accorded constitutional recognition by the U.S. Supreme Court only in 1965 in *Griswold v. Connecticut*. For this purpose, we need to understand the dissenting feminist tradition on which Sanger built, her organizational genius and advocacy of groups such as Planned Parenthood, and how and why the character of her arguments was finally accorded constitutional recognition by an all-male Supreme Court in 1965.

Certainly, as recently as 1961, the Supreme Court had unanimously affirmed in *Hoyt v. Florida* the measure of women's rights and responsibilities in their ascribed status "as the center of home and family life," an argument first- and second-wave feminists challenged. Even the three justices who had dissented from the enforcement of this conception in *Goesaert v. Cleary* in 1948 assumed that, in principle, truly benign protective legislation of women would be constitutional (for example, laws that women could not work while pregnant). However, subsequent cases interpreted relevant constitutional principles in a different way that gave expression to and indeed forged a judicially enforceable conception of women's legal status grounded in the rights-based principles central to second-wave feminism. These principles had two dimensions. First, an argument of toleration required respect for the diverse ways people exercised their basic human rights. It was this argument the abolitionist feminists in the antebellum period applied to both racism and sexism, calling for equal respect for inalienable human rights (conscience, free speech, intimate life, and work) that could only be legitimately abridged when required by compelling secular purposes (a person's basic right to marry did not, for this reason, extend to killing one's spouse, because this flouted the secular purpose of protecting life). Second, because both racism and sexism unjustly regarded race/ethnicity or gender as grounds for abridging the basic human rights of whole classes of persons, abolitionists and some suffragists regarded those grounds as inadequate to rationalize such abridgments of basic rights.

The argument for toleration revealed that the political power of U.S. racism and sexism rested on dehumanizing cultural stereotypes that abridged basic human rights of moral personality, including conscience, speech, and intimate life. Systematic abridgment of these rights undermines constitutional democracy precisely because of the role the free exercise of such rights plays in self-respect for the freedom to originate claims and forge and sustain the cultural forms of life that give enduring meaning to living moral agency. Persons systematically deprived of such rights in a constitutional system such as the United States that otherwise respects such rights are denationalized both as persons and citizens. They may be considered useful as tools are useful (as women were considered chattel), lovable and amusing as pets are (a common reason for educating women was to entertain men), but not equal subjects of and thus members of the democratic community. Accordingly, any serious attention to such injustice requires correlative attention to guaranteeing on equal terms each of these basic rights.

The tradition of rights-based feminism theorized by Mary Wollstonecraft, Lucy Stone, Sarah and Angelina Grimke, Lucretia Mott, Elizabeth Cady Stanton, Matilda Joslyn Gage, Susan B. Anthony, and others had given central weight consistent with the centrality of the inalienable right to conscience in the argument for toleration to claims for correlative rights to equal educational opportunity and participation at the polls (including, as Wollstonecraft argued, coed public education). These early feminists' arguments focused on the equal right of women to be scholars, theologians, and ministers and thus to bring their moral agency to criticism of misogynist bible interpretation and the political power it had unjustly allowed men. Women had in nineteenth-century U.S. culture used constitutional guarantees of religious liberty not only in forging, as the Grimkes, Mott, and Stone did, abolitionist feminist dissent within Quakerism, which traditionally accorded a more central role to women in works of conscience, but in generating either highly personal forms of spirituality like that of Sojourner Truth or religious organizations founded by women such as Shakerism, Christian Science, and spiritualism. Stanton published her controversial *Woman's Bible* in 1895 much to the alarm of her less radical suffragist sisters. The censure of Stanton over Susan B. Anthony's anguished objections by the suffrage organization she had founded and been a leader of for five decades, by then known as the National American Woman's Suffrage Association, suggests the degree to which feminism had compromised the argument for toleration that had made such a movement normatively possible, cramping the scope of acceptable feminist conscience to the sectarian measure on matters of religion and sexuality of a Frances Willard (who thought women's "purity" should be mobilized on behalf of the temperance movement — and for that reason they should be able to vote — but they should maintain their traditional sphere in the home).

Thus, echoing the theories of the early rights-based feminists, an important background condition for the emergence of second-wave feminism after World War II was the increasingly powerful insistence of the Supreme Court during this period that, consistent with the guarantees both of free exercise and antiestablishment of religion in the First Amendment, the government not engage in or support sectarian religious teaching but extend respect to all forms of conscience, secular and religious. This development was articulated in cases about the separation of church and state such as *Engel v. Vitale* (1962) and *Lemon v. Kurtzman* (1971). Although these doctrinal developments did not deal specifically with issues of gender roles, they affirmed limits on legitimate state power in the enforcement of sectarian purposes. These limits were of generative importance in the constitutional legitimation of new forms of conscientious dissent, both antiracist and antisexist, that rested on such grounds. We can see the impact of such protest on the elaboration of the constitutional right to privacy by the U.S. Supreme Court.

The abridgment of the basic human right to intimate life had played a pivotal role in the racist dehumanization of African Americans both under slavery and in later patterns of state-supported segregation and antimiscegenation laws. A measure of the depth of the comparable dehumanization of women was that the very proposal of such a right was the subject of obscenity prosecutions (including, for their advocacy of the right to contraception, prosecution of Emma Goldman and Margaret Sanger). Against this background, the struggle of rights-based feminism could reasonably be measured by the seriousness with which U.S. constitutional culture was willing to take the protection of the human right to intimate life. Margaret Sanger thus played a particularly important intellectual and organizational role in the long struggle to secure constitutional recognition of the right to privacy. And it was a woman, Estelle Griswold, executive director of Planned Parenthood of Connecticut, who, on the shoulders of Sanger's resistance, opened birth control clinics in Connecticut that provided services criminal under Connecticut's anticontraception law. Griswold's arrest persuaded the Supreme Court that, in contrast to *Poe v. Ullman* (1961), *Griswold v. Connecticut* involved a real case or controversy (namely, a law was in fact enforced against a citizen, whereas in *Poe* the law had not been enforced). As we shall see, in *Poe v. Ullman*, which involved the same Connecticut statute later struck down in *Griswold*, Justice John Marshall Harlan not only dissented to the majority's jurisdictional grounds (no case or controversy) for not taking the case but also offered his reasons for believing such statutes were unconstitutional, which he brought to bear as well in his concurring opinion in *Griswold*, which we will examine later.

The judicial elaboration and protection of the constitutional right to privacy can be traced to two cases that survived the otherwise discredited *Lochner* era of judicial intervention into matters of economic policy, namely, *Meyer v. Nebraska* (1923) and *Pierce v. Society of Sisters* (1925). Both opinions described what they were protecting as the role of parents in family relationships from the overreaching authority of the state that failed to accord the constitutionally required weight to the place of parents in both the formation and transmission of values that should not, without compelling reason, be dictated by the state.

That the underlying right in question extended to sexual relations leading to procreation was implicit in *Skinner v. Oklahoma* (1942) in a state requiring compulsory sterilization for some crimes but not others, a practice the Supreme Court struck down on equal protection grounds.

In 1965 the Supreme Court in *Griswold v. Connecticut* constitutionalized the basic human right to contraception, a decision Sanger lived to see. (*Griswold* was, however, decided some six years before the Supreme Court signaled in *Reed v. Reed* growing constitutional concern with the use of gender classifications in laws and policies.) The diverse opinions in *Griswold*, although undoubtedly influenced by Sanger's arguments, were not phrased in the more explicitly feminist terms of later opinions elaborating the constitutional right to privacy — in particular, as we shall see in the next chapter, to abortion. To understand this historical development, we need both to be clear about the background arguments of basic rights made by Sanger and Goldman, and then examine closely the form these arguments took in the diverse opinions of the Supreme Court in *Griswold*.

The issue of contraception had been framed prior to World War II by Sanger and Goldman in terms rooted in rights-based feminism. Sanger's opponents certainly made that point clear. When her then husband, Bill Sanger, was convicted of obscenity for distributing one of his wife's publications, the judge emphasized that the dispute was over women's role:

> Your crime is not only a violation of the laws of man, but of the law of God as well, in your scheme to prevent motherhood. Too many persons have the idea that it is wrong to have children. Some women are so selfish that they do not want to be bothered with them. If some persons would go around and urge Christian women to bear children, instead of wasting their time on woman suffrage, this city and society would be better off.

Sanger's and Goldman's arguments had two prongs, both of which were articulated in the Supreme Court's decisions in *Griswold* and later cases: first, a basic human right to intimate life and the right to contraception as implicit in that right; and second, the assessment of whether laws abridging such a fundamental right met the heavy burden of secular justification required.

The fundamental human right to intimate life was, as Lydia Maria Child, Stephen Andrews, and Victoria Woodhull had made clear in the nineteenth century as free love advocates, as inalienable a right of moral personality (respect for which is central to the argument for toleration) as the right to conscience. Thomas Emerson's brief for the petitioners in *Griswold* made the same point when he connected the argument for a free-standing right to constitutional privacy to the values of the First Amendment. Like the right to conscience, this amendment protects intimate moral resources (thoughts and beliefs, intellect, emotions, self-image, and self-identity) and the way of life that expresses and sustains them in facing and meeting rationally and reasonably the challenge of a life worth living — one touched by enduring personal and ethical values. The right to intimate life centers on protecting these moral resources as they bear on the role of loving and being loved in a tender and caring relationship in which one finds one's moral self as a person in love for, and in the love of, another moral self.

The human right of intimate life was not only central to the argument for toleration central in U.S. constitutionalism, but interpretively implicit in its historical tradition. In both of the two great revolutionary moments that shaped the trajectory of this constitutionalism (the American Revolution and the Civil War), the abridgment of the right to intimate life rendered political power illegitimate and gave rise to the Lockean right to revolution.

At the time of the American Revolution, the literature on human rights known to and assumed by the revolutionaries and founding constitutionalists included what the influential Scottish philosopher Francis Hutcheson called "the natural right each one to enter into the matrimonial relation with anyone who consents." Indeed, John Witherspoon, whose lectures Madison heard at Princeton, followed Hutcheson in listing as even more basic the "right to associate, if he so incline, with any person or persons, whom he can persuade (not force) — under this is contained the right to marriage." Accordingly, political leaders at the state conventions to ratify the Constitution — both those for and against adoption — assumed that the government could not interfere in the domestic sphere. Alexander Hamilton of New York denied that federal constitutional authority did or could "penetrate the recesses of domestic life, and control, in all respects, the private conduct of individuals." Patrick Henry of Virginia spoke of the core right to liberty as the sphere where a man "enjoys the fruits of his labor, under his own fig-tree, with his wife and children around him, in peace and security." The human rights arguments both of leading proponents (Hamilton) and opponents (Henry) of adoption of the Constitution thus converged on the private sphere of domestic married life.

The founding generation thus assumed that the Constitution would not overreach into matters of intimate life such as marriage and divorce, which would be within the jurisdiction of the states, not the federal government. Because the Bill of Rights of 1791 only imposed enforceable constitutional constraints on the national government, it makes sense that it would not include the right to intimate life as among the specifically guaranteed rights, as it was not a matter in which the federal government had any competence (the law of marriage was a state matter, and the Bill of Rights did not apply to the states). However, the drafters would certainly have assumed that it was one of the unenumerated rights protected by the Ninth Amendment if it were ever at threat. The matter was raised in that very light, however, by the growing antebellum constitutional crisis culminating in the Civil War and the victory of the Union and leading to the Reconstruction amendments. Slavery was at the heart of the crisis, and slavery was a state-based institution. Accordingly, abolitionist arguments about the way the slave states abridged basic rights crystallized American thinking about rights that the states had abridged. Those amendments clearly drew upon the abolitionist arguments objecting not only to slavery but to its supporting ideology of racism. It was because, as we shall see, slavery and racism abridged, among other rights, the basic human right to intimate life that resistance to them is relevant to understanding the clauses of the Reconstruction amendments that constitutionalize these arguments, including their conception of basic human rights protected, inter alia, by the Privileges and Immunities Clause of the Fourteenth Amendment against abridgment by the states.

At the time of the Civil War, the understanding of marriage as a basic human right took on a new depth and urgency because of the antebellum abolitionist rights-based attack on the peculiar nature of U.S. slavery. Slavery failed to recognize the marriage or family rights of slaves, and indeed inflicted on black families the moral horror of breaking them up by selling family members separately. One in six slave marriages thus were ended by force or sale. No aspect of slavery more represented its radical evil for abolitionists than its brutal destruction of intimate personal life, including undermining the moral authority of parents over children as they were also sold away from their families at young ages. Africans who were enslaved, the abolitionist Theodore Weld argued, had "as little control over them [children], as have domestic animals over the disposal of their young." Slavery, thus understood as an abomination against intimate personal life, stripped persons of essential attributes of their humanity. My colleague Peggy Davis has powerfully argued that the racist attack on the intimate life of people enslaved was at the heart of the atrocity of U.S. slavery and thus justified the abolitionist political morality that condemned it. It was precisely because the southern states had thus abridged so fundamental a human right that this morality, which underlies the Reconstruction amendments, required a new constitutionally enforceable legal status for blacks that would protect this right against both state and federal power.

Against this historical background (as well as that of eighteenth-century rights-based political theory), it makes interpretive sense to regard the right to intimate life as one of the unenumerated rights protected both by the Ninth Amendment and the Due Process and Privileges and Immunities Clauses of the Fourteenth Amendment, as Justice Harlan implicitly argued in his concurrence in *Griswold*. The Supreme Court interpreted the Fourteenth Amendment in particular as protecting this basic human right against unjustified state abridgment, and, as Sanger and Goldman had urged, regarded the use of contraceptives as an instance of this right. The right to contraception was, for Sanger and Goldman, so fundamental a human right for women because it would enable women, perhaps for the first time in human history, to decide reliably whether and when their sexual lives would be reproductive, thus making possible their self-determination. This principle was crucial to the more basic right of intimate life in two ways. First, it would enable women to exercise control over their intimate relations to men, which included the significant economic and personal consequences of having children. Second, it would secure for women the right to decide whether and when they would form the intimate relationship to a child for which they might or might not be emotionally or financially equipped. Both forms of self-determination threatened the traditional gender-defined role of women's sexuality as both exclusively and mandatorily procreational and maternally self-sacrificing, which benefited men by providing a continuous source of free labor, and were resisted, as by Bill Sanger's judge, for that reason.

But second, this human right, like other such rights, may only be regulated or limited in terms of state reasons not hostage to an entrenched political hierarchy (for example, compulsorily arranged marriage) resting on the abridgment of such rights. For example, from the perspective of abolitionist criticism of slavery and racism, the southern slaveowners' justifications for destroying the family lives of blacks were transparently inadequate.

Such arguments were in their nature essentially racist:

His natural affection is not strong, and consequently he is cruel to his own offspring, and suffers little by separation from them.

Another striking trait of negro character is lasciviousness. Lust is his strongest passion; and hence, rape is an offence of too frequent occurrence. Fidelity to the marriage relation they do not understand and do not expect, neither in their native country nor in a state of bondage.

The blind moral callousness of southern proslavery thought was nowhere more evident than in its view of what were in fact agonizing family separations:

He is also liable to be separated from wife or child . . . but from native character and temperament, the separation is much less severely felt.

With regard to the separation of husbands and wives, parents and children, . . . Negroes are themselves both perverse and comparatively indifferent about this matter.

The irrational racist sexualization of blacks was evident in the frequent justification of slavery in terms of maintaining the higher standards of sexual purity of southern white women. Distorted by the polemical prism of such thought, the relation of master and slave was itself regarded as an intimate relationship like husband and wife that should be similarly immunized from outside interference. In this Orwellian world of truth mutated by power, the justification of slavery became the defense of freedom. Arguments of these sorts rested on interpretations of facts and values hostage to entrenched political institutions of which the stability required the abridgment of basic rights of blacks and of any whites who ventured reasonable criticism of such practices.

If the antebellum experience of state abridgments of basic rights informs a reasonable interpretation of the Privileges and Immunities Clause, the protection of intimate personal life must be one of the basic human rights thus worthy of national protection. The remaining question is whether there is any adequate basis for the abridgment of so basic a right — in the case of contraception, the right to decide whether or when one's sexual life will lead to offspring, and indeed, to explore one's intimate sexual life as an end in itself.

That abridgment can only be justified by a compelling state reason, not on the grounds of reasons that are today sectarian. In fact, the only argument that previously sustained obscenity laws such as Comstock's (namely, the Augustinian and Thomistic view that it is immoral to engage in nonprocreative sex) is not today a view of sexuality that reasonably can be enforced in the public at large. Such a view may once have made sense when there was massive infant and adult mortality and a correspondingly desperate need to have large numbers of children, at least some of which might survive to perform needed tasks in a basically agrarian way of life. But such a context is no longer present in industrialized societies with modern health care; enforcing such a procreational model to legitimate sex in contemporary circumstances is now anachronistic. Indeed, many people regard sexual love as an end in itself and the control of reproduction as a reasonable way to regulate when and whether they have children consistent with their personal ethics about their children and the larger issue of an overpopulated society. Even the question of having children at all is today a highly personal matter of genuine choice, not of social or moral necessity. From the perspective of women in particular, as Sanger and Goldman made so clear, the enforcement of compulsory maternity not only harms women's interests (as well as those of an overpopulated society more generally), but deprives them of the rational dignity of deciding as moral agents consistent with their other legitimate aims and personal ambitions (including the free exercise of all of their basic human rights), whether, when, and on what terms they will have children. Enforcement of procreational morality rests on a now conspicuously sectarian conception of gender hierarchy in which women's sexuality is defined only by reproduction. That conception, the basis of the construction of gender hierarchy, cannot reasonably be the measure of human rights today. Its enforcement through law is unjust for the same reason antebellum southern racist assumptions about black sexuality were unjust: they rest on dehumanizing certain classes of persons as lacking the capacity or need for responsible control over their intimate lives and associations.

Armed with this way of understanding Sanger's and Goldman's pathbreaking arguments of why the prohibition of contraception abridged a basic human right, we turn now to the diverse opinions in *Griswold v. Connecticut,* the first opinion of the Court that articulated and defended a free-standing constitutional right to privacy applicable to sexual conduct. *Griswold* was decided seven to two, with Justice William O. Douglas writing for the Court and concurring opinions by Justice Goldberg (writing also for Chief Justice Earl Warren and Justice William J. Brennan), Justice John Marshall Harlan, and Justice Byron R. White. There were two dissenting opinions, one by Justice Hugo L. Black (in which Justice Potter Stewart concurred), and another by Justice Stewart (in which Justice Black joined). Only Justice Tom C. Clark did not write an opinion, but concurred in the majority opinion for the Court. Douglas's opinion was joined by Clark, Goldberg, Warren, and Brennan. Justices Harlan and White concurred in the result, but wrote separate opinions in support of their views. The argument for a free-standing right of constitutional privacy had been questioned in an important memorandum for Chief Justice Warren by his law clerk John Hart Ely. Ely urged Warren to declare the unconstitutionality of the Connecticut anticontraception criminal statute on an equal protection ground that the law had been enforced only against birth control clinics, thus bearing only on low-income women, not on the ground of a free-standing constitutional right to privacy, which Ely argued was not there. As it turned out, Warren decided to support the argument for such a right (Ely later, as a law professor, questioned the legitimacy of the elaboration of the right to privacy to cover abortion services; see discussion in next chapter).

As earlier suggested, there are two analytically important parts of the inference, understanding, and elaboration of the constitutional principle of privacy: first, the source, nature, and scope of the basic right in question; and second, the source and weight of the kind of justification required to abridge such a basic right. Of the opinions in *Griswold*, the opinion for the Court of Justice Douglas focused almost entirely on the first issue, whereas the concurring opinions of Justices Goldberg and White dealt with both issues, although with the latter issue somewhat schematically (as we shall see). Only the opinion of Justice Harlan grappled with both issues in an analytically powerful though somewhat incoherent way. The two dissents (by Justices Black and Stewart) were preoccupied entirely with what they perceived as the lack of support for inferring such a basic right from the text and history of the U.S. Constitution.

Justice Douglas's opinion for the Court opened with a warning that the Court does "not sit as a super-legislature to determine the wisdom, need, and propriety of laws that touched economic problems, business affairs, or social conditions." What distinguished this case, however, was that the criminal law in question "operates on an intimate relation of husband, wife, and their physician's role in one aspect of that relation." The opinion ended as well with a similar emphasis on the right of marriage:

> We deal with a right of privacy older than the Bill of Rights—older than our political parties, older than our school system. Marriage is a coming together for better or for worse, hopefully enduring, and intimate to the degree of being sacred. It is an association that promotes a way of life, not causes; a harmony in living, not political faiths; a bilateral loyalty, not commercial or social projects. Yet it is an association for as noble a purpose as any involved in our prior decisions.

Certainly, Douglas aimed to show that the right to marriage, or some more general right of which marriage is an example, is and has always been a constitutionally protected basic right. His argument, however, appealed to the two cases earlier mentioned, *Pierce v. Society of Sisters* and *Meyer v. Nebraska*, both of which protect aspects of parents' right to decide where and how their children are educated – in *Pierce*, in a parochial as opposed to a public school; in *Meyer*, their desire that their child learn a foreign language (German). Neither deals with sexual conduct as such, and both may be more narrowly understood as grounded in values of conscience and speech protected by the First Amendment.

The remaining argument of the majority opinion dealt entirely with the ways in which various provisions of the Bill of Rights protect aspects of privacy, understood as the right to control information about oneself from more public dissemination. The most elaborate discussion was of the Court's inference and protection of a right to protect the privacy of one's associations. For example, Douglas cited a case protecting the NAACP from a state requirement of disclosure of membership lists on the ground that such an infringement of privacy would threaten the First Amendment rights of persons freely and without fear of intimidation to join groups that protest injustices, such as racial segregation in the South, both popular and prone to such violent intimidation of dissenters. Douglas claimed such precedents "suggest that specific guarantees in the Bill of Rights have penumbras, formed by emanations from those guarantees that help give them life and substance," and then, adding to his previous discussion of the First Amendment, showed how aspects of privacy are protected by the Third Amendment (forbidding quartering of soldiers in homes), the Fourth Amendment (protecting persons from unreasonable searches and seizures), and the Fifth Amendment (protecting persons from having to incriminate themselves). The only analytical attempt, however, to connect the right to privacy announced in *Griswold* to these amendments was a query arising from imagining how a law criminalizing use of contraceptives would be enforced: "Would we allow the police to search the sacred precincts of marital bedrooms for telltale signs of the use of contraceptives?" Of course, the force of the rhetorical query assumed the issue in dispute, namely, that there would be something outrageous in regarding such a search as reasonable, presumably because a basic right is being infringed when there is no harm to the state that could justify such infringement. It would be quite a different case, surely, if the issue involved homicide, assault, or rape (because of the feminist movement, interspousal rape is now criminal in many jurisdictions). Douglas implied that real harms can justify even infringements of marital privacy, just as human sacrifice would not be protected by the constitutional right of free exercise of religion.

The analytical problem with Douglas's opinion for the Court was thus twofold. It nowhere explained why the right to marriage should be protected as a free-standing constitutional right, which was the issue in dispute in *Griswold*. And, it assumed without explaining the harms that would justify the infringement even of such a fundamental right, and failed to show why no such harms could justify the infringement in this case.

On both of these points, the opinion of Justice Goldberg (joined by Chief Justice Warren and Justice Brennan) was at least much less conclusory. On the issue of the inference of the basic right to privacy, Justice Goldberg appealed to a provision only mentioned but not discussed by Justice Douglas, namely, the Ninth Amendment of the Bill of Rights. Both the text and history of the Ninth Amendment make quite clear, Goldberg argued, that James Madison, its author, "proffered [it] to quiet expressed fears that a bill of specifically enumerated rights could not be sufficiently broad to cover all essential rights and the specific mention of certain rights would be interpreted as a denial that others were protected." (Goldberg had developed his historical arguments on the basis of the research of his law clerk Stephen Breyer, who was later appointed a justice of the Supreme Court.) Goldberg referenced statements to this effect by both James Madison and Justice Joseph Story "that the Framers did not intend that the first eight amendments be construed to exhaust the basic and fundamental rights which the Constitution guaranteed to the people." Goldberg's emphasis on both text and history was directed against Justice Black, who, in his dissent, questions on both grounds the majority's inference and protection of a constitutional right to privacy. Goldberg supported the specific inference of a free-standing right to marriage, among other constitutionally protected rights, largely by reference to dicta of the Supreme Court that referred to such a right and to Justice Harlan's argument for such a right in his dissent in *Poe v. Ullman*, in which the Court refused to decide the issue of the constitutionality of anticontraception on alleged jurisdictional grounds. After Goldberg thus justified such an independent right to marriage, he addressed the question of what compelling state reason could justify the abridgment of such a fundamental right. At this point, Goldberg adduced only one such legitimate purpose, "the discouraging of extramarital relations," but argued that the anticontraception law in question was unconstitutional because it failed to satisfy the general requirement for laws abridging basic constitutional rights, namely, that they not sweep under their prohibition the many cases that did not meet this purpose, including the use of contraceptives by married couples who were faithful.

Justice White's concurring opinion in *Griswold* assumed that a basic right to marriage existed and questioned the constitutionality of the statute because of the means chosen to pursue its alleged end: "The State's policy against all forms of promiscuous or illicit sexual relationships be they premarital or extramarital, concededly a permissible and legitimate legislative goal." The use of contraceptives by married couples did not implicate this purpose at all, and was "at most . . . of marginal utility to the declared objective." Like Justice Goldberg, Justice White concluded such a statute could not meet the required burden that abridgment of a fundamental constitutional right requires.

Justice Harlan's concurring opinion distinguished itself from the opinion of the Court because it assumed the abridgment in question must be "found to violate some right assured by the letter or penumbra of the Bill of Rights," an assumption Harlan found much too close to the reasons for dissent of Justices Black and Stewart. Harlan always objected to Justice Black's view that all of and only the Bill of Rights was incorporated against the states under the Fourteenth Amendment, because he believed that the best reading of both the text and history, *pace* Black, was that the Fourteenth Amendment protected basic constitutional rights against the states, which included some but not all of the Bill of Rights, and also included basic rights not enumerated in the Bill of Rights. Harlan's opinion in *Griswold* largely made this point, appealing to his argument about the unconstitutionality of anticontraception statutes in his dissenting opinion in *Poe v. Ullman*, an opinion to which all the other justices in the *Griswold* majority (Douglas, Goldberg, White) appealed at various points in their opinions. Why did Harlan's interpretive argument in *Poe* carry such weight for them?

In *Poe v. Ullman*, which involved the same Connecticut statute later struck down in *Griswold*, Justice Harlan dissented not only to the majority's jurisdictional grounds for not taking the case (no case or controversy) but also offered his reasons for believing such statutes were unconstitutional (Harlan's arguments on this point were shaped by a memorandum from his law clerk Charles Fried, who later both as a solicitor general and a law professor questioned the extension of the right to abortion services). Harlan argued that the protection of basic rights under the Constitution was not limited to those specified in the Bill of Rights and elsewhere, but involved all basic human rights, "which are . . . fundamental; which belong . . . to the citizens of all free governments." That expansive conception of constitutionally protected rights was, Harlan argued, the proper normative metric for interpreting the rights protected by the Fourteenth Amendment, which he found in the Due Process Clause but which could plausibly also be based on the Privileges and Immunities Clause. The right to marriage was such a free-standing constitutional right, aspects of which the Court had already acknowledged in *Pierce v. Society of Sisters* and *Meyer v. Nebraska*. Harlan conceded that both cases could be more narrowly grounded on "concepts of freedom and expression and conscience assured against state action by the Fourteenth Amendment." But the fundamental right to marriage was, Harlan argued, long historically recognized in U.S. legal tradition, subject, of course, to abridgment when compelling state purposes so required. Many such abridgments Harlan did not question, in particular, "laws forbidding adultery, fornication, and homosexual practices which express the negative of the proposition, confining sexuality to lawful marriage" (he later included in this list abortion as well as "fornication and incest"); but Harlan did question whether the purpose underlying anticontraception laws could reasonably justify such laws.

The historical dimension of Harlan's argument for a free-standing right to marriage can be further supported by a good historical understanding of the view of the founding generation, the antebellum controversies over the constitutional issues of slavery and racism, and the post–Civil War constitutional debates over race that increasingly connected U.S. racism to abridgment of the basic right of marriage across the ethnic/racial divide by antimiscegenation laws. Such compelling historiography shows that the right to marriage has a deeper historical grounding than even Harlan supposed, which secures his normative argument even more deeply in the U.S. constitutional tradition.

{ *Chapter 2* }

Harlan's interpretive argument was more on track than those of the other justices in the majority in *Griswold* because his arguments supported a free-standing constitutional right to an intimate life grounded in the basic human rights. Harlan recognized that protecting intimate life is an essential part of a democratic society, which has to be tolerant of differences because the United States has so many different cultures and peoples. Such a right is independent even from the privacy concerns Justice Douglas affirmed. The right to intimate life is as worthy of protection as the rights of conscience and free speech central to the First Amendment of the Bill of Rights. Indeed, many reasonable people take no interest in religion and even less in the skills of reading and writing unless and until those interests connect to an interest that absorbs both their minds and hearts, namely, love in intimate life. If anything normatively gives a human life enduring meaning, it is this. Harlan's argument thus was more powerful than the appeal of other justices to the text and history of the Ninth Amendment because it showed how and why, specifically, a right to intimate relationships is one of the rights that requires protection of rights beyond the Bill of Rights. Finally, Harlan's argument showed that the protection of constitutional privacy does not have to be grounded in the Due Process Clause, of which the text and history is more procedural than substantive. Rather, both the text and history of the Privileges and Immunities Clauses both of Article IV and of the Fourteenth Amendment support the protection of such free-standing substantive rights, including the abolitionist antebellum arguments against slavery and racism as the abridgment of the basic human right of intimate life of people of color. Harlan's argument is both deeply conservative (this free-standing basic right was historically assumed in the U.S. legal tradition) and liberal (such a basic right must be extended to all on fair terms, an argument central to the abolitionist moral ground constitutionalized in the Fourteenth Amendment).

But there is another, perhaps more important, dimension to Harlan's argument, namely, his treatment of the compelling purposes that could justify abridgment of such a fundamental right. Harlan's argument is so important because, unlike the way Justices Goldberg and White treated this issue, he did not argue that these purposes could be justified as easily as Goldberg and White supposed. Goldberg and White argued that the only legitimate purpose such a statute could

have is to stem extramarital and premarital sex acts, and then condemned the Connecticut statute because it bore so heavily on marital
sex acts and only marginally on others. But the traditional moral purpose of such statutes was, as earlier suggested, to condemn all forms
of nonprocreational sex, a purpose that applied equally to sex inside
and outside marriage and heterosexual relations. From this perspective, the Connecticut statute did not overinclusively sweep marital sex
under its prohibitions; rather, it forbade all forms of nonprocreational
sex, marital or not. Why was this purpose not constitutionally acceptable? It is this kind of problem that may explain why Harlan struggled
with the issue in *Poe* and *Griswold* in a way other justices did not. His
struggle was demonstrated in his expressed reluctance to assess "simply, and in abstraction, whether the moral judgment implicit in the
application of the present statute to married couples was a sound one,"
and then to confront his duty as a constitutional judge when persons
were subject to criminal penalties to advance such a purpose. What
Harlan said at this point is striking: "The secular state is not an examiner of consciences: it must operate in the realm of behavior, of overt
actions, and where it does so operate, not only the underlying, moral
purpose of its operations, but also the *choice of means* becomes relevant
to any constitutional judgment on what is done." It was the distinction between means and ends that Harlan argued distinguished anticontraception statutes from prohibitions he did not question:

> Adultery, homosexuality, and the like are sexual intimacies which
> the State forbids altogether, but the intimacy of husband and wife
> is necessarily an essential and accepted feature of the institution of
> marriage, an institution which the State not only must allow, but
> which always and in every age it has fostered and protected. It is
> one thing when the State exerts its power either to forbid extra-
> marital sexuality altogether, or to say who may marry, but it is quite
> another when, having acknowledged a marriage and the intimacies
> inherent in it, it undertakes to regulate by means of the criminal
> law the details of that intimacy.

Of course, the traditional purpose of anticontraception laws meant
exactly what Harlan refused constitutionally to credit, namely, that
all forms of nonprocreational sex (marital and not) were intrinsically

wrong and to be condemned and prohibited. Harlan said that such a purpose cannot constitutionally be applied to sex acts in marriage not because it condemns means but not ends but because its end is not constitutionally acceptable. "The secular state is not an examiner of consciences" suggests what must have been the basis of Harlan's argument, namely, that the prohibition of nonprocreational sex is, in the modern world, no longer supported by the compelling secular purposes the Constitution requires. If this argument was right, it would be more difficult to cabin the principle of constitutional privacy in some of the ways Harlan suggests (not applying to abortion, or consensual homosexuality). But that is exactly what the judicial elaboration of the principle exemplifies, which shows that Harlan's normative argument of principle has had staying power and appeal well beyond his own expectations in 1965.

The dissent of Justice Black, joined by Justice Stewart, argued that judicially enforceable constitutional rights must be limited to "some specific constitutional provision." For Justice Black, there was no difference between the constitutionally discredited use of natural law in *Lochner v. New York* and its use in *Griswold*. Justice Black was, of course, justly famous for his appeal to both text and history in the enforcement of basic rights, including free speech and religious liberty, as well as incorporation of the Bill of Rights against the states. His argument for full incorporation of the Bill of Rights rested on an appeal not only to the text of the Fourteenth Amendment but to the history of the ratification debates in the Reconstruction Congress. Those debates certainly showed, as Black argued they did, that incorporation was contemplated. But they also showed something Black omitted to mention, namely, that the rights to be protected against the states were, as Justice Harlan argued, construed to apply beyond the Bill of Rights to all basic human rights. So, text and history at this point did not sustain what Black claimed they did. This was Harlan's devastating critical point against Black's vaunted fidelity to text and history.

The Supreme Court first recognized the constitutional right to privacy in *Griswold* in a married couple, but subsequently extended the right in 1972 in *Eisenstadt v. Baird* to all persons, married or single, and in 1977 in *Carey v. Population Services International* to sexually active teenagers. Justice Brennan marked the distance the Supreme Court had come from *Griswold* when in 1972 he wrote for the Court in *Eisen-*

stadt v. Baird: "If the right of privacy means anything, it is the right of the *individual,* married or single, to be free from unwarranted governmental intrusion into matters so fundamentally affecting a person as the decision whether to bear or beget a child." These interpretive developments suggest that the constitutional principle of privacy must be located in some right that includes marriage certainly, but extends to sexual relations beyond marriage. If this was true of the cases dealing with contraception (where the Supreme Court first inferred and protected a free-standing constitutional right to privacy inhering in sexual relation), it was true, *a fortiori,* of the two later elaborations of constitutional privacy we must now discuss, abortion and consensual homosexuality.

The Constitutional Right to Privacy
Abortion

We saw in the previous chapter that although the basic normative arguments for a right to contraception had been made by feminist pioneers such as Margaret Sanger and Emma Goldman even before World War II (drawing on the previous arguments of Elizabeth Cady Stanton and others), the Supreme Court's constitutionalization of their argument in 1965 placed no particular emphasis on the rights of women, rather grounding the argument in a basic right of sexual privacy in marital relationships, in which men have as strong an interest as women. Notably, the very terms in which marriage was characterized in the opinion for the Court of Justice Douglas suggested an idealization of marriage ("Marriage is a coming together for better or for worse, hopefully enduring, and intimate to the degree of being sacred . . . an association for as noble a purpose as any involved in our prior decisions"). Idealization often shadows loss (Douglas married and divorced three times, marrying his fourth wife when he was sixty-seven and she twenty-three), and his idealization was from a man's point of view rather remote from a feminist analysis and critique rooted in women's experience. It does not follow from the opinion, of course, that women (in particular Margaret Sanger) were not crucial in sustaining organizations such as Planned Parenthood that mobilized support for a right to contraception and brought and argued cases such as *Poe v. Ullman* and *Griswold v. Connecticut,* and that the right eventually recognized benefited women enormously, enabling them to regulate their reproductive lives consistently with their other aims in life. A great case such as *Griswold* had staying power and authority because it expressed an overlapping normative consensus of men and women, who found in the case a respect for the dignity of their sexual choices and lives. But it is surely not accidental that the issue of women's rights was muted in the opinions for the majority in

Griswold, a case decided well before the Supreme Court had begun to take seriously gender as a classification arguably as important as race.

The issue of abortion is, of course, quite different: only women have abortions. It is a more starkly gendered question than contraception, and for this reason, views of abortion – both pro and con – are much more acutely sensitive to the degree to which traditional conceptions of gender roles are uncritically accepted or critically contested. The issue of abortion moved to a central position in U.S. political and constitutional debate as a consequence of two social movements that emerged in the wake of the civil rights and antiwar movements, both of which transformed not only politics but constitutional law (see chapter 2). No small part of this transformation was the expanding protection of dissenting speech that the civil rights movement persuaded the U.S. Supreme Court to affirm. That brilliant display of free speech made possible new forms of resistance and cooperation not only across the racial/ethnic divide but the gender divide as well as women moved into new relationships with each other and with men.

What resulted was the emergence of the transformative social movement called second-wave or rights-based feminism, which challenged in a way anticipated by the abolitionist feminists of the antebellum period the cultural force of gender stereotypes that rested on the repression of the free voices both of women and men that might and would reasonably challenge the unjust power such stereotypes engendered. The new relationships of women with each other and with men made possible by the new freedoms of conscience and speech forged by the civil rights and antiwar movements empowered women to begin speaking and hearing one another speaking in what Carol Gilligan called in a different voice and Nelle Morton called hearing each other into speech. This was a voice rooted in women's experience of their lives and their relationships. This consciousness-raising and the different voice to which it gave rise expressed itself in feminists' claim for women of basic rights, including the right to an abortion, as we shall see; their view received the important support of the Model Penal Code in 1961, calling for revising all state abortion laws. The movement claimed as well that gender as a basis for laws and policies should be constitutionally suspect for the same reasons race was. Feminists urged ratification of the Equal Rights Amendment (which had been first introduced in Congress in 1923) to make this latter point. Ratification failed in the 1970s, but many second-wave feminist arguments were adopted by the Supreme Court in its interpretation of the Equal Protection Clause of the Fourteenth Amendment.

I begin with *Roe v. Wade*, in which the constitutional right to privacy recognized in *Griswold* and its progeny was extended to abortion services. In contrast to *Griswold*, the Supreme Court by 1973, when *Roe* was decided, had already begun to acknowledge that gender discrimination was to some degree constitutionally suspect (*Reed v. Reed*, which struck down the exclusion of women from administering estates, had been decided in 1971). *Roe* itself addressed the criminalization of abortion applied not to a married couple, but an unmarried woman, which starkly made the point that the right in question here, in contrast to the right to contraceptives, was the right of an individual woman. Sarah Weddington made the oral argument in *Roe* before the Supreme Court both times it was argued (the case was reargued to allow two new justices, Lewis Powell and William Rehnquist, to participate in the decision), and spoke to the Court from her experience as a woman (in fact, she had secretly had an abortion herself). She thus spoke of the burdens of pregnancy: "It disrupts her body, it disrupts her education, it disrupts her employment, and it often disrupts her entire family life and . . . because of the impact on the woman, this certainly, inasfar as there are any rights which are fundamental, is a matter . . . of such fundamental and basic concern to the woman involved that she should be allowed to make the choice as to whether to continue or terminate her pregnancy." No one—none of the seven men on the bench when she first made her oral argument at the age of twenty-six—interrupted her as she spoke to this point, a point at the heart of the rights-based feminism Weddington embodied.

Roe, decided seven to two, struck down a Texas statute criminalizing all abortions except those to save the life of the mother. Justice Harry Blackmun wrote the opinion for the Court (in which Chief Warren E. Burger and Justices Douglas, Brennan, Stewart, Thurgood Marshall, and Powell joined), with concurring opinions by Justice Stewart, Justice Douglas, and Chief Justice Burger. Justice Rehnquist and Justice White each wrote dissenting opinions. Justices White and Stewart changed positions from those taken in *Griswold*: White concurred in *Griswold* but dissented in *Roe*; Stewart dissented in *Griswold* but concurred in *Roe*.

The opinion for the Court of Justice Harry Blackmun, after initially considering various jurisdictional issues, turned to assessing the claim of the unconstitutionality of the Texas statute by a single woman. Blackmun prefaced his constitutional analysis, however, with a long and quite learned discussion of the history of the treatment of abortion, stretching back to ancient Greece and Rome, including, inter alia, the Hippocratic Oath, common law, English statutory law, U.S. law, and the views on the issue of various professional organizations (medical, health, and legal). Blackmun showed that the statutory pattern of criminalizing abortion arose relatively late in U.S. history (largely after the Civil War), which raised the question of why. Blackmun considered three reasons, the first of which (discouraging illicit sex) he rejected as unreasonable, and the remaining two (saving a woman's life and protecting potential life) more weighty. Abortion thus was criminalized during a period when the procedure was hazardous to women, so that its prohibition was justified as a way of saving a woman's life. However, "modern medical techniques have altered this situation. . . . Mortality rates for women undergoing early abortions, where the procedure is legal, appear to be as low as or lower than the rates for normal childbirth." Although prohibiting abortions could thus no longer be justified on this ground, Blackmun conceded that abortions might be regulated to secure their safety for women, and also mentioned the weight accorded to protecting potential life. With these historical considerations as background, Blackmun turned to his constitutional analysis of the Texas statute.

There were two prongs to Blackmun's analysis: first, the nature and weight of the basic right; and second, the weight and nature of the compelling state purposes that justify abridgment of such a basic right.

The basic right, Blackmun argued, was *Griswold*'s free-standing constitutional right protecting sexual acts "founded in the Fourteenth Amendment's concept of personal liberty and restrictions on state action." This right

> is broad enough to encompass a woman's decision whether or not to terminate her pregnancy. The detriment that the State would impose upon the pregnant woman by denying this choice alto-

{ *Chapter 3* }

gether is apparent. Specific and direct harm medically diagnosable even in early pregnancy may be involved. Maternity, or additional offspring, may force upon the woman a distressful life and future. Psychological harm may be imminent. Mental and physical health may be taxed by child care. There is also the distress, for all concerned, associated with the unwanted child, and there is the problem of bringing a child into a family already unable, psychologically and otherwise, to care for it. In other cases, as in this one, the additional difficulties and continuing stigma of unwed motherhood may be involved.

Blackmun's characterization of the right in these circumstances was in a different moral world altogether from Justice Douglas's idealization of marriage in *Griswold*. It is true that, in *Roe*, Blackmun accorded more weight to the professional judgment of the medical profession than he would in later opinions, appealing more directly there to women's right to reproductive autonomy. But, the point exists even in *Roe*, put in a way that shows the influence of rights-based feminism. Blackmun characterized the right in *Roe* in terms rooted in a woman's conscience and experience of sexuality with consequences (pregnancy) men do not bear in the same way. There was no idealization of women or motherhood here, but rather a breaking from the disassociation that gives rise to idealization, trying to think through how a basic human right of intimate life owed to all persons should be reasonably understood and recognized in the distinctive experience of women in all its human complexity, including painful choices among lesser evils. Carol Gilligan's important study of women's morality in making the abortion choice speaks precisely to this issue, namely, that the right recognized in *Roe* empowered women to experience moral agency in a decision such as having a child, not ceding to society or the state that authority. For many women, *Roe* gave a constitutional framework to a sense of moral responsibility in and for relationships, breaking the disjunction with their experience on which the traditional concepts of women in procreational roles rested. How, Gilligan asked, can women have ethical responsibility when unreasonable demands of maternal self-sacrifice deprive them of any sense of self and thus of real relationship? Blackmun's analysis of the basic constitutional right insisted, as a matter of principle, that the right to moral control of intimate life not be limited to men's experience but extended on fair terms to women's distinctive moral experience in matters of sexuality and child-bearing.

Having thus robustly articulated the basic right infringed by the criminalization of abortion, Blackmun turned to the second question of his analysis: the nature and weight of the compelling interests that might justify abridgment or limitation of such a basic right. At this point, Blackmun drew a sharp distinction between a case such as *Griswold*, where there is no such compelling interest, and *Roe*, where several purposes have significant weight in justifying constraint and even abridgment of this right — "important interests in safeguarding health, in maintaining medical standards, and in protecting potential life." The structure of Blackmun's argument soon became apparent:

> At some point in pregnancy, these respective interests become sufficiently compelling to sustain regulation of the factors that govern the abortion decision. The privacy right involved, therefore, cannot be said to be absolute.
>
> Everything will turn on the constitutional weight attached to these interests.

Before Blackmun turned to his assessment of this question, he rebutted the argument for the strongest constitutional weight that could be given these interests, namely, that a fetus is a person within the text and history of the Fourteenth Amendment whose life therefore may be protected by strong antiabortion laws such as that of Texas. Blackmun found no support for this interpretation in the text, precedents, and constitutional history, stating "that throughout the major portion of the nineteenth century prevailing legal abortion practices were far freer than they are today." Whatever personhood fetuses had been accorded under U.S. law was "contingent upon live birth."

If the life of the fetus was not to be accorded normative weight, the question central to *Roe* was what weight its potential life, if any, should be accorded by the state and why. Blackmun's invocation of "protecting potential life" as one legitimate purpose assumed that life must be accorded some weight. When, however, he came to consider what constitutional weight should be accorded this state interest, he posed the question in the terms Texas did in arguing that there was a compelling purpose to protect life at the time of conception. Blackmun did not accept this interpretation of the beginning of life, claiming, in a passage that caught the particular attention of his critics: "We need not resolve the difficult question of when life begins. When those trained in the respective disciplines of medicine, philosophy, and theology are unable to arrive at any consensus, the judiciary, at this point in the development of man's knowledge, is not in a position to speculate as to the answer."

Blackmun then went on to review a range of views on when life begins, including live birth (the Stoics and many Jews and Protestants), quickening (Anglo-American common law), viability (that is, when the fetus is "potentially able to live outside the mother's womb, albeit with artificial aid" (one of the views endorsed by physicians and scientists), mediate animation (once the view of the Catholic Church), and conception (now the view of the Catholic Church). Blackmun then adopted, as the constitutional measure of when there is a compelling state interest, viability (at about seven months, twenty-eight weeks but sometimes earlier, even twenty-four weeks) "because the fetus then presumably has the capability of meaningful life outside the mother's womb."

There were then two purposes Blackmun identified as compelling: the health and life of the mother and the potential life of the fetus at viability. Because "until the end of the first trimester mortality in abortion may be less than mortality in normal childbirth," the state could regulate abortions for health reasons only after the first trimester (before that, presumably, abortions must take place without such regulations). Because at the point of viability (during the second trimester), the weight accorded the potential life of the fetus was now compelling; at this point the state could prohibit abortions. Because the Texas statute failed to comply with these requirements, it was unconstitutional.

The concurring opinions by Justice Stewart and Chief Justice Burger did not add much to Blackmun's opinion. Justice Douglas's concurring opinion, however, clarified the roots of Blackmun's argument in the idea of basic human rights not named in law. Justice Douglas, under the influence of a memorandum from Justice Brennan in 1971, had come to interpret the constitutional right to privacy expansively and in women's rights broadly conceived, and now wrote of this right as one of the most basic rights in the U.S. Constitution. Nor—in light of the controversy *Roe* elicited—did either of the dissents (by Justice White and Justice Rehnquist) fundamentally question the opinion in the way its critics did. White's argument was an appeal to democracy: the issue was too much in the domain "over which reasonable men [*sic*] may easily and heatedly differ" to be subject to judicial review in the way *Griswold* was. Although Justice Rehnquist accepted that rights exist beyond the Bill of Rights and would have struck down a Texas statute that forbade an abortion that jeopardized a mother's health, he found the broad sweep of Blackmun's opinion too legislative both in its basis and its holding (the trimester framework). It was, Rehnquist argued, much more like *Lochner v. New York* (the now repudiated incursion of the judiciary into economic and social policy) than the majority supposed.

There is an analytical problem at the heart of *Roe*—a problem any serious defense of *Roe* must address and solve—namely, what we may call Blackmun's rather startling non sequitur. Having previously claimed the Court need not decide the issue of when life begins, Blackmun proceeded to decide the issue, identifying viability as the turning point. In light of ongoing philosophical, religious, and medical controversies over this issue, can one reasonably defend the kind of constitutional argument Blackmun made?

There were two suggestions of such a defense in the Blackmun opinion. First, in discussing the range of historical and contemporary views on abortion, Blackmun observed that, among ancient philosophers, only the Pythagoreans as "a matter of dogma" took the view that the embryo was a person from the moment of conception, leading them to condemn both abortion and suicide, a view influential on the "emerging teachings of Christianity." And later in the opinion, Blackmun noted the range of different religious views on when life begins. Both of these discussions suggest that, consistent with the constitutional demand that basic rights may only be abridged when supported by a compelling secular state purpose, Blackmun looked for a measure of when constitutional protection of potential life is compelling on a secular basis free from sectarian religious disagreements. And second, when discussing the historical views of the American Medical Association supporting antiabortion laws, Blackmun quoted

{ *Chapter 3* }

one such moral view, "calling 'the attention of the clergy of all denominations to the perverted views of morality entertained by a large class of females — aye, and men also, on this important question." This quotation suggests that in Blackmun's view a misogynist moral ground for such antiabortion laws was questionable as a basis for laws and policies because it reflected and enforced unjust gender stereotypes, which the Court had begun to strike down as constitutionally suspect just as it had racial and ethnic discrimination.

Neither of these arguments was made explicitly in *Roe*, but both of them were made in *Planned Parenthood of Southeastern Pennsylvania v. Casey* (1992) by two justices concerned with protecting and defending the full *Roe* framework. Justice John Paul Stevens, for example, insisted that "the State's interest must be secular; consistent with the First Amendment the State may not promote a theological or sectarian interest." Justice Blackmun himself argued that "a State's restrictions on a woman's right to terminate her pregnancy also implicate constitutional guarantees of gender equality." We could elaborate both arguments as follows.

First, antiabortion laws, grounded in the alleged protection of a neutral good such as potential life, unreasonably equate the constitutional weight of the life of a fetus in the early stages of pregnancy with that of a person, and thus equate abortion with murder. Such laws fail to take seriously the weight that should be accorded a woman's basic right to reproductive autonomy in making highly personal moral choices central to her most intimate bodily and emotional life against the background of the lack of reasonable public consensus that fetal life, as such, can be equated with that of an adult moral person. Society has legitimate interests in according legal weight at some point to fetal life as part of recognizing the importance of taking the lives of children seriously and caring for them. This is somewhat analogous to the interest society may have in securing humane treatment for the irretrievably comatose and thus approaching cautiously the requests of their families to terminate their lives. But such interests do not constitutionally justify forbidding abortion throughout all stages of pregnancy. Rather, such interests can be accorded their legitimate weight after a reasonable period has been allowed for the proper scope of a woman's exercise of her decision whether to have an abortion. The *Roe* doctrine of allowing criminalization only at viability may be regarded as identifying this turning point: giving a reasonable period of freedom to women in which to choose to have an abortion, subject to making a decision by a time that marks for the state legitimate concerns for valuing children. However, some women's morality has been unreasonably constrained by this trimester framework when they discovered in the third trimester that the fetus was in a condition that would relegate it to a life of unbearable suffering or death shortly after birth, thus leading to controversy over late-term abortions and so-called partial-birth abortions.

Second, the moral arguments for the prohibition of abortion cluster around certain traditional conceptions of the natural processes of sexuality and gender. However, when one takes seriously the constitutional precedent that fetal life is not a compelling public interest sufficient to outweigh a woman's right of reproductive autonomy, the argument for criminalizing abortion is not a reasonable argument for regarding abortion as homicide, but a proxy for powerfully sectarian ideology about proper sexuality and gender roles often no longer reasonably believed in the society at large. From this perspective, the prohibitions on abortion encumber what many now reasonably regard as a highly conscientious choice by women regarding their bodies, their sexuality and gender, and the nature and place of pregnancy, birth, and child rearing in their personal and ethical lives. Traditional laws against abortion, like comparable anticontraceptive laws, failed at a deep level to recognize women as free and rational persons, instead lending legal force to sectarian theological ideas of biological determination of destiny and gender hierarchy that denied the constructive moral agency of women to establish the meaning of their sexual and reproductive lives. The underlying conception of the antiabortionists appears to be at one with the sexist idea that women's minds and bodies are not their own but the property of others, namely, men or their masculine God, who may "husband" them, like cattle on the farm, for the greater economic good. The abortion choice is thus one of the choices essential to the moral independence of women. The abortion choice is a just application of the right to intimate life, because that right protects women from the degradation of their moral empowerment reflected in the traditional assumptions underlying antiabortion laws.

In the history of antiabortion laws lies a normative view of gender roles. The little weight accorded women's rights and the decisive weight accorded the potential life of the fetus in antiabortion laws make sense only against the background of the still powerful traditional conception of mandatory procreational, self-sacrificing, nurturing gender roles for women. It is the symbolic violation of that normative stereotype that imaginatively transforms abortion into murder. The enforcement of such gender stereotypes through law is now condemned as constitutionally suspect for reasons analogous to those that render racial/ethnic classifications constitutionally suspect. Just as the constitutional suspectness of racial classifications influenced the recognition of the unconstitutionality of antimiscegenation laws, the suspectness of gender stereotypes shaped the unconstitutionality of both anticontraception and antiabortion laws, both of which presumed, on grounds of gender hierarchy rooted in injustice, to tell women what their role and nature were.

Roe, as written, was vulnerable because of Blackmun's non sequitur. It is important to be clear that some of the constitutional criticism of *Roe* came from otherwise liberal constitutional scholars who, as a matter of democratic politics, believed that abortion should be decriminalized in the United States. The notable intellectual leader of those scholars was Professor John Hart Ely, the former law clerk of Chief Justice Warren who had objected to a free-standing right of constitutional privacy as the basis for *Griswold*. Ely conceded that there was a plausible interpretive case to be made for the legitimacy of *Roe* based on the text and history of the Constitution, but he argued that a sound understanding of the modern Supreme Court required that, when a result was not commanded by specific texts, the bench should only exercise its power of judicial review over democratic politics when that review secured a democratically more representative politics. Ely's models for such legitimate judicial review had been the Warren Court's decisions in both racial and reapportionment cases. Because African Americans historically had been deprived of the participation they deserved in U.S. politics, it was legitimate for the Supreme Court to strike down the use of racial classifications to disempower them, such as in state-supported racial segregation; in contrast, Ely defended the use of racial classifications in ameliorative affirmative action programs because such programs did not disempower but fairly empowered African Americans. Malapportionment in electoral districts unfairly accorded some persons more political power than others, and the judiciary had performed an appropriate role in striking down such redistricting, thus securing a fairer system of political representation. Ely's theory questioned the very legitimacy of the principle of constitutional privacy, in contrast to other constitutional scholars such as Charles Fried and Kent Greenawalt who did not object to the principle of constitutional privacy in general but rather to its application to abortion services (in light of the weight of fetal life), as opposed to contraception and consensual homosexuality.

The criticism of *Roe* by Ely as well as Charles Fried and Kent Greenawalt was within the discipline of constitutional law and theory. But because *Roe* challenged the hegemonic power of traditional gender stereotypes of women's roles as wives and mothers, it also occasioned the reemergence into U.S. politics of fundamentalist religion, which rested on a highly patriarchal conception of religion being challenged increasingly successfully by the arguments of rights-based feminists. One of their greatest such successes was, of course, *Roe v. Wade*, which led to a sometimes virulently antifeminist movement that warred on the ERA (which was never ratified) as well as *Roe*. The hypermasculinity of some prolife forces sometimes took the form of lethal violence against women's health clinics, and, in its more moderate forms, attacked the decision in *Roe v. Wade* as fundamentally wrong and mobilized a political movement largely centered in the Republican Party to appoint justices to the Supreme Court that would overrule the decision.

The legal expression of this political movement was originalism, an attitude toward law that tied judicial interpretation to the situations in the world to which the generation who wrote and ratified the relevant constitutional provisions would have applied the term. The great appeal of originalism was that it regarded the constitutional successes of the feminist movement as interpretively wrong, because a decision like *Roe v. Wade* clearly did not express the view of either the founders of the Constitution of 1787 or the Reconstruction Congress that wrote and ratified the Fourteenth Amendment. President Reagan nominated for appointment to the Supreme Court a federal judge and former law professor, Robert Bork, who not only publicly took this position but questioned the legitimacy of the principle of constitutional privacy, including *Griswold v. Connecticut*. Two other originalist justices, Antonin Scalia and Clarence Thomas, were successfully appointed, though the issue of their view of privacy was not as central to the debates over the appointments as it was in the case of Bork. A number of other justices had been appointed by Republican presidents hostile to *Roe v. Wade*, including Justice Sandra Day O'Connor and Justice Kennedy (both appointed by President Reagan) and Justice David H. Souter (by the first President Bush).

There is no doubt that the new appointments to the Supreme Court led to a shift in the decisions of the Court with respect to abortion, allowing regulations of abortion services — for example, tests for fetal viability, upheld in *Webster v. Reproductive Health Services* (1989) — that the *Roe* Court regarded and would have regarded as unconstitutional. The question was whether the new appointees — who now constituted a majority on the Supreme Court — would exercise their power not just to uphold more regulations than the *Roe* Court would have but to overrule *Roe v. Wade* itself. Of the justices who had participated in the *Roe* decision, only one justice in the *Roe* majority, Harry Blackmun, remained and two other justices (now Chief Justice Rehnquist and Justice White) who had dissented in *Roe;* the rest of the justices on the *Webster* Court were Justices Stevens, O'Connor, Kennedy, Souter, Scalia, and Thomas.

In 1992, two decades after *Roe* had been decided, in *Planned Parenthood of Southeastern Pennsylvania v. Casey*, this new Court addressed a case in which many expected that *Roe* might be overruled, making possible not only much broader regulation of abortion services than the *Roe* Court was prepared to allow, but even its criminalization. The Pennsylvania statute at issue in *Planned Parenthood* involved five provisions of the Pennsylvania Abortion Control Act of 1982: (1) requirements that a woman seeking an abortion be provided with certain information at least twenty-four hours before the abortion and give informed consent; (2) a requirement that at least one parent give informed consent before a minor had an abortion, subject to a judicial by-pass procedure; (3) a command that a woman have notified her husband before an abortion; (4) various emergencies that suspended the requirements of 1–3; and (5) reporting requirements on facilities providing abortion services. The Court did allow somewhat broader regulation, upholding provisions 1 and 5, but followed earlier precedent in upholding 2 and disallowing 3. On the issue of criminalization, however, the Court reaffirmed five to four the central principle of *Roe v. Wade*, namely, that abortion could only be criminalized after viability.

On this point, two justices remained committed to *Roe* as the earlier Court had elaborated it, namely, Justices Blackmun and Stevens. These two joined three justices (O'Connor, Kennedy, and Souter), who reaffirmed the central principle of *Roe*, but also allowed somewhat more regulation aimed at encouraging birth over abortion. What is striking about the opinion of the three justices, which is the opinion for the Court, is the extent to which they worked within the framework of *Roe v. Wade* both on the issue of the underlying basic right and their conception of compelling state purposes (the health and life of the mother, and potential life of the fetus).

On the issue of the basic right, the three justices appealed to both the method and substance of the reasoning of Justice Harlan in *Poe v. Ullman*, but were clearly concerned to preserve what they perceived as the integrity and legitimacy of the inference and elaboration of the constitutional right to privacy in *Griswold* and its progeny: "We have no doubt as to the correctness of those decisions." Foreshadowing the later decisions that extended the right to privacy beyond sexual relations in marriage, the three justices characterized the basis of the right in much broader, normatively freighted terms:

> These matters, involving the most intimate and personal choices a person may make in a lifetime, choices central to personal dignity and autonomy, are central to the liberty protected by the Fourteenth Amendment. At the heart of liberty is the right to define one's own concept of existence, of meaning, of the universe, and of the mystery of human life. Beliefs about these matters could not define the attributes of personhood were they formed under compulsion of the State.

Both the language and the spirit here derive from the inalienable right to conscience as the basic right protected by both the religion clauses and free speech and press guarantees of the First Amendment, echoing Harlan's prescient observation in *Poe v. Ullman:* "The secular state is not an examiner of consciences." The choice whether to use contraceptives in sexual relations is in this way as intimately personal, about the meaning of love and relationship, as any choices persons make, indeed defining a person's sense of the enduring values in a well-lived human life. If that is the case with contraceptives (a choice open to men and women under *Griswold*), it is, the three justices argued, true as well of the role the choice of an abortion has in a woman's life:

> The mother who carries a child to full term is subject to anxieties, to physical constraints, to pain that only she must bear. That these sacrifices have from the beginning of the human race been endured by a woman with a pride that ennobles her in the eyes of others and gives to the infant a bond of love cannot alone be grounds for the State to insist she make the sacrifice. Her suffering is too intimate and personal for the State to insist, without more, upon its own vision of the woman's role, however dominant that vision has been in the course of our history and our culture. The destiny of the woman must be shaped to a large extent on her own conception of her spiritual imperatives and her place in society.

The appeal here was to the free exercise of one's own moral convictions in making a choice of this sort especially when that choice had been so unjustly burdened by the "dominant . . . vision" of a woman's destiny.

If the right to intimate life was thus normatively understood as deriving from the fundamental role of the right to conscience among constitutionally protected values, then any state burden on such a right must take the form of a compelling secular state purpose that is not itself a sectarian imposition inconsistent with basic values the Constitution protects. The three justices expressed "no doubt" that the prohibition of contraceptives in the modern world was such a sectarian imposition, and the question, of course, is whether the weight the state accords fetal life as a basis for criminalization of abortion was also such an imposition.

The three justices acknowledged the broad range of views on the weight to be accorded fetal life, and addressed the question of overruling *Roe* as one that would require them to find that the weight *Roe* accorded this interest was so clearly wrong, so unworkable and so incoherent in its principle and application, that it must be overruled. On the issue of workability, the three justices argued that *Roe* had proven workable, that is, it had given rise to legitimate reliance interests of women upon it, and was not out of line with other developing bodies of law. They contrasted the proposed overruling of *Roe* with the overturning of other highly controversial opinions of the Supreme Court, namely, *Lochner v. New York* and *Plessy v. Ferguson*; these cases were properly overruled because their underlying principles and their application were wrong when decided, as the Court later reasonably came to see. But the plurality regarded the inference and elaboration of the principle of constitutional privacy in *Griswold* and its progeny as wholly correct, and regarded the issue in question in *Roe* not as the legitimacy of its principle, as Ely and the originalists argued, but the way in which the Court struck the balance between the basic right and the compelling state purposes. Because this was so, overruling *Roe* might and would be regarded as illegitimate because the judiciary, in so acting, would not be interpreting and applying constitutional principles but acting politically. Although the three judges might have given different weight to compelling state purposes were *Roe* now coming before the Court as an original matter, they were not, at least on the issue of criminalization, prepared to say now that viability was the wrong constitutional line to draw, and thus they affirmed the central principle of *Roe*, that abortions may only be criminalized after viability.

However, working within the framework of Blackmun's opinion for the Court in *Roe*, the three justices accorded potential life greater weight than Blackmun (without reference to Blackmun's trimester system) on the issue of permissible state regulations, permitting those that, without placing an undue burden on a woman's right to an abortion, expressed a preference for childbirth over abortion. It is on this ground that the three justices, joined by the four dissenters who would have overruled *Roe* entirely, upheld some of the Pennsylvania regulations, but nonetheless joined with Blackmun and Stevens in striking down the spousal notification requirements because they unduly burdened a woman's right to an abortion.

In a later case dealing with a state prohibition on so-called partial birth abortions, *Stenberg v. Carhart* (2002), the three justices divided over whether potential life was sufficient to justify such a prohibition (Justices O'Connor and Souter joining the majority to strike the prohibition down, Justice Kennedy joining the four dissenters). In *Gonzales v. Carhart* (2007), after the retirement of Chief Justice Rehnquist (replaced by Chief Justice John G. Roberts) and of Justice O'Connor (replaced by Justice Samuel A. Alito), Justice Kennedy wrote for the Court, now giving effect to his view about potential life, in striking down a federal statute. Justice Kennedy's opinion accepted *Casey* on the issue of criminalization of abortion in general, and was joined on this point by Chief Justice Roberts and Justice Alito (Justice Thomas wrote separately for himself and Justice Scalia in questioning *Roe* and *Casey*). Justice Ruth Bader Ginsburg wrote a vigorous dissent for herself and Justices Stephen G. Breyer, Souter, and Stevens.

In *Casey*, both Justices Stevens and Blackmun wrote separate opinions, concurring with the opinion of the Court upholding the central holding of *Roe v. Wade*, but dissenting from its willingness to uphold at least some of the Pennsylvania regulations.

Four justices dissented – Chief Justice Rehnquist and Justices White, Scalia, and Thomas. Both Rehnquist and Scalia wrote separate dissents in which the other dissenters concurred. Chief Justice Rehnquist assumed the authority of *Griswold* and its progeny, but argued that, because of the weight of fetal life, *Roe* was distinguishable. The dissent of Justice Scalia was, as one would expect with an originalist, much more radical: there was no constitutional right of a woman to abortion services because "the Constitution says absolutely nothing about it." Scalia's dissent is of interest to our study of the background of *Lawrence v. Texas* because of his questioning of the coherence of the majority in view of the failure of any of justices who joined it even to mention *Bowers v. Hardwick*, in which the Court in 1986 declined to extend the constitutional right in question to the protection from criminalization of gay/lesbian sex acts. Certainly, such sex acts could be regarded equally as an expression or instance of the right to intimate life, yet they were, in Scalia's view, properly held criminal because, like abortion, "it is our unquestionable constitutional tradition that they are proscribable." Chief Justice Rehnquist had also cited *Bowers*, arguing that the same reasons applied to abortion that led Justice White, writing for the Court, to refuse to recognize a right to sodomy: "The Court is most vulnerable and comes nearest to illegitimacy when it deals with judge-made law having little or no cognizable roots in the language or design of the Constitution." Both of these dissents suggest that *Bowers* must be understood in the context of the ongoing interpretive debates over *Roe* that raged at the time of its decision, and that *Planned Parenthood of Southeastern Pennsylvania v. Casey* raised fundamental questions about whether, now that the central principle of *Roe* had been reaffirmed, *Bowers* could any longer be regarded as good law.

Bowers v. Hardwick

Background, Briefs, and Oral Arguments

A possible challenge to a state sodomy statute (in particular, Virginia's) was first discussed by a group of gay rights activists after an open forum with Supreme Court Justice William O. Douglas held at Staten Island College just after *Roe v. Wade*. Douglas opined during the forum that a sodomy challenge might succeed if the litigants could show that they were in real jeopardy of persecution under the law and that they lived otherwise impeccable lives. One of the members of the group was Bruce Voeller, who at that time was president of Gay Activists Alliance and would later become one of the cofounders of the National Gay Task Force. Voeller became one of the plaintiffs and was the main force behind the suit, initiating the suit to test Douglas's hypothesis. In 1975 the two plaintiffs in the case asserted that they regularly engaged in private, consensual conduct falling within the provisions of Virginia's statute. (One of the two, in fact, had previously been prosecuted under the statute.) They filed suit against Virginia local and state authorities, requesting an injunction against that state's law, which made oral and anal sex felonies. Relying on *Griswold*, the attorneys for the plaintiffs maintained that the Virginia law violated their right to privacy. The three-judge panel split two to one against the litigants. The federal court's majority opinion refused to extend the right of privacy to this situation, holding that *Griswold* only addressed the matter of privacy in a "marital situation." Furthermore, the majority ruled that the state's interests justified passing the legislation because homosexual conduct "is likely to end in a contribution to moral delinquency." The dissenting district court judge, Robert Merhige, Jr., saw no problem in extending the principle of *Griswold* to cover sex between consenting adults: "To say as the majority does, that the right of privacy, which every citizen has, is limited to matters of marital, home, or family life is unwarranted under the law." Merhige argued that the majority "misinterpreted the issue" by stressing morality and decency when it should more properly have focused on the constitutional right of privacy.

The plaintiffs appealed to the Supreme Court, but without comment, by a vote of six to three in *Doe v. Commonwealth's Attorney* (1976), the Court summarily upheld the two-person majority opinion of the federal district court. It is not surprising that, as early as 1975, the federal judiciary should have at least considered, albeit rejected, the argument that the constitutional right to privacy extended or should extend to gay/lesbian sex acts, or that the ruling against it was summarily affirmed by the Supreme Court in the next year. The Supreme Court had, after all, decided *Roe v. Wade* in 1973. If the Court was willing to give the underlying right so broad an interpretation and to regard the weight of fetal life as inadequate to justify criminalization, the privacy of gay/lesbian sex might on both counts seem, if anything, clearer.

The summary affirmation by the Supreme Court is subject to various interpretations. One of them is that the Court's view of the case may reflect its deference to state discretion in criminal matters, so long as it does not disfavor anyone in the categories forbidden by the Civil Rights Act of 1964. The act did not include sexual orientation, which may have limited the Court's sense of what it could do from a judicial standpoint. Another interpretation is that six justices of the Court agreed on the merits with the lower federal court (the Rule of 4 requires that at least four justices must agree to take jurisdiction), or, even if some justices did not agree, such justices preferred that such a case should come to them as a live case and controversy in which a state had actually sought a criminal conviction for sodomy against a putative defendant. All of these interpretations raise the question of the timing of constitutional arguments — why some are historically feasible when others are not (some would even argue that *Roe* was decided before it was historically feasible).

It was only after World War II that U.S. constitutional institutions became more responsive even to hearing arguments for gay rights. As we earlier saw (chapter 2), it was only after the judiciary more expansively protected free speech (narrowing obscenity laws) that gay rights arguments could be made without censorship by the state, and this new freedom undoubtedly energized, in the wake of the successes of the feminist movement with contraception and abortion, gay voices arguing for comparable recognition of their rights. Such voices had been encouraged as well by the decision of the Model Penal Code in 1955 to recommend decriminalization of consensual sex acts in private, the comparable recommendation of the Wolfenden Report in Great Britain in 1957 (leading to decriminalization in 1967), and the decriminalization of such acts by Illinois in 1961. Illinois remained alone in its stance until 1971, when both the Model Penal Code and the emergence of gay activism at Stonewall in 1969 led Connecticut to become the second state in the nation to erase sodomy statutes from its books. Within three years, five additional states followed the path of Illinois and Connecticut: Colorado (1972), Oregon (1972), Delaware (1973), Hawaii (1973), and Ohio (1974). By 1979, Stonewall's tenth anniversary, twenty-one states had invalidated their sodomy laws. By 1983, the number of states with operational sodomy laws had dropped from forty-nine to twenty-four. Thus by the time *Bowers* was decided in 1986, twenty-six states had removed sodomy laws from their criminal codes.

Bowers v. Hardwick must be discussed, analyzed, and criticized in its historical context. We begin with background issues, and then turn to its facts, the briefs by the State of Georgia and the briefs for the defendant, Hardwick, and then turn to the amici briefs and the oral argument.

As we have now discussed at some length (chapter 2), in the post–World War II period, under the influence of various protest movements, the U.S. Supreme Court had interpreted basic constitutional principles, including guarantees of human rights as well as equal protection of laws, to support the claims of justice of religious minorities, people of color, and women. There was, I have argued, a connection of deeper principle between two such developments: those striking down the use of racial/ethnic and gender stereotypes that reflected the history of cultural dehumanization I have called moral slavery, and those extending basic human rights on fair terms to groups afflicted by that history. The connection is this: the evil of moral slavery is to dehumanize a whole class of persons from their status as full bearers of basic human rights (such as conscience, speech, intimate life, and work). That evil has two dimensions: the unjust ground (moral slavery) on which persons have not been accorded their basic rights, and the abridgment of their basic rights on such inadequate grounds. These two dimensions are mirror images of one another. The growing con-

{ *Chapter 4* }

stitutional concern for this evil in the post–World War II period accordingly takes two forms: the striking down as unconstitutional of certain grounds for laws or policies (suspect classification analysis under the Fourteenth Amendment) and the corresponding protection of basic human rights that had been unjustly denied on such grounds. It was on such grounds that the Supreme Court had struck down laws reflecting unjust racial/ethnic stereotypes, and had also struck down laws that abridged the basic right of intimate life (for example, the antimiscegenation cases). Similarly, the Court's growing skepticism about gender discrimination as suspect for the same reasons as race/ethnicity was reflected as well in its recognition of various basic rights of women, prominent among which was the right to intimate life reflected in the constitutional privacy cases.

For reasons earlier discussed, the gay/lesbian protest movement, at least in the United States, came relatively late in these historical developments. Although there had been a long history of protest by people of color and women in the United States (dating back at least to antebellum radical abolitionism and suffragism), the voice of gay protest, though given brilliant expression in the poetry and prose of Walt Whitman, had been repressed and marginalized until the developments of robust judicial protection of free conscience and speech in the post–World War II period. The United States was, for this reason, much more culturally homophobic than Britain and many European nations, several of which had decriminalized gay/lesbian sex long before *Bowers* in 1986 or *Lawrence* in 2003 — France and the Netherlands as early as 1810, Belgium in 1867, Italy in 1889, Spain in 1932, the Scandinavian countries between 1930 and 1970, Britain in 1967, and Germany in 1968–1969. Indeed, five years before *Bowers*, the European Court of Human Rights in *Dudgeon v. United Kingdom* held that laws proscribing gay/lesbian sex acts were invalid under the European Convention on Human Rights, a decision authoritative in all countries that are members of the Council of Europe (twenty-one nations then, forty-five nations now). Nonetheless, despite U.S. cultural homophobia, it was clear to gays and lesbians by 1974 that they could reasonably build on constitutional developments in other countries, and that their protesting voices had a just place in the constitutional principles Americans now, under the leadership of the Supreme Court, had come to regard as basic. That is to say, by this time in U.S. constitutional history, the arguments of liberal political philosophy that had led many ethically to question traditional homophobic moralism had now been recognized as underlying the best interpretation of basic constitutional rights such as conscience, speech, and intimate life and associated guarantees of equal protection of laws. It was now a question of showing by reasonable arguments that gays and lesbians must, on grounds of principle, be accorded just recognition in terms of these rights and guarantees, which are the birthright of all Americans.

It was clear to many lawyers and activists that the starting point for their arguments for such recognition must be the constitutional right that more than any other was denied to gays and lesbians, the right to be free of criminal sanctions directed at the sexual lives of consensual adult gay men and lesbians. There was reason to believe that such arguments, appealing to already judicially accepted principles of constitutional privacy and equal protection, might be given a just hearing by a judiciary committed to arguments of principle as the ground for the legitimacy of its powers of judicial review in the United States. For example, the highest court of New York, the New York State Court of Appeals, had accepted in 1980 in *People v. Onofre* arguments that the right to privacy protected by the New York Constitution rendered unconstitutional New York's sodomy statute. If respected state courts had accepted such arguments, why not the Supreme Court?

The problem was that when in 1982 Michael Hardwick filed a challenge to Georgia's sodomy statute, the first period of rapid sodomy reform was drawing to a close, perhaps under the initial stigma of AIDS, even as *Bowers* was starting its litigation journey. Of the twelve states considering the Model Penal Code in the years from 1984 through 1991, not a single one repealed its sodomy statute. Indeed, a spate of bills attempted unsuccessfully to recriminalize sodomy; there was backsliding as the Fifth Circuit reinstated Texas's sodomy law (a federal district court had earlier held it unconstitutional). This repression stands in stark contrast to the period from 1971 to 1983, when nearly two-thirds of the states considering the Model Penal Code repealed their sodomy statutes. Legislative repeal, in fact, tapered off after 1980. The only state to repeal its sodomy statute in the 1980s was Wisconsin, which did so in 1983.

In addition, by the time the issue was posed to the U.S. Supreme Court in *Bowers v. Hardwick*, there had been increasingly politicized criticism of the Supreme Court's application of the constitutional right to privacy to abortion services in *Roe v. Wade* in 1973, which was manifested in the increasingly conservative appointment of judges to the Supreme Court, who might overrule *Roe*. Although a majority of the Supreme Court still supported the principle of *Roe* at the time *Bowers* came before the justices, it was not clear, with new judicial appointments, that this majority would last for long; and clearly the criticism of *Roe* had an impact on members of the Court when they considered *Bowers*. It was perhaps the likelihood of such appointments that may explain why, as a matter of strategy, litigators on behalf of gay rights chose to make their case at the time they did.

Even if we accept the legitimacy and application of the right to constitutional privacy as a wholly valid development within U.S. constitutional law, as the Supreme Court now clearly does, there were reasonable questions raised about the way in which the Court in *Roe* struck the balance between its identification of a basic constitutional right and the compelling state purposes that might justify the abridgment of such a basic right. Why, if fetal life is accorded weight as potential life, should the operative line be drawn at viability as opposed to a range of other points at which the fetus develops moral relevant features, for example, sentience or brain activity? Why not draw the line (which determines when criminalization will and will not be constitutional), if not earlier, then later? Ultimately, three justices of the Supreme Court, all appointed by Republican presidents who claimed to be prolife, decided not to restrike the balance struck by the Court in *Roe*, reaffirming the core principle of that opinion that abortion could not be criminalized before viability, but allowing more regulation before that point than the *Roe* Court allowed. But these issues were still open at the time *Bowers* came to the Supreme Court, and undoubtedly made the case interpretively more difficult for prochoice justices (notably, as we shall see, Justice Lewis Powell) than it should have been.

The facts of *Bowers v. Hardwick* were also appealing to advocates litigating gay rights, as a state criminal statute apparently had been enforced (on this point, see discussion below) and the enforcement targeted acts taking place in the home, an area that a number of constitutional provisions protected (the case did not involve a public bathroom, for example). The Georgia criminal statute was an act-defined statute, applying by its terms to sexual acts of sodomy defined as when a person "performs or submits to any sexual act involving the sex organs of one person and the mouth or anus of another," subject, upon conviction, to a term of imprisonment of not more than twenty years. Georgia prohibited any but the missionary position in sexual conduct, and also criminalized adultery (Michael Bowers, then Georgia attorney general, had conducted an adulterous relationship with a secretary for years, including at the time of *Bowers v. Hardwick*). In August 1982, Michael Hardwick, then a twenty-eight-year-old gay man living in Atlanta, was issued a citation for carrying a beer from a bar and drinking it in public. Hardwick paid a fine, but because he failed to appear in court, he was confronted one night in his apartment by a police officer with a warrant for his arrest. A guest had let the police officer into the apartment, where Hardwick and a male companion were engaging in oral sex. The officer observed the sex act and proceeded to arrest Hardwick under the Georgia sodomy statute that had been passed in 1968. After a preliminary hearing, the district attorney decided not to present the case to the grand jury. Hardwick, however, accepted the offer of the American Civil Liberties Union (ACLU) to represent him in challenging the constitutionality of the Georgia statute. Hardwick then brought suit in federal district court challenging the constitutionality of the Georgia statute insofar as it criminalized consensual sodomy between adults. Although the district court dismissed the suit for failure to state a claim on the basis of the ruling in *Doe v. Commonwealth's Attorney*, the Court of Appeals for the Eleventh Circuit reversed and remanded, holding that the Georgia statute violated the respondent's constitutional rights.

The level of Georgia's enforcement of its sodomy statute was, on the facts of *Bowers*, not entirely clear. On the one hand, Hardwick had been arrested by a police officer for consensual sex acts in his home. On the other, the district attorney decided not to seek an indictment, which raised a number of questions about Georgia's policy in enforcing its antisodomy statute. Did the district attorney's decision reflect the fact that grand juries routinely refused to indict for this offense? Did the state attorney general routinely decline to prosecute? Was the statute a dead letter — still on the book, but never enforced? Georgia had at this time laws prescribing missionary position sex and punishing adult sex out of wedlock, but never prosecuted these. Did the attorney general think the statute was unenforceable? Unfair? Unconstitutional under the Georgia Constitution? Questions along these lines were understandably raised by Supreme Court justices during the oral argument. One thing was clear: Georgia chose to argue that the statute was itself constitutional as applied to a defendant like Bowers, though not, as it conceded in oral argument, to married couples.

Because the decision by the Eleventh Circuit Court had been favorable to gay rights, liberals on the Supreme Court like Justices Brennan, Marshall, Stevens, and Blackmun were not inclined to grant cert, and Powell's instinct as well was to duck the case. Initially, only Justices White and Rehnquist—long hostile to *Roe v. Wade*—wanted to take the case, clearly to refute any expansion of the scope of the right to privacy. White refused to drop the matter. He circulated a written dissent to the denial of cert, which Rehnquist immediately joined. Surprisingly, Justice Brennan added his name, perhaps because he calculated that a majority of five votes for Hardwick were possible or not improbable. When the justices took a second vote on whether to grant cert, Marshall joined, providing the necessary fourth vote to grant cert. Blackmun at this point urged Brennan to reconsider, as he was concerned not only that a majority would not extend the right to privacy to gay/lesbian sex, but might undermine the authority of *Roe v. Wade*. Brennan did not.

The brief of petitioner Michael J. Bowers argued that the lower court failed to give proper weight to the Supreme Court's summary affirmation of *Doe v. Commonwealth's Attorney*, which had upheld the constitutionality of Virginia's sodomy statute, and that there had been no significant doctrinal developments since *Doe* that undermined its authority. On the merits, the brief did not question the existence of a right of personal privacy under the Constitution, but it did question whether there was any good basis for extending the right to homosexual sodomy largely because history and tradition ran so strongly against recognition of such a right. Whereas the other cases protecting the privacy right were rooted in the traditional values of family life, homosexual sodomy was not so rooted; and, in contrast to *Stanley v. Georgia* (which recognized a right to use obscene materials in the privacy of one's home), "homosexual sodomy as an act of sexual deviancy expresses no ideas. It is purely an unnatural means of satisfying an unnatural lust, which has been declared by Georgia to be morally wrong." The brief also argued that gay sex often took place in public places and was not limited to the home, and mentioned that "the legislature should be permitted to draw conclusions concerning the relationship of homosexual sodomy in the transmission of Acquired Immune Deficiency Syndrome (AIDS) and other diseases."

The brief for the respondent was coauthored, among others, by Professor Laurence Tribe of the Harvard Law School (who orally argued the case) and Professor Kathleen Sullivan, then of Harvard Law School, later Dean of Stanford Law School. The brief defined the issue narrowly in terms of the unconstitutionality of the criminalization of same-sex adult consensual relations in the home, and argued that the Court's elaboration of the constitutional right to privacy over time rested on the flexible interpretation of our history in light of our basic values, and that sexual intimacy between unmarried couples for purposes other than procreation had been recognized as one of those values, as the cases dealing with contraception clearly show. A law like that of Georgia that criminalized sexual intimacy could only be justified if supported by a compelling secular state interest, which the Georgia statute lacked. The brief conceded such interests did exist, including "protecting public sensibilities, . . . protecting vulnerable persons such as minors from possible coercion, . . . restricting commercial trade in activities offensive to public decency," but none applied to the facts of this case. The brief concluded with a discussion of laws that would be constitutional under its analysis including "criminal laws banning public indecency, prostitution, pimping, and pandering" (protecting society's public places and commercial exchanges), laws "protecting unconsenting citizens — including children — from sexual force or coercion," and "criminal laws against adultery or polygamy" (protecting monogamous marriage). As for the threat of AIDS, the brief argued this question was not apposite when the issue was the appropriate standard of review, but should be decided on remand in terms of scientific evidence. The brief suggested, however, that this is "a possible post hoc rationalization for a law Georgia has until now sought to defend solely as the morals measure it was when it was first enacted. If so, it would then be incumbent on the State to explain how a threat of criminal prosecution could serve as an effective public health measure, rather than driving underground the very information that medical authorities need most, by fostering fear that a visit to a doctor will mean prison for the patient."

{ *Chapter 4* }

The reply brief of the petitioner observed that the respondent brief "rejects the historical approach to identifying fundamental rights." A historical analysis was what the Court had previously used in recognizing such rights, and it was because the analysis did not support recognition of a right of homosexual sodomy that it should not be recognized in the current case. The brief concluded: "Without history, the line drawn by the Court's previous privacy decisions might be difficult to comprehend and Respondent's difficulties may stem from his having left history outside the door." Citing Justice Harlan's narrow reading of the right to privacy in *Poe v. Ullman,* the brief argued that, if the respondent prevailed, the same analysis would extend to "polygamy, homosexual marriage, fornication, adultery, and some cases of incest."

There were three amicus briefs in support of the petitioner, from the Rutherford Institute et al., David Robinson, Jr., and the Catholic League for Religious and Civil Rights. The brief of the Rutherford Institute was almost entirely historical, arguing that because gay/lesbian sex had always historically been condemned, it should not be constitutionally protected. Robinson of the George Washington Law School focused almost entirely on health risks — epidemiological concerns, evidenced by the AIDS tragedy, were inconsistent with recognition of a constitutional right to privacy. And the brief of the Catholic League argued that a reasoned analysis of the Court's precedents compelled reaffirmation of *Doe.*

Amicus briefs for respondent included, among amici curiae, the American Psychological Association and American Public Health Association, the National Organization for Women, the Presbyterian Church (U.S.A.) and other religious groups, the Lambda Legal Defense and Education Fund et al., the Association of the Bar of the City of New York, the Lesbian Rights Project et al., the American Jewish Congress, and the National Gay Rights Advocates et al. The range of perspectives of these briefs is notable, including two religious groups, several gay/lesbian groups, the leading feminist organization (NOW), and a bar association. None of them, however, critically addressed the historical questions the brief for the petitioner and the supporting Rutherford Institute amicus brief so prominently emphasized. One of them, that of the American Psychological and American Public Health Association, turned from history to contemporary science, in particular, the reasonable consensus among scientific professionals about the origins and incidence of sexual orientation, the repudiation of the disease model of homosexuality, and the importance of sexual intimacy to the lives and happiness of gays and lesbians. Perhaps the most important evidence it discussed was that bearing on health risks, questioning the scientific basis of the claim of the petitioner's brief and the amicus brief of David Robinson that the Georgia statute could be reasonably based on the health risk of AIDS transmission because such criminal statutes made candor with physicians and researchers more difficult, detrimentally affected research efforts, and interfered with educational efforts designed to encourage safe-sex practices.

Senior Assistant Attorney General of Georgia Michael E. Hobbs orally presented the case for Attorney General Bowers before the Supreme Court. Under questioning, Hobbs offered no explanation as to why an indictment had not been brought. Justice Powell pressed Hobbs on whether the statute was criminally enforced in Georgia in general and, in particular, on married couples. Hobbs responded that the statute had been enforced against consenting adult homosexuals for sex in the home (recalling such prosecutions "back in the 1930s or 40s"), but he knew of no such prosecution of a married couple. Pressed by Justice Powell, Hobbs argued that the statute would be unconstitutional as applied to a married couple because of *Griswold v. Connecticut*. On further questioning, Hobbs emphasized that, in contrast to other cases extending the right to privacy to families related by blood, there was no link in this case to this historical tradition, and expressed ignorance as to why Georgia had not further prosecuted this case. Hobbs concluded that striking down the Georgia statute would undercut "the legitimacy of statutes which prohibited polygamy, homosexual, same-sex marriage, . . .incest, prostitution, fornication, adultery, and possibly even personal possession in private of illegal drugs."

Professor Laurence Tribe of the Harvard Law School argued the case for Michael Hardwick. Justice Powell immediately challenged Tribe to articulate the limiting principles of his argument, distinguishing this case from "bigamy involving private homes or incest or prostitution." Tribe responded that there were two limiting principles: where the acts took place (in the home) and sexual acts "of a kind that are not demonstrably physically harmful that are consensual and noncommercial in the home." When further challenged by Chief Justice Burger on the issue of incest, Tribe appealed to genetic harms and to the question of consent in such relationships, including, among questionable forms of consent, sex between a parent and adult child. In response to a comparable challenge from Justice Rehnquist about criminal prohibitions of polygamy and cohabitation with one person already married, Tribe responded that state interests (protecting existing relationships) would justify such statutes. In response to a query from Justice O'Connor, Tribe argued for a higher standard of review when harmless sex acts took place in the home. To a continuing query from Justice Powell about the extent of protection Tribe proposed, Tribe denied his analysis would apply to a public toilet, but it might to a hotel room. Justice Stevens pressed Tribe about his second limiting principle: if Tribe was willing to allow the protection of state-sanctioned relationships as a legitimate state purpose, why couldn't this purpose justify criminalizing extramarital relationships between men or women in order thus to foster marriage (fornication laws)? Tribe's response was that strict or substantially heightened scrutiny of such laws would be called for and that they would be dubious under this test. Tribe at this point cited various cases, including those dealing with gender, in which the Court had not slavishly followed history, and cited even Harlan's dissenting opinion in *Poe v. Ullman* as consistent with this evolutionary view of legal development. Justice Rehnquist queried that if states were in fact decriminalizing sodomy, why not trust this issue to democracy? Tribe responded that if a basic right was indeed at stake, the Court had never ceded its protection to democracy. Tribe also acknowledged that Harlan in *Poe* had expressly disavowed the application of constitutional privacy to homosexuality, but argued that Harlan's interpretive approach was consistent with, in contemporary circumstances, extending such a right to gays and lesbians on the concrete facts of the case before the Court, as a state criminal statute threatened them with a twenty-year prison sentence for their sexual lives at home. On questioning, Tribe conceded to Rehnquist that his argument about the sodomy statute was limited to the home. Justice White then asked several questions about the textual and methodological basis for inferring a constitutional right to consensual sodomy, and Tribe responded that it was the right under-lying *Griswold* and *Roe* and other cases and protected by the Third, Fourth, and Ninth Amendments. Both Justices White and Powell queried Tribe about the implications of their opinions in *Moore v. City of East Cleveland* (Powell had defended extending the privacy right to an extended family, but White had questioned the extension), to which Tribe responded that Powell's view was more favorable to his current case than White's. In conclusion, Chief Justice Burger cited two pur-poses for the statute: protecting traditional marriage and avoiding health risks. Tribe responded that, if the issue were homosexual mar-riage, there would be a close connection between that issue and the first purpose, but the current statute was much too sweeping. With respect to health risks, in response to a question on this point by Jus-tice O'Connor, Tribe cited the brief of the American Public Health Association as to the irrationality of such an argument.

Michael Hobbs, in his rebuttal argument, emphasized that Geor-gia conceded "it cannot invade the privacy of the home and regulate each intimate activity which takes place there," but nonetheless argued that the Georgia statute, as applied to gay/lesbian sex acts, had "the legitimate purpose of maintaining a decent and moral society." The Constitution protected "ordered liberty," not "licentiousness."

To summarize, *Bowers v. Hardwick* came before the Supreme Court after twenty-six states had decriminalized sodomy. There was, however, on and off the Supreme Court growing hostility to the application of the right to privacy to abortion services in *Roe v. Wade*, and these debates influenced at least two justices who shared this hostility (namely, White and Rehnquist), to want to take the case to limit the authority of *Roe*. More liberal justices such as Brennan and Marshall agreed to take the case perhaps because they believed a decision of five justices favorable to Hardwick was within sight. The crucial swing justice on the Court was Justice Powell, and both the briefs and oral arguments engaged with the question of whether the expansion of privacy to gay/lesbian sex could be both principled and limited, not undermining the legitimacy of other criminal laws forbidding forms of consensual adult sex (for example, bigamy, adultery, incest, prostitution, etc.).

Bowers v. Hardwick

The Debate among the Justices, Justice Powell's Shift, and the Opinions of the Court

It had always been clear to Laurence Tribe that the justice whom he needed most to persuade was Justice Lewis Powell, a strong supporter of *Roe v. Wade* who might on that basis be reasonably responsive to an argument of principle that the constitutional right to privacy should be extended to consensual adult sex acts of gays and lesbians in their homes. Of the other justices, four were likely in favor of such an extension (Justices Blackmun, Brennan, Marshall, and Stevens); in fact, Justice Marshall regarded the matter as quite clear, reminiscing to his clerks about the role of Bayard Rustin, a gay man in the civil rights movement who worked with Martin Luther King, Jr., to orchestrate the 1963 march on Washington. Four other justices were likely opposed (Chief Justice Burger and Justices O'Connor, Rehnquist, and White). Powell would be, Tribe believed, a swing vote, as he was without a settled view either way but open to reasonable argument. It is unsurprising, from this perspective, that so much of Tribe's oral argument centered on extended colloquies with Justice Powell.

Tribe could not have known that Powell's law clerk, Michael Mosman, a Mormon, had submitted to Powell on the Saturday before the *Hardwick* oral argument a twelve-page bench memorandum that argued against the extension of constitutional privacy to gay/lesbian sex. Mosman's memo did not communicate how much he was personally upset by *Roe v. Wade*, a decision Justice Powell supported. He argued that if the Court ruled in favor of Hardwick, it might be opening the doors to unchecked sexual freedom, including prostitution, because "no limiting principle comes to mind." Reading Mosman's memo, Powell wrote "no limiting principle," a phrase that haunted him.

Powell responded to Mosman in a memorandum dated March 31,

1986 — the day of oral argument in *Bowers v. Hardwick* — but more likely dictated on Saturday March 29. The memo reveals the state of Powell's thinking, in particular, how much he bridled at the suggestion in Tribe's brief that the right that Tribe argued should protect gay/lesbian sex had anything to do with the values Powell associated with home life:

> This case, that we should not have taken [Powell began], involves the validity of the Georgia statute that makes sodomy a misdemeanor. The facts are straightforward (if one can use that term in this case!). . . . (Possibly the crime is a felony of some level.)
>
> . . . Professor Tribe, with his usual overblown rhetoric, does focus his claim in the narrowest possible language: "Whether the state of Georgia may send its police into private bedrooms to arrest adults for engaging in consensual, noncommercial sexual acts, with no justification beyond the assertion that those acts are immoral . . ."
>
> In view of my age, general background, and convictions as to what is best for society, I think a good deal can be said for the validity of statutes that criminalize sodomy. If it becomes sufficiently widespread, civilization itself will be severely weakened as the perpetuation of the human race depends on normal sexual relations just as is true in the animal world.
>
> Despite the foregoing, if I were in the state legislature I would vote to decriminalize sodomy. It is widely prevalent in some places (e.g., San Francisco), and is a criminal statute that is almost never enforced. Moreover, police have more important responsibilities than snooping around trying to catch people in the act of sodomy . . .
>
> As the briefs all recognize, there is nothing explicit in the Constitution on this subject. Yet, this Court has frequently recognized that there are human rights that can be derived from the concept of liberty in the Fourteenth Amendment. The most dramatic example is Roe v. Wade. . . . One of the best discussions of this subject that I am familiar with is Justice Harlan's dissent in Poe v. Ullman. . . . He explicitly refers to homosexuality as not within the right of privacy that he found to exist with respect to the use of contraceptives. . . .
>
> It is clear that, as in Roe v. Wade, the issue here is whether there

is a substantive due process right—within the meaning of liberty and privacy—to engage in private, consensual sodomy. At present, I think substantial argument can be made on both sides of the question. The weight of modern thinking at least supports decriminalization.

It is tempting to accept the very narrow argument made by Professor Tribe. Apart from other considerations, it is impossible in any realistic sense to detect and later convict adult citizens who engage consensually in homosexual conduct in a truly private setting—e.g., what fairly may be called home. "Home" is one of the most beautiful words in the English language. It usually connotes family, husband and wife, and children—although, of course, single persons, widows and widowers, and others also have genuine homes.

A problem would be to identify some limiting principle if we are inclined to agree with the court of appeals and Professor Tribe. A number of examples come to mind: would the term "home" embrace a hotel room, a mobile trailer (yes, I think), a private room maybe available in a house of prostitution or even in a public bar, the "sanctity" of a toilet in a public restroom?

And if sodomy is to be decriminalized on constitutional grounds, what about incest, bigamy, and adultery. Incidentally, is there a Supreme Court decision holding that bigamy is unconstitutional? It is not easy for me to see why a husband in the privacy of two homes should not lawfully have two wives if liberty and privacy derived from the Fourteenth Amendment require invalidation of antisodomy laws. . . .

As you can see, Mike, I am not talking very much like a lawyer. . . . Both parties rely on my decision in Moore v. City of East Cleveland [striking down a zoning ordinance that barred a woman from living with two grandsons because they were not brothers]. If that case is relevant to any extent, it would support reversal.

In sum, Mike, I am sorry you had to be burdened with this case. . . .

LFP, JR.

Powell's memo to his clerk reveals his thinking before the oral argument. At the oral argument, Powell took notes, rating Hobbs a "good lawyer." His summary of Hobbs's argument concluded: "No limiting principle."

Powell's papers contain an undated note that appears to be Powell's handwritten crib sheet of questions he wanted answered at oral argument:

> limiting principle
> Fundamental right??
> Incest?
> Prostitution?
> Adultery
> In a hotel room
> (privacy of home)
> In an automobile
> In a toilet

Powell placed a bracket around the four listed sex crimes and drew an arrow from them to the question that was uppermost in his mind, "limiting principle." Powell was struggling to find a way to rule narrowly against Georgia's sodomy law.

Tribe's oral argument failed to impress Powell. Atop his notes on Tribe's argument, Powell wrote: "Tribe . . . (torrent of words!)". Tribe had no idea of Powell's horrified reaction to his use of "home" in his written brief. In fact, he thought the argument "might . . . have tentatively . . . moved someone like Powell just a bit."

Between the time Justice Powell returned to his chambers on March 31 and the court's conference vote two days later, there were a number of memos as Powell sought to find an acceptable way of invalidating Georgia's antisodomy law. Surprisingly, in view of his reaction to "home" in Tribe's brief, Powell raised the possibility with Mosman that the Constitution might protect homosexual relationships that resemble marriage — stable, monogamous relationships of members of the same sex. Mosman warned Powell that such an approach would erode the traditional limitation of marriage to heterosexuals, and would make it very difficult for states not to recognize such relationships as marriages, or the right to adopt and raise children, or to forbid homosexuals to be public school teachers. Mosman's memo pulled Powell away from recognizing a constitutional privacy argument: "I think Mike is

{ *Chapter 5* }

right. I'll forget this possible rationale." Instead, Powell found "considerable logic" in using the Eighth Amendment's ban on "cruel and unusual punishment." The theory of this approach was that if Hardwick was powerless to change his sexual orientation, it was wrong to punish him for acting on it. Powell could rely, Mosman suggested, on the Court's 1962 *Robinson v. Powell* and 1968 *Powell v. Texas* decisions.

When the justices gathered alone in their conference room on Wednesday, April 2, 1986, Chief Justice Burger neutrally summarized *Bowers*, then strongly pushed for reversal. There was no fundamental right to engage in sodomy, an activity that had been criminalized "for centuries," Burger argued. A privacy decision in favor of Hardwick would undermine laws against incest and prostitution.

Brennan spoke next and sided, as expected, with Hardwick.

White said he agreed with Burger, and wanted to reverse.

Marshall agreed with Brennan, arguing the case was controlled by *Stanley v. Georgia* (which constitutionally protected the use of obscene materials in the privacy of one's home).

Blackmun then praised Judge Johnson's ruling in favor of Hardwick, stressing that it was limited to the home. He agreed that *Stanley* controlled, and also found relevant the 1967 *Loving* decision, which struck down laws against interracial marriage.

Having found a way to avoid his worries about a "limiting principle" for the right of constitutional privacy, Powell voted to affirm. Powell said it would be cruel and unusual punishment to imprison someone like Hardwick for "private conduct based on a natural sexual urge and with a consenting partner." Powell also remarked to his colleagues that he had never known a homosexual. Blackmun responded: "But surely, Lewis, you were approached as a boy?" Blackmun said nothing else at the conference, but later told his clerks that he considered saying: "Of course you have. You've even had gay clerks." In fact, one of Powell's four clerks, Cabell Chinnis, was a gay man who lived with a lover, but had not come out to Powell as gay. Chinnis had been quite concerned about how Powell would vote in this case, had argued to him that the statute was unconstitutional, and had talked with his lover about coming out to Powell if he were going to vote for reversing the court of appeals. Chinnis, knowing that Powell would vote in conference for affirming the lower court decision, decided not to rock the boat.

Rehnquist voted against Hardwick.

Stevens cast the crucial fifth vote for affirming. He signaled he might agree with Powell's "cruel and unusual punishment" approach.

O'Connor, voting last, stated the right to privacy was not unlimited and Georgia's law was not unconstitutional.

As senior justice in the majority, Brennan assigned Blackmun to write the decision affirming that Georgia had infringed on Michael Hardwick's fundamental rights. When word of the preliminary vote reached Cabell Chinnis, he "declared victory."

Powell's vote was, however, not secure. His clerk Mike Mosman continued to argue for reversal. More importantly, the day after the conference, Chief Justice Burger personally delivered a letter urging Powell to provide the crucial fifth vote for reversal:

Dear Lewis:

I have some further thoughts on your suggestion at conference that Hardwick cannot be punished because of his "status" as a homosexual. . . .

You will remember my "degree" in psychiatry, which led me to be very skeptical about that breed of M.D.'s. [Burger, whose "degree" was earned writing an opinion on psychiatric testimony, was leery of having "the shifting sands of scientific opinion" influence courts.] I have never heard of any responsible member . . . of the A.P.A. [American Psychiatric Association] who recognized homosexuality as an "addiction" in the sense of drug addiction. It is simply without any basis in medicine, science, or common sense. In fact these homosexuals themselves proclaim this is a matter of sexual "preference." Moreover, even if homosexuality is somehow conditioned, the decision to commit an act of sodomy is a choice—pure and simple—maybe not so pure!

. . . The Fourteenth Amendment argument goes too far because there is no limiting principle that would allow the states to criminalize incest, prostitution, or any other "consensual" sexual activity. Moreover, it would forbid the states from adopting any sort of policy that would exclude homosexuals from classrooms or state-sponsored boys' clubs and Boy Scout adult leadership.

The Eighth Amendment argument . . . creates a potentially greater mischief. . . . Surely homosexuals are not "sex crazed" automatons who are "compelled" by their "status" to gratify their sexual appetites only by committing sodomy. Heterosexuals, after all, manage to live in a society where sexual activities are often proscribed except within the bonds of marriage.

The record simply does not remotely support a conclusion that sodomy is compulsive. . . . It is extremely unlikely that what Western Civilization has for centuries viewed as a volitional, reprehensible act is, in reality, merely a conditioned response to which moral blame may not attach. Are those with an "orientation" towards rape to be left off merely because they allege that the act of rape is "irresistible" to them? Are we to excuse every "Jack the Ripper?"

Hardwick merely wishes to seek his own form of sexual gratification. Undoubtedly there are also those in society who wish to see gratification through incest, drug use, gambling, exhibitionism, prostitution, rape, and what not. . . . As Justice [Oliver Wendell] Holmes put it, "pretty much all law consists in forbidding men to do something that they want to do." . . .

April 13, an unlucky day, will mark my 30th year on the bench. This case presents for me the most far-reaching issue of those 30 years. I hope you will excuse the energy with which I have stated my views, and I hope you will give them earnest consideration.

Powell wrote "Incredible statement!" by the chief justice's assessment that *Bowers* raised the "most far-reaching issue" of his career. Powell later wrote atop Burger's letter: "There is both sense and nonsense in this letter — mostly the latter." But Powell's notes after reading Burger's missive are telling, showing that Powell was reconsidering his vote:

I sought a "middle ground" to avoid a court holding that would be w/o [without] a limiting principle. I would not agree that every person has a fundamental right to engage in sodomy any time, any place. There are men who can gratify their sexual desire only with another man. [In the margin, Powell wrote, "Mike—Any medical or other support for this?"] Given this fact, I find it difficult to lawfully imprison such a person who confines his abnormality to a private setting with a consenting homo. No one is adversely affected by such conduct.

Incest is different because of genetic consequences. Rape obviously is different.

Possibly I could remand [send the case back to a lower court] to determine whether Hardwick suffers from this abnormality.

Powell decided to change his vote, firing off a memo announcing that he was switching his vote to reverse. He explained: "I did not agree that there is a substantive due process right to engage in conduct that for centuries has been recognized as deviant, and not in the best interest of preserving humanity." He still thought that imprisonment for homosexual sodomy would be cruel and unusual punishment. However, since the question argued centered on due process privacy rights — not his Eighth Amendment scheme — "further study" had led him to

conclude that my "bottom line" would be to reverse rather than affirm. The only question presented by the parties is the substantive due process issue, and—as several of you noted at Conference—my Eighth Amendment view was not addressed by the court below or by the parties.

In sum, my more carefully considered view is that I will vote to reverse but will write separately to explain my view of this case generally. I will not know, until I see the writing, whether I can join an opinion finding no substantive right or simply join the judgment.

Gay clerk Cabell Chinnis was heartsick.

Suddenly in the majority, Chief Justice Burger assigned Byron White to write the Court's *Bowers* opinion, in which Chief Justice Burger and Justices Powell, Rehnquist, and O'Connor concurred. Chief Justice Burger and Justice Powell filed as well concurring opinions. Justice Blackmun filed a dissenting opinion, in which Justices Brennan, Marshall, and Stevens concurred. Justice Stevens also filed a dissenting opinion, in which Justices Brennan and Marshall joined.

The opinion for the Court of Justice White certainly suggests a general skepticism about the constitutional right to privacy, rooted in his dissent in *Roe v. Wade* and perhaps in the worries about *Roe* suggested by liberal constitutionalists such as John Hart Ely and others. This skepticism is shown by the fact that White's arguments apply more plausibly to constitutional privacy generally, rather than only to the expansion of the constitutional right to privacy to gay/lesbian sex. White was not, however, in a position to overrule the entire line of constitutional privacy cases, so he made his critical point rather unreasonably by postulating "We think it evident that none of the rights announced in those cases bears any resemblance to the claimed right of homosexuals to engage in acts of sodomy that is asserted in this case." Nothing could be less evident, as at least two of the leading constitutional privacy cases, *Griswold v. Connecticut* and *Roe v. Wade*, rested on a right to conduct one's intimate sexual life without procreating, which is exactly the constitutional principle to which Hardwick appealed.

White had concurred in *Griswold*, but had dissented in *Roe v. Wade*, and had come by the time of *Bowers* to a general position of hostility to substantive due process arguments. White was the earliest justice to want to take *Bowers* in order to overrule the Eleventh Circuit. When the decision for the majority had been assigned to him, White initially assigned it to a law clerk who struggled to write an opinion that upset doctrine as little as possible. Twelve days after receiving the assignment, he presented his lengthy draft opinion to White, who replied that he got tired of waiting and wrote his own opinion last night. It was this basically curt, conclusory, and angrily dismissive opinion that was to be Justice White's opinion for the Court. In the place of the considered discussion of his objections to substantive due process that it might have been, the opinion impressed even White's otherwise sympathetic biographer, Denis J. Hutchinson, as "an intellectual hit-and-run incident."

We can see that White's quarry really was constitutional privacy itself when we consider the two arguments he offered for identifying basic rights: namely, those so implicit in ordered liberty that justice could not exist if they were sacrificed, and those deeply rooted in the nation's history and traditions. White believed neither argument would justify protecting acts of consensual sodomy because historically sodomy was always criminal in the United States. Indeed, even making such an argument "is, at best, facetious." But the same point could be made about *Griswold* and *Roe*, both of which departed from a long history hostile to the legitimacy of nonprocreational sex. White was not in a position to overrule these cases, which clearly regarded criminalizing nonprocreational sex as a constitutionally unacceptable purpose in contemporary circumstances. White's argument, with all its polemical excesses, came down to insisting on a distinction among cases when, as Justice Kennedy would observe in *Lawrence v. Texas*, there was no reasonable distinction worth making.

White put his point about not expanding constitutional privacy to cover gay/lesbian sex in terms that echo Ely's theory of the legitimacy of judicial review: "The Court is most vulnerable and comes nearest to illegitimacy when it deals with judge-made constitutional law having little or no cognizable roots in the language or design of the Constitution." Once again, White was questioning the legitimacy of the judicial inference of a right when no such right is expressly guaranteed, in contrast, to the rights of religious liberty and of free speech guaranteed explicitly by the First Amendment. It is correct, from this viewpoint, to protect enumerated rights, but wrong to protect unenumerated rights, as if U.S. tradition drew a sharp line between these rights when, in fact, both the Ninth Amendment of the Bill of Rights and the Privileges and Immunities Clause of the Fourteenth Amendment offer text, history, tradition, and political theory that expressly and for compelling reason deny that the protection of enumerated rights should in any way prejudice the protection of unenumerated rights.

All of these points had been made cogently by Justice Harlan in *Poe v. Ullman* (see chapter 3). There is quite clear text and history in the Bill of Rights of 1791 (notably, the Ninth Amendment) that rejected the inference that rights specifically protected by the Bill of Rights exhausted the rights worthy of protection. Also there was a good reason why the right to intimate life would not have enjoyed specific protection by the Bill of Rights, namely, questions of marriage and divorce were clearly not federal but rather state matters, and the Bill of Rights only addressed federal powers. And there was abundant history and text in the Reconstruction amendments, which clearly are directed against state power, that the rights now guaranteed protect against threats to the basic right to intimate life. The Reconstruction amendments, which ended slavery and condemned, inter alia, the cultural racism that supported it, reflected an antebellum abolitionist political morality that regarded its abridgment of the rights of African Americans to marry or to have custody of their children as one of its

{ *Chapter 5* }

worst atrocities. It was against this background that Harlan argued that the Due Process Clause and arguably the Privileges and Immunities Clause as well of the Fourteenth Amendment clearly protected the right to intimate life as a constitutional right rooted in a basic human right, and that any abridgment of such a basic right must satisfy at least the same heavy burden of secular justification required for the abridgment of other such basic rights, for example, the right to religious liberty. It is quite consistent with that text and history that the U.S. Supreme Court strike down abridgments of so basic a right no longer supported by the kind of burden of justification required, as it did in *Griswold v. Connecticut*.

There is as reasonably compelling a tradition of respect for the right to intimate life in the United States as there is a tradition of respect for the rights to conscience and speech, and the judiciary, whose power of judicial review is grounded in arguments of principle, may be as uniquely positioned to secure respect, on grounds of principle, for the right to intimate life as it has been to secure respect for variant religious and irreligious interpretations of the right to conscience and the expansive forms of conscientious speech that now enjoy unprecedented protection from the Supreme Court. There appears to be no good reason for regarding a right like that of intimate life as less a right than the right of conscience or free speech: such ties of intimate life are as central to what makes us human and thus bearers of human rights as our conscience or our expressiveness. The founders would not have understood a distinction between such rights, and U.S. historical experience in the antebellum period shows clearly how important abridgment of the right to intimate life was to a growing understanding of the atrocity of slavery. We may say, paraphrasing Lincoln on slavery, if the right to intimate life is not a basic right, nothing is. Accordingly, exercise of the power of judicial review is legitimate if we regard the institutional task of the judiciary to be a forum of principle in which persons may reasonably be heard for claims they should enjoy on equal terms such basic human rights owed all persons as equal persons and bearers of human rights. There is, from this perspective, arguably something Orwellian in Justice White's appeal to legitimacy in *Bowers*. Rather, what is clearly illegitimate is for the Supreme Court, in the unfortunate spirit of Justice White's opinion in *Bowers v. Hardwick*, to extend a basic right such as intimate life to all forms of heterosexual coupling but then to dismiss such claims as illegitimate precisely when they come from a class of persons (gays and lesbians) whose rights of intimate life have been most egregiously abridged by a cultural tradition that, until well after World War II, refused even to allow their ethical voices to be heard, let alone in a forum of principle. Judicial review makes the moral contribution to contemporary constitutional understanding when it gives a fair hearing to the previously unjustly silenced voices of Americans who make claims to the basic principles of U.S. constitutional law. White's appeal to legitimacy in *Bowers* is a parody of this mission.

Another way of understanding White's argument would be to interpret it as urging different styles of judicial interpretation when constitutional rights are specifically protected as opposed to when they are more inferential. Justice White was certainly not an originalist in his general approach to how history matters in constitutional interpretation. For example, in *Williams v. Florida* (1970), Justice White wrote the opinion for the Court interpreting how the constitutional guarantees of a trial by jury in criminal cases, which date from the Constitution of 1787 and the Bill of Rights of 1791, should be interpreted in the twentieth century. There was, of course, an available originalist interpretation of "jury": namely, a jury was the historical institution assumed by the founders in 1787 and 1791, which consisted of twelve men and required unanimity as its rule of decision. White expressly rejects such an originalist interpretation, arguing that the jury guarantee should be interpreted in terms of a more abstract intention: a reasonably representative group of one's peers — sufficiently large to resist intimidation from judges and prosecutors but not so small as not to allow dialogue — that would be required to interpose its judgments of guilt or acquittal between a criminal defendant and the state authorities who are criminally prosecuting him or her. This mode of interpretation appeals to Justice White precisely because it releases the interpretive judgment of the contemporary Supreme Court from an unreasonably slavish tracking of how the founders would have applied a constitutional term in its historical context. The appeal of a more abstractly connotative approach is that it allows a contemporary generation to construe a constitutional term reasonably in light of its facts and circumstances. For example, Justice White could have assessed whether in contemporary circumstances the essential purposes of the jury guarantee might be realized with a somewhat smaller jury size (say, nine instead of twelve) or by a decision rule less demanding than unanimity (say, two-thirds).

One way of understanding Justice White's illegitimacy claim in *Bowers v. Hardwick* is that, whereas specific guarantees call for this abstractly connotative approach, an inference of a constitutional right such as constitutional privacy should stay closer to originalist history. The problem, of course, is that again the objection is directed at the principle of constitutional privacy itself, which often questions earlier historical understandings. Presumably, the Supreme Court in *Loving v. Virginia* (1967) came constitutionally to reject antimiscegenation laws, which abridged the right to intimate life, precisely because the historical understanding of the legitimacy of such laws rested on cultural racism, and rejected anticontraception (*Griswold*) and antiabortion (*Roe*) laws because the historical understanding of such laws rested on a view of the intrinsic evil of nonprocreational sex that was by contemporary standards unreasonable, indeed quite anachronistic. There is no reason to distinguish interpretive strategies in the way Justice White's opinion suggests, at least if we think there is any good sense in having a right to constitutional privacy at all. To the contrary, the judiciary may best perform its mission when it tests all claims to basic human rights by the most reasonable contemporary understanding of what the reasonable connotative meaning of those rights is in current circumstances.

After Justice White dismissed the idea that there could be any right to privacy reasonably enjoyed by gays and lesbians, he accorded anti-sodomy laws the broadest judicial deference. According to him, common moral opinion would be enough to justify such laws even if they harm no one. White concluded his opinion by raising questions about line-drawing: if the Court protected gay/lesbian consensual adult sex, what about other consensual conduct that takes place in the home?

Victimless crimes, such as possession and use of illegal drugs, do not escape the law where they are committed at home. . . . And if respondent's submission is limited to the voluntary sexual conduct between consenting adults, it would be difficult, except by fiat, to limit the claimed right to homosexual conduct while leaving exposed to prosecution adultery, incest, and other sexual crimes even though they are committed in the home.

{ Bowers v. Hardwick: *Opinions of the Court* }   97

White's rather harsh, impersonal decision holding sodomy laws constitutional was initially tempered a bit: "Rather than resorting to the courts, those claiming rights involved in this case should take their case to the states, where they have often been successful. As presently advised, however, this Court is of the view that it has insufficient constitutional authority to declare laws against homosexual sodomy unconstitutional." But White removed these sentences, leaving the rather brusque denial that gays' and lesbians' claim to constitutional privacy could have any legitimacy.

When White circulated his first draft on April 21, 1986, Blackmun responded, "In due course, I shall try my hand at a dissent in this case." The next day, Powell was the first justice to sign on to the White opinion, saying, "I will join the judgment but will probably write separately." Marshall indicated he would join the dissent. Rehnquist agreed to the White opinion on April 23. The four remaining justices didn't take a final stand for another two months.

Justice Powell, the swing justice, was potentially in the position to speak for the Court. His memorandum to the conference, changing his vote, had reserved the question of "whether I can join an opinion finding no substantive due process right or simply join the judgment." The second opinion would have been a strongly written, concurring opinion in the judgment that would have invalidated sodomy laws by forbidding imprisonment for private, consensual oral or anal sex. But clerk Mike Mosman urged Powell not to write a concurrence strong enough to halt enforcement of sodomy laws, pushing Powell to opt for the first option, joining White's opinion, not just the result. Powell's tepid concurrence said, "In my view, a prison sentence for such conduct — certainly a sentence of long duration — would create a serious Eighth Amendment issue. . . . In this case, however, [Hardwick] has not been tried, much less convicted and sentenced."

In a footnote, Powell observed that sodomy laws were so rarely enforced that they were "moribund." It is a remark not supported by facts, some of which Powell had earlier been told: Florida's prisons chief informed Powell in 1972 that at least eighty-five people were serving sentences of up to twenty years for crimes against nature. Further, the Court had, during Powell's tenure there, turned away men sentenced up to fifteen years in prison for oral sex.

Compared to Powell's relatively mild concurrence, Chief Justice

Burger's was rhetorically shrill, including noting with approval that homosexuals had once been put to death:

> Decisions of individuals relating to homosexual conduct have been subject to state intervention throughout the history of Western civilization. Condemnation of those practices is firmly rooted in Judaeo-Christian moral and ethical standards. Homosexual sodomy was a capital crime under Roman law. . . . [Eighteenth-century English legal scholar Sir William] Blackstone described the "infamous crime against nature" as an offense of "deeper malignity" than rape, a heinous act "the very mention of which is a disgrace to human nature," and "a crime not fit to be named." . . . To hold that the act of homosexual sodomy is somehow protected as a fundamental right would be to cast aside millennia of moral teaching.

On June 23, 1986, the day after Burger circulated his concurrence, Blackmun finally circulated his dissent from White's opinion. Burger and Blackmun had been close friends since their kindergarten years in a working-class neighborhood of St. Paul, Minnesota. Blackmun had been best man at Burger's wedding, and had been elevated to the Supreme Court in 1970 by Nixon at Burger's suggestion. But, as their divergent responses to Hardwick's claim show, they had developed as judges in quite different ways. Burger's opinion endorsed the historical view of homosexuals as beyond the pale. Blackmun depicted them as victims of prejudice and as individualists worthy of the constitutional respect due their conscientious choices.

Justice Blackmun's dissenting opinion was written by the justice who authored *Roe v. Wade*. In contrast to the majority opinion, Blackmun assumed not only that constitutional privacy was a legitimately inferred and protected constitutional right but that *Roe v. Wade* was a justified application of that right. The concern of his opinion, like that of Justice Stevens's dissenting opinion, was almost entirely with the character, substance, and scope of the basic constitutional right that is constitutional privacy, rather than with the question of how and why the grounds that rationalize Georgia's sodomy statute failed to meet the standard of compelling secular state purposes that justify abridgment of basic rights.

Justice Blackmun's dissenting opinion is powerful precisely because of his opening comparison of the Georgia sodomy statute with the way Justice White's opinion for the Court postured the case: "The Court's almost obsessive focus on homosexual activity is particularly hard to justify in light of the broad language Georgia has used." Georgia's statute was an act-centered statute: certain sex acts are criminal irrespective of the gender of the partners. The statute thus criminalized heterosexual and homosexual fellatio, cunnilingus, and anal discourse: "The sex or status of the persons who engage in the act is irrelevant as a matter of state law." Such statutes make sense historically if we understand their origins in the sexual morality of Augustine and Thomas Aquinas, which condemned all nonprocreational sex, heterosexual and homosexual, and which was not for this reason specifically homophobic but rather skeptical of the value of sexuality as such. But Justice Blackmun's opinion made clear that only the prohibition of homosexual forms of nonprocreational sex now interested Georgia prosecutors. Indeed even common moral opinion now rejected the criminalization of heterosexual forms of nonprocreational sex, perhaps regarding such sex acts as protected by constitutional privacy (this apparently was the view, for example, of a majority of the justices in *Bowers v. Hardwick*, including Justice Powell). Blackmun's analysis clarified that Justice White's opinion — by accepting constitutional privacy in the full range of its heterosexual applications and then abruptly, indeed dismissively, refusing *any* homosexual applications — was itself the cultural agent of contemporary, modernist homophobia, seeing any evil in nonprocreational sex *only* in its homosexual forms. Perhaps, the closest historical analogy to the Supreme Court's playing such an ugly role in the cultural validation of irrationalist political prejudices is *Plessy v. Ferguson*, in which the Court in interpreting the Equal Protection Clause, which clearly condemned the expression of irrational racial hatred through law, refused to find state-imposed segregation by race an expression of such hatred, thus ratifying and supporting a pattern of U.S. apartheid that unconstitutionally dehumanized persons of color, as the Supreme Court was to acknowledge in 1954 when it unanimously overruled *Plessy* in *Brown v. Board of Education*. *Bowers*, both in its style and its result, gave gay people a brutal sense of what African Americans experienced in *Plessy*, a sense of irrationalist exclusion from human community. Its holding also set back making the case for gay rights in other areas, for, if gay/lesbian sex could legitimately be subject to criminal penalties, the fact of legitimate criminalization could be a rational basis for other forms of unjust treatment (for example, discrimination in employment).

Justice Blackmun's dissenting opinion was so constitutionally important, certainly in terms of the recognition of the human rights of gays and lesbians, because of the sense of humane justice he brought to interpreting the meaning of the right to constitutional privacy, just as he had earlier done in recognizing that the right to intimate life included for women access to abortion services. Blackmun's empathy clearly showed in his dissent in *Bowers v. Hardwick:*

> Only the most willful blindness could obscure the fact that sexual intimacy is "a sensitive, key relationship of human existence, central to family life, community welfare, and the development of personality." . . . The fact that individuals define themselves in a significant way through their intimate sexual relationships with others suggests, in a Nation as diverse as ours, that there may be many "right" ways of conducting those relationships, and that much of the richness of a relationship will come from the freedom an individual has to choose the form and nature of these intensely personal bonds.

Justice Blackmun, in contrast to Justice White, not only believed in the principle of constitutional privacy but in its applications, including in *Roe v. Wade,* and he thus succeeded in doing what White did not even attempt to do — to offer the most plausible normative reading of the earlier constitutional privacy cases as grounded in a basic human right to intimate life when there is no compelling secular basis that could justify the abridgment of such a right. It is because he made much better sense of the existing case law that he could so clearly see that the same right was owed all Americans, including gays and lesbians.

After a compelling case had been made, as Justice Blackmun did, for reading the legitimacy of the principle of constitutional privacy as protecting a basic human right, owed equally to heterosexuals and homosexuals, the force of arguments of principle as grounds for the legitimacy of judicial review justified his argument for extending constitutional privacy to gay/lesbian sex. The Georgia criminal statute, criminalizing such sex, clearly abridged a basic constitutional right, and could not, Blackmun argued, any more present a compelling secular justification than it could to justify the prohibition of the sale and use of contraceptives in the modern period of overpopulation pressing on scarce resources "because of demographic considerations or the Bible's command to be fruitful and multiply." Blackmun thus responded to Justice White's worries about line-drawing by drawing reasonable lines: "Drugs and weapons are inherently dangerous," "adultery is likely to injure third persons," and "the nature of familial relationships renders true consent to incestuous activity sufficiently problematical that a blanket prohibition of such activity is warranted."

Powell was angry that Blackmun's dissent dared mention the *Moore v. East Cleveland* decision, Powell's 1977 ruling striking down a zoning ordinance that had barred a grandmother from sharing her "single-family" house with two grandchildren if they were cousins, not siblings. Powell wrote in a footnote: "I find it more than a little curious to . . . analogize *Moore*'s focus on the importance of the 'family' to the conduct of sodomy in private. The fundamental reason for the condemnation of sodomy has been its *antithesis* to family. The preservation of civilization depends upon family and the bearing of children." On further thought, he decided against keeping the footnote. Powell viewed as fully constitutionally protected both contraception and abortion, both of which interfered directly with procreation. It is precisely such inconsistency, which Powell later acknowledged, that may explain his anger and the role in his thought process of a conception of family life (earlier observed) that apparently disabled him from seeing or taking account of the inconsistency.

Stevens, Brennan, and Marshall immediately joined Blackmun's dissent. Stevens also wrote a separate dissent, which Brennan and Marshall joined. His dissenting opinion took as its premise, as did Justice Blackmun's, the authority and meaning of the cases that protected the constitutional right to privacy. It was from this perspective that Justice Stevens put his constitutional analysis in terms of two questions: first, whether a state such as Georgia could prohibit all nonprocreational sex acts irrespective of the gender of the parties, and second, if not, if a state could save the statute by announcing that it would only enforce its ban against partners of the same sex? With respect to the first question, Justice Stevens answered that the principle of the privacy cases so far decided by the Supreme Court clearly protected the right of intimate sexual life of both married and unmarried persons, and protected that right whenever the parties "are isolated from observation from others," grounded in "the right to engage in nonreproductive, sexual conduct that others may consider offensive or immoral." The right, thus recognized by existing case law, clearly forbade the Georgia criminal statute targeting nonprocreational sex acts. With respect to the second question, Justice Stevens argued that any selective application of such a statute against homosexuals but not heterosexuals "must be supported by a neutral and legitimate interest — something more substantial than a substantial dislike for, or ignorance about, the disfavored group." But in his opinion there were two reasons for believing that the state of Georgia itself did not believe there was such an interest: first, it did not choose only to ban gay/lesbian sex, and second, its prosecutors had chosen not to pursue criminal actions against such conduct.

The dissenting opinions of both Justices Blackmun and Stevens made clear that, when a constitutionally guaranteed right applies, any general argument that appeals to dominant or conventional moral opinion, majoritarian offense, or long-standing religious tradition cannot suffice to justify serious abridgment of a basic human right unsupported by a compelling secular state purpose. It was at this point that their argument drew, at least implicitly, upon a form of John Stuart Mill's harm principle: the right of personal autonomy in Mill's liberal political philosophy is at least instantiated by the right of constitutional privacy, and Mill's point was, of course, that conventional moral opinion cannot suffice to abridge such a basic right in the absence of the conduct in question meeting the requirements of the harm principle (for example, imposing harms on third parties). This connection is even clearer in *Lawrence v. Texas*, in which the justices in the majority clearly regarded a showing of such harms as a necessary condition for the constitutional legitimacy of a statute criminalizing gay/lesbian sex acts.

On Monday, June 30, 1986, the justices filed into their courtroom and announced their five-to-four decision against respecting the sexual privacy of gay/lesbian Americans. White chose to read aloud large portions of his opinion. Blackmun did as well, his voice expressing anger at what he saw as the majority's willful nescience. It was the only time Blackmun read from the bench that term. Blackmun's papers contain a handwritten note to him from Thurgood Marshall about his reading of his dissent that day: "You was great."

Justice Powell was central to the Court's decision in *Bowers v. Hardwick*. After he left the Court, Justice Powell, responding to a question posed to him at a public occasion at my law school, in effect confessed his error in his change of mind and reversal of vote. It is reasonably clear why: Powell, unlike other justices in the majority, was clearly committed to the principle not only of *Griswold* but of *Roe v. Wade* itself; indeed, Powell's strong convictions about women's rights influenced Justice Blackmun to ground the argument of *Roe* so securely in a woman's right to choose whether to carry a child to term. When we accept, as Powell evidently did, both the general principle of constitutional privacy and the correctness of its application to contraception and abortion, the failure to apply it to gay/lesbian sex raises questions about how principled a justice's conception of constitutional law really was. Powell clearly saw the issue in this way, as he confirmed to a reporter about his recantation: "I do think it was inconsistent in a general way with *Roe*. When I had the opportunity to reread the opinions a few months later, I thought the dissent had the better of the arguments." There can be no more fundamental criticism of any justice, and Powell came conscientiously to accept this criticism of himself.

There is an illuminating background that suggests the sometimes fatal role the closet plays in homophobic silencing of ethical voice in sustaining such injustices. When one of Powell's clerks (Cabell Chinnis, a gay man, his homosexuality unknown to Powell) had urged him to hold the statute unconstitutional, Powell remarked to his astonished clerk, "I don't believe I've ever met a homosexual," a remark he evidently repeated at the conference of the justices on the case. Justice Blackmun later told his clerks that he thought of remarking, "Of course you have. You've even had gay clerks," but like Powell's current clerk, he didn't point this out to Powell. The cultural tradition underlying homophobia rests on the unspeakability of homosexuality. In such circumstances, a failure to break the silence ratifies the unjust authority of the tradition, not exposing a person like Powell, striving to do justice, to the voices he most needs to hear in order to do justice.

What such unspeakability shows is, of course, the continuing repressive political power of the closet, which not only silenced Justice Powell's law clerk but also Justice Blackmun, who did not speak to Powell about what he knew about his clerks. Such reticence is, under circumstances of continuing homophobia, certainly understandable, but it is a matter that, as the reticence of Powell's clerk and Blackmun shows, compromises and indeed may cripple the case for gay rights. *Bowers v. Hardwick* may be a model case study for such distorting effects of the closet on an ethical voice that would otherwise resist injustice.

Everyone who knew Powell, including his former clerk Paul M. Smith, who was successfully to argue *Lawrence v. Texas*, attested to his personal goodness and liberal open-mindedness. When a man like this confessed both to a clerk and to his fellow justices, "I don't believe I've ever met a homosexual," he was doing something quite unusual in a culture in which the closet was still hegemonic: he was breaking the silence about homosexuality and worrying about what the effects of this might be on the impartiality of his judgment in a case involving homosexuality. In fact, Smith observed to the author (telephone interview) that Powell had mentioned to him that, while a soldier serving in France in World War II, he had met Gertrude Stein and Alice B. Toklas, a famous lesbian pair known to Powell as such. So, Powell had in fact met homosexuals, in the form of a long-standing, rather famous lesbian couple, which may explain why, at one point in his reflections, he mentioned to his clerk, Mike Mosman, that some homosexuals form relationships as stable and committed as heterosexual marriages, and that this element of personal relationship might call for constitutional protection. If Powell was open to such an analogy, it must mean that he was seeking both from his closeted gay clerk and from his fellow justices some conversation that might enable him to think through the question with some measure of impartiality. We know now what Powell's preconceptions were, namely, that nothing about male homosexuals like Michael Hardwick was within his conception of what home and family were. When Powell confessed not knowing homosexuals, he meant not lesbians, but gay men and, in particular, the only gay man he could imagine, namely, Michael Hardwick. He was, I believe, inviting dialogue; what in fact he got, from both his gay clerk and Harry Blackmun, was silence about his relationships to the gay men and lesbians who had been his clerks, a silence that proved unequal to the rather aggressive lobbying of his Mormon clerk and Chief Justice Warren Burger. In effect, Powell was hearing only one side of the argument if the argument rests, as it does, on protecting loving sexual relationships or the right to form such relationships. It is unsurprising that, after *Bowers v. Hardwick* came down, Powell learned of the homosexuality of various clerks over time, and that such knowledge opened his mind to ethical dimensions he had not previously seen. To that extent, *Bowers* changed conventions of reticence among the justices and clerks that had disserved the search for justice under the rule of law.

The oral argument in *Bowers*, in contrast to the argument in *Lawrence*, was remarkable not only for its reticence about sex (which was, after all, what the case was about), but for its focus essentially on forbidden forms of sex in bedrooms and other more public locales. The case for Hardwick was ably made before the Supreme Court by a very distinguished academic and constitutional lawyer, Laurence Tribe, an argument that clearly initially moved Powell to vote for Hardwick's side of the case. But Tribe's very attempt to ground the right in question in something like the personal relationships of family life clearly antagonized Powell, as we now know. Would this have been less psychologically possible if Tribe, in fact a straight man, had been a gay man or lesbian and known as such, speaking from the experience of the role of gay/lesbian sex in valued personal relationships? Would the oral argument in *Brown v. Board of Education* have been the same if not argued by Thurgood Marshall speaking from his experience as a southerner and man of color? Would the argument in *Roe v. Wade* have had the same cogency if not argued by Sarah Weddington, speaking from her own experience as a woman about what counted as a fundamental human right? What Tribe did in *Bowers v. Hardwick* was pathbreaking, not least because he courageously brought to bear his own public stature and voice as a leading U.S. constitutional scholar, responsibly challenging, as he had in many other cases, constitutional injustice. Perhaps, in that time and place and milieu, no one, gay or straight, could have done better, or even as well. It would be neither reasonable nor right nor wise to limit constitutional advocacy to persons actually suffering the injustice. But *Bowers v. Hardwick*, dealing with a problem where cultural silencing played such a powerful role in sustaining the injustice, suggests that the voice of personal grievance may be one way of breaking through the sound barrier of silencing that sustains deep injustices, finding in this way a more responsive audience for one's claims. Strikingly, the oral argument in *Lawrence v. Texas* was made by Paul Smith, a former clerk of Powell's in the early 1980s, who, like some other men of his generation, later married and had children only to discover that his true feelings lay elsewhere. Smith divorced his wife, though he remains close with her and his children, and now centers his life in a long-standing gay relationship. Smith's life, as both a man and a lawyer, illustrates the choices gay men and lesbians during this period came to make to center their lives in the new forms of love gay rights made possible in life. Smith argued *Lawrence* as an out gay man.

Between *Bowers* and *Lawrence*

The Supreme Court's decision in *Bowers* was a devastating blow to U.S. gays and lesbians. Thomas Stoddard, then executive director of the Lambda Legal Defense and Education Fund, expressed the experience in terms of a historical analogy: "For the gay rights movement, this is our *Dred Scott* case." He was referring to the Court's now infamous 1857 decision upholding slavery and ruling that blacks were "of an inferior order, so far inferior that they had no rights which the white man was bound to respect." Moreover, the tone of Justice White's majority opinion in *Bowers* was gratuitously contemptuous, and Chief Justice Burger's concurrence expressed emotional hostility toward lesbian and gay people: condemnation of sodomy, he wrote, was based on "millennia of moral teaching." Tom Stoddard opined that the tone of the decision was actually more damaging to gay/lesbian people than the content: "The most important judicial body in the United States has expressed a certain distaste for gay men and women and suggested that they may be treated differently from other Americans."

Courts in the wake of *Bowers* certainly treated gays and lesbians differently; indeed, lower courts appealed to *Bowers* in denying arguments of unconstitutional discrimination against gays and lesbians on the ground that a group constitutionally subject to criminal penalties could be reasonably distinguished from other groups. These consequences were as bad as had been expected. But although *Bowers* did indeed have a negative effect on the rights of gay and lesbian persons, one fear was not realized. Not a single state recriminalized sodomy in response to *Bowers*. In fact, efforts to eliminate sodomy laws began regaining force within a few years of the Supreme Court's decision. In 1992, Kentucky became the first post-*Bowers* state to invalidate its sodomy law, inaugurating a new period of sodomy law reform. Kentucky was followed in short order by Nevada, the District of Columbia, Tennessee, Montana, Georgia, Rhode Island, Maryland, Arizona, Minnesota, Massachusetts, and Arkansas. Repeal was accomplished legislatively in four instances (the District of Columbia, Nevada, Rhode Island, and Arizona). In the other eight, repeal was accomplished by legal challenge under state constitutional law (on the model of *Onofre*). The renaissance of sodomy law reform culminated in 2003 when the U.S. Supreme Court in *Lawrence v. Texas* invalidated all remaining state sodomy laws as impermissibly infringing on the right of privacy. Thirteen states had retained sodomy laws, of which four only enforced their laws against homosexual conduct. All were now invalid.

Matters may have looked quite dark for the future of gay rights in the United States at the time of *Bowers*, since it seemed unlikely that the composition of the Court in the future would be any more liberal than it was at the time of *Bowers*. Nonetheless, *Bowers v. Hardwick*, decided in 1986, was overruled by *Lawrence v. Texas*, decided in 2003. It took some sixty years for the U.S. Supreme Court to reconsider and overrule *Plessy v. Ferguson* (1896) in *Brown v. Board of Education* (1954), and nearly thirty years to overrule *Lochner v. New York* (1905) in *Nebbia v. New York* (1934). Whereas the periods from *Plessy* to *Brown* and from *Lochner* to *Nebbia* were marked by appointments to the Supreme Court of more liberal justices (reflecting shifts in public opinion), the membership of the Supreme Court from *Bowers* to *Lawrence* became, if anything, more conservative, reflecting a number of appointments by Republican presidents committed to overruling *Roe v. Wade* (including the elevation of Justice Rehnquist to chief justice and the appointments by President Reagan of Justice Antonin Scalia and Justice Anthony Kennedy, and by the first President Bush of Justice David Souter and Justice Clarence Thomas). By the time of *Lawrence*, a number of justices on the Court at the time of *Bowers* had retired, including Chief Justice Warren E. Burger and Justices William Brennan, Thurgood Marshall, Byron White, Harry Blackmun, and Lewis Powell.

There was, however, one important moment of successful public resistance to the proposed new Supreme Court appointments of President Reagan that bears on our topic. In 1987, the year after *Bowers v. Hardwick*, liberal worries were crystallized when President Reagan nominated Judge Robert Bork to the High Court. Judge Bork had written in no uncertain terms about his hostility to the principle of constitutional privacy on grounds that seemed to many constitutional scholars to lack any historical and normative understanding of either the text or enduring principles of U.S. constitutionalism bearing on the protection of basic human rights. His nomination to the Supreme Court would politicize an issue of basic constitutional principle in ways that threatened what seemed the most important ground of judicial review in the United States, the protection of the basic human rights owed all Americans, including political minorities who could not otherwise secure the hearing and the respect that was their due. A Constitution of which the legitimacy rested on majority rule and the protection of minority rights was in peril from such ill-advised, ideologically driven appointments. It was for this reason that I testified with Professor Kathleen Sullivan (then of the Harvard Law School, who had been counsel with Lawrence Tribe in *Bowers*) before the Senate Judiciary Committee, expressing worries about Judge Bork's insensitivity to an important constitutional principle of law such as the right to privacy. Other law professors made comparable arguments on the same basis or on the basis of other concerns. Judge Bork's nomination was defeated.

President Reagan's second nominee, federal appeals court Judge Douglas Ginsburg, lasted just days. The anti-drugs Reagan administration was embarrassed by the revelation that Ginsburg had smoked marijuana as a Harvard law professor. Ginsburg quickly withdrew his name from nomination.

The president then turned to a Californian, Anthony Kennedy, born and raised in Sacramento, who had been a Boy Scout and a Roman Catholic altar boy. An oft-repeated anecdote about him was that he was such a good boy that his hard-drinking father, a liquor industry lobbyist, unsuccessfully offered him $100 if he would do something bad enough to get in trouble with the police. After Kennedy took over his father's law practice, he drafted a tax-cut initiative for then-governor Reason. As a favor to Reagan, President Ford appointed Kennedy at the age of thirty-eight to the Ninth Circuit in 1975, making him the youngest federal appellate judge at that time. Kennedy got most satisfaction from teaching a Monday night class in constitutional law. Displaying a flair for the theatrical, he sometimes delivered a lecture dressed as James Madison, the father of both the Constitution and the Bill of Rights.

At his Senate confirmation hearings in December 1987, Kennedy stressed that the Constitution protects rights — including privacy — not explicitly listed in it. He said that "there is a zone of privacy, a zone of protection, a line that is drawn where the individual can tell the government: Beyond this line, you may not go." The rather eloquent Kennedy did not sound like a Bork, or, for that matter, a Rehnquist or Scalia. Although his nomination was opposed by some leading liberal groups, Laurence Tribe, the attorney who had lost *Bowers*, urged Kennedy's confirmation, saying Kennedy's writings indicated that he was "deeply committed to an evolving understanding of the Constitution."

Kennedy won confirmation, ninety-seven to zero, on February 3, 1988. Justice Kennedy was to write the opinion for five justices in *Lawrence v. Texas* that would overrule *Bowers v. Hardwick.*

President Reagan's attempt to appoint Robert Bork to the Supreme Court had been rejected by the Senate in part because of Bork's attack on the principle of constitutional privacy, and President Bush's nomination of Clarence Thomas almost failed, although the issue of his interpretive attitude to constitutional privacy was not the basis for his problems. President Clinton successfully appointed two justices, Ruth Bader Ginsburg and Stephen Breyer, who were on the Court at the time of *Lawrence*.

The conservative majority of the Supreme Court (Chief Justice Rehnquist and Justices O'Connor, Kennedy, Scalia, and Thomas) at the time of *Lawrence* had decided many cases in ways the majority on the Court in *Bowers* would not. The Rehnquist Court was skeptical of racial classifications to the extent of rarely upholding them, even when ameliorative in otherwise reasonable affirmative action programs, and it developed doctrines regarding the Commerce Clause and other areas that have limited the powers of Congress in ways the previous membership of the Court rejected. Why, then, was *Bowers* so critically vulnerable?

Much happened between 1986 and 2003, not least the growing visibility in the United States of gays and lesbians living in relationship, some quite long-term, some caring for children and even parents. The closet had clearly had an impact on *Bowers v. Hardwick*, as our discussion of Justice Powell's struggle shows. After *Bowers*, the closet not only eroded among the clerks on the Court but as a condition of acceptable gay/lesbian life generally, though President Clinton was compelled to accept a form of it, "Don't Ask, Don't Tell" as the condition for gay/lesbian presence in the military services. The AIDS health crisis, as earlier noted (chapter 2), though a tragedy for the gay men afflicted by it, was not fatal to the further progress of gay rights (whatever its effect on *Bowers*). For one thing, the crisis shattered forever the unspeakability of homosexuality and humanized the lives of the gays and lesbians who struggled responsibly to care for those they loved and for whom they grieved. The protests of gays and lesbians about public nescience regarding AIDS became a model for more visible gay/lesbian activism generally, activism that increasingly protested *Bowers v. Hardwick* as a betrayal of the mission of U.S. constitutional law to recognize the universal human rights of all Americans.

About 500,000 gay men and lesbians marched through the nation's capital on October 11, 1987, setting a record for a gay-rights rally. Two days later, in a carefully staged six-hour display of civil disobedience, Michael Hardwick and 571 other demonstrators were arrested in front of the Supreme Court. The protestors shouted "Shame! Shame! Shame!" and they were dragged to police cars. Lesbian Pat Norman, an organizer of Sunday's march, shouted: "Every day we commit an act of civil disobedience by loving each other." Most protestors wore "Silence = Death" T-shirts of the AIDS protest group ACT-UP. Gay gallows humor was directed at the white plastic gloves the police wore as protection from the AIDS virus: "Your gloves don't match your shoes. Your gloves don't match your shoes."

The indignation of gays and lesbians at *Bowers* showed itself as well in financial support for activist gay rights organizations. Individual contributions to Lambda, for example, more than tripled between 1985 and 1986, jumping from $181, 239 to $553,402. This dramatic increase suggests that Lambda used a litigation defeat to mobilize support for its work.

The two-term presidency of William Clinton also had its impact. Clinton saw gays and lesbians as an important political group supporting him, and tried, however haplessly, to repeal their exclusion from the military. His appointments to the Supreme Court (Justices Ginsburg and Breyer) were clearly favorable to some measure of constitutional recognition of gay rights as judicially enforceable rights. And the public absorption in his wayward sexual life (including the

{ *Chapter 6* }

Monica Lewinsky scandal that nearly ended his presidency) eroded whatever remaining reticence the American people had about discussing sex acts not confined to heterosexual marriage.

Finally, the overwhelming majority of law review commentary on *Bowers v. Hardwick* supported the dissenters in that case. There were at least three reasons why commentators found *Bowers* so inconsistent with the holdings of *Griswold*, *Roe*, and *Casey*.

First, the quality of the arguments of the justices in the majority in *Bowers* was, to say the least, highly questionable, as many scholars argued. There was, first of all, Justice White's appeal to legitimacy allegedly on the ground of history. But scholars pointed out that history evidently did not bar the development and elaboration of the constitutional right to privacy in the areas of contraception and abortion, and that, in fact, the failure to extend the principle of constitutional privacy to gay/lesbian sex—after extending it to every incident of heterosexual sexual life—was unprincipled in precisely the way that made any Supreme Court opinion an illegitimate exercise of the judicial power.

Second, scholars questioned the uncritical role historical argument played in the thinking both of Justice White and Chief Justice Burger in failing to take seriously the traditional concern with nonprocreational sex, a concern applicable equally to heterosexual and homosexual sex. The use of history both by White and Burger was not just inaccurate but selective in a way that bespoke prejudice, in particular, homophobia. As Janet Halley and Nan Hunter acidly observed, the Court took an act-based statute (directed at all forms of nonprocreational sex, heterosexual and homosexual) and homophobically underwrote the state's stigmatizing of homosexual identity. It is not surprising, in light of criticisms of this sort, that the briefs in *Lawrence*, both those for the petitioner and various amicus briefs, so prominently developed and elaborated highly sophisticated historical arguments of a sort that were not in play in *Bowers v. Hardwick*. Such scholarly historical research both by legal and social historians made clear how many different strands there were in the historical record and how important it was to make a responsible normative choice among them in light of contemporary circumstances, including the relatively recent development of a specifically homophobic animus in U.S. politics.

Third, several of the justices in the conservative majority on the

Court at the time of *Lawrence* showed, long before *Lawrence*, a concern for the principle of constitutional privacy that had distinguished them from other justices in the majority. Their interpretive work suggested that the principles of constitutional privacy transcend partisan political divisions, and it touched on deeper matters of constitutional essentials on which they shared common ground with more liberal justices. There were two important cases decided after *Bowers v. Hardwick* that suggested these judges might join with more liberal judges to reconsider *Bowers:* first, *Planned Parenthood of Southeastern Pennsylvania v. Casey* (1992), and second, *Romer v. Evans* (1996).

Bowers v. Hardwick was decided in a period of considerable debate in the nation and on the Supreme Court itself about the legitimacy of *Roe v. Wade,* which clearly showed in Justice White's opinion for the Court in *Bowers,* reflecting skepticism not only about *Roe v. Wade* but about the principle of constitutional privacy. Because of recent judicial appointments by Republican presidents (Reagan and Bush), there was by 1992 a majority on the Supreme Court that could, if it wished, have overruled *Roe* (including Chief Justice Rehnquist and Justices White, Scalia, Thomas, O'Connor, Kennedy, and Souter). Only two justices clearly committed to *Roe* remained on the High Court (Justices Blackmun and Stevens). To the surprise of many, three justices in the likely overruling group (namely, Justices O'Connor, Kennedy, and Souter) chose not to overrule *Roe,* rather preserving its essential principle (no criminalization before viability), although allowing more regulation before that point than the *Roe* Court had been prepared to allow (see chapter 4).

There was, strikingly, no mention in *Casey* in the opinion for the Court of the three justices, nor in the concurring opinions on this point of Justices Blackmun and Stevens, of *Bowers v. Hardwick* (though Justice O'Connor had concurred in the Court's opinion). Only the dissents of Chief Justice Rehnquist and Justice Scalia cited *Bowers,* questioning how *Bowers* could be squared with the reaffirmation of the central principle of *Roe v. Wade.* The opinion of Justice White for the Court in *Bowers* expressed a general skepticism about the right of constitutional privacy, only incidentally involved in that case. The three justices writing the opinion for the Court in *Casey* put that skepticism to rest, and indeed reaffirmed the application of the principle in *Roe,* a case crucially involving the weight to be accorded state interests in fetal life. Arguably, there was more of an issue about legitimate state interests in *Roe* than there was in *Bowers*, which would suggest that the principle of constitutional privacy might reasonably be regarded as even more egregiously violated by a criminal ban on gay/lesbian sex.

Romer v. Evans was not, like *Casey*, only implicitly about the continuing authority of *Bowers*. The continuing meaning of *Bowers* was at the heart of the interpretive issue in the case, as Justice Scalia made clear in his dissent. The issue was this: in response to political successes of gay groups in Colorado, laws had been legislatively approved by various municipalities in the state that protected gays and lesbians from discrimination on the ground of sexual orientation (on the analogy of the state and federal laws that forbid discrimination on grounds of religion, race/ethnicity, and gender). Sodomy was no longer criminal in Colorado, but groups aggressively opposed to gay rights did something quite extraordinary, something so unusual, indeed extreme that they unconsciously prepared the way for the first major victory for gay rights in U.S. constitutional history. They did not just seek and secure repeal of such statutes, which would have been in the tradition of U.S. politics, but took a step that many lawyers regarded as quite unprecedented in U.S. constitutional history. With Colorado being one of the easiest states in which to place constitutional amendments on the ballot, they secured passage of Colorado Amendment Two, which not only repealed such antidiscrimination ordinances, but forbade any such antidiscrimination laws or policies ever to be effective anywhere in Colorado. As it turned out, the Supreme Court agreed with the constitutional lawyers. There had never been anything like this, a successful attempt constitutionally to wall off a named group from any antidiscrimination protection. Its passage clearly shocked members of the Supreme Court, notably, Justice Anthony Kennedy, as the oral argument made clear. Its unprecedented character suggested to the Court irrational animus, which was to be the basis for striking it down. *Bowers*, which allowed the criminalization of gay/lesbian sex, was implicated in the arguments for Colorado Amendment Two because, if the conduct central to a group's identity could be criminal, then it seemed reasonable that a state, which could constitutionally wholly forbid such conduct, might take the less restrictive option of not criminalizing it, but discouraging its public acceptability by forbidding any protections of gays and lesbians from people's desire not to associate with them.

Justice Kennedy's opinion for the Court was joined by five justices (including Justices O'Connor, Souter, Stevens, Ginsburg, and Breyer); Justice Scalia wrote in dissent for himself and Chief Justice Rehnquist and Justice Thomas. Kennedy's opinion nowhere mentioned *Bowers*, whereas the authority of *Bowers* was at the center of Justice Scalia's argument in *Romer*: "In holding that homosexuality cannot be singled out for disfavorable treatment, the Court contradicts a decision, unchallenged here, pronounced only 10 years ago, see *Bowers v. Hardwick*."

Romer was such a turning point in the Court's recognition of the constitutional rights of gays and lesbians because of its sense, from the opening of Justice Kennedy's opinion for the Court, that populist support for Colorado Amendment Two was analogous to support for state-endorsed racial segregation in *Plessy v. Ferguson*. Earlier I observed that, as Justice Blackmun's dissenting opinion argued in *Bowers*, Justice White's opinion for the Court was so objectionable because its endorsement of distinctions on no basis other than irrational prejudice made the U.S. Supreme Court, in violation of its constitutional responsibilities to treat persons as equals, the agent of the cultural construction of prejudice, such as racism in *Plessy* and homophobia in *Bowers*. Although Justice Kennedy's opinion in *Romer* did not mention *Bowers*, its opening appeal to Justice Harlan's dissent in *Plessy* (the Constitution "neither knows nor tolerates classes among citizens") strikingly aligned that powerful dissent with Justice Blackmun's dissent in *Bowers*. It was not only the style of Kennedy's opinion that questioned the continuing authority of *Bowers*, but the substance. Colorado Amendment Two was unconstitutional, Kennedy argued, because it lacked any rational relationship to legitimate state interests, reflecting unconstitutional prejudice. Kennedy did not recognize as legitimate what Justice Scalia, in his dissent, argued *Bowers* established as legitimate: an evil in gay/lesbian sex that justified criminalization. If such an evil was a legitimate basis for outright banning, it must, Scalia argued, be a rational basis for drawing distinctions. Kennedy's denial of this point suggested *Bowers* was not legitimate.

There was a rather brilliant argument in Justice Kennedy's opinion that clearly attempted to answer Justice Scalia's argument, again without mentioning or discussing *Bowers*. This was Kennedy's discussion of earlier cases dealing with the Mormons. These cases were of two sorts: those like *Reynolds v. United States* that constitutionally allowed laws that banned Mormon polygamy despite the fact that polygamy was rooted in the right of religious liberty; and those like *Davis v. Beason* that allowed Mormons to be deprived of the right to vote. Justice Kennedy did not question the authority of the case upholding a ban on polygamy (presumably, on the ground that banning a practice rooted in a basic right such as religious liberty would be justified by a compelling state interest, such as gender equality; but the latter case, he argued, was no longer good law because it rested on the now constitutionally unacceptable view "that persons advocating a certain practice may be denied the right to vote." Just because a religious practice might be constitutionally banned, it did not follow that advocacy of such a practice might be a ground for depriving the advocates of a constitutional right such as voting. The analogy to gays and lesbians was evident: gays and lesbians now publicly claimed their basic rights on fair terms with other Americans. It might be, if *Bowers v. Hardwick* was good law, that conduct rooted in their conscientious exercise of their right to intimate life might be banned because a compelling state purpose supported such a ban; but it did not follow that their public claims and lives as gays and lesbians might for that reason be the subject of discrimination.

What the analogy showed is how far, in the view of six justices of the Supreme Court, gays and lesbians had come in twenty years, bringing their ethical voices to bear on U.S. politics and constitutional law. Although opposition to gay rights was often grounded in traditional religious views that condemned gay/lesbian sex as the unspeakable crime against nature not to be mentioned, the growing public presence of gays and lesbians in intellectual and public life led the six justices of the Court to recognize the claims of gays and lesbians as being as much rooted in ethical conviction and principled argument at the core of the constitutional protection of liberty as the arguments of their opponents. The analogy of the Mormons was thus striking in recognizing the voices of gays and lesbians as ethical, as much entitled to respect as any religious voices in the United States. The opinion also suggested that what may have moved the Court in *Romer* was a sense of religious discrimination against gays and lesbians—a sectarian cultural war on the personal and ethical convictions of gays and lesbians analogous to traditional Christian discrimination against Jews and no better justified on constitutional grounds of equal treatment of all forms of conscience, whether it was traditional religious minorities or contemporary ethical voices challenging such claims.

If I am right about these reasons for the suspectness of sexual orientation as a basis for discrimination in *Romer v. Evans*, such reasons would explain and clarify both the substance and rhetorical excesses of Justice Scalia's dissent, for Scalia's originalism may be rooted in his own highly patriarchal, indeed fundamentalist religious views. Scalia insisted that, because *Bowers v. Hardwick* was still good law, the compelling state interest that sustained laws criminalizing sodomy against constitutional attack must extend to the legitimacy of that state's moral purpose in sustaining the less intrusive demands of Colorado Amendment Two. Justice Kennedy's analogy to religious discrimination, of course, addressed and answered that argument, and the very power of the argument was, I believe, exemplified by the terms of Scalia's dissent, namely, that even were gay/lesbian sex decriminalized, there would be a legitimate state purpose in laws like Colorado Amendment Two as democratically legitimate self-defense, that gays and lesbians were not really politically unpopular because, despite small numbers, the "group. . .enjoys enormous influence in American media and politics," and, lastly, that the Court majority illegitimately depended on the elitist views of the law schools and legal profession.

In fact, lesbians and gay men are a small minority of the U.S. population. Although relatively affluent in some cases and sometimes influential, their political gains have been comparatively small and, as publicly identified gay men and lesbians, they remain radically underrepresented in key government positions and still quite vulnerable to violent hate crimes. Against this factual background, making an argument of legitimate state self-defense against gay advances exemplified a use of facts and values all too familiar in the history of intolerance. Thus, the argument remarkably transforms the minority status of homosexuals, analogous to the similar irrationalist appeals central to political anti-Semitism, into a secret and powerful conspiracy against which politics must be protected. In effect, the very attempt by homosexuals or Jews to make any basic claims of equal citizenship and any small gains thus secured (including relative affluence and occasional influence) are interpreted as an illegitimate attack on dominant majorities. Normative outrage at the very idea of an outcast's claim of rights remakes reality to rationalize nullification of such rights.

If motivated by such sectarian anxieties, Justice Scalia was much less impartial in this matter than he claims to be. Certainly, in the view of his critics, Justice Scalia was an active player in this cultural war, his originalism arguably masking, at least in the areas of sexuality and gender, his own rather reactionary brand of Catholic religious fundamentalism based on the current views of the papacy (of course, many American Catholics disagree with these views). His appeal to democracy was thus brigaded with an anti-intellectualism more familiar in Protestant fundamentalism than in a learned Catholic like Scalia when he condemned the intellectual culture of academic and professional law because, as it seems, this culture questions the reasonableness of sectarian views Scalia was unable and unwilling to question.

Nothing in Justice Kennedy's argument reflected that *Bowers v. Hardwick* was still good law; indeed, his failure even to mention *Bowers* suggested, as Justice Scalia claims, that the Court had doubts about the authority and weight of *Bowers* (as we later learned it clearly did). Kennedy's argument showed that *Romer* did not require, though it might permit the overruling of, *Bowers*. It did not require it because that matter would turn, as the Mormon case did, on the weight of the state purpose underlying the criminal bans; it might permit it if the Court found both that a basic right had been violated, and that no such compelling purpose existed. Kennedy's argument plausibly suggested that *Bowers* would be overruled on the premise that a fundamental right as basic as the religious liberty rights of the Mormons was as much owed gays and lesbians. Recall that Justice White's argument in *Bowers* denied any basic right was owed gays and lesbians. Justice Kennedy took a different view in *Romer*, which suggested that White's dismissal of gay/lesbian rights, as rights, no longer commanded a majority of the Supreme Court, which is to say that the authority of *Bowers* was now in doubt.

There were two later cases that, although unfavorable to the claims made by gays and lesbians, showed the growing seriousness with which the ethical voices of gays and lesbians were taken in U.S. democratic politics, in particular at the state level. The first such case was *Hurley v. Irish-American Gay, Lesbian, and Bisexual Group of Boston (GLIB)*, decided in 1995, and the second was *Boy Scouts of America v. Dale*, decided in 2000. Both cases involved constitutional issues relating to the application of state laws, forbidding discrimination on grounds of sexual orientation. In *Hurley*, a Massachusetts law forbade discrimination on the basis of sexual orientation in a place of public accommodation, which GLIB had successfully argued in state courts applied to its exclusion from the Boston St. Patrick's Day parade. In *Boy Scouts of America*, a New Jersey law forbade discrimination on the basis of sexual orientation in public accommodations, which the highest court of the state held required admission to the Boy Scouts of a gay man who had publicly advocated gay rights. In *Hurley*, Justice Souter, writing for a unanimous Supreme Court, held that the state statute was unconstitutional as applied to the expressive decisions of a private parade, appealing to the free speech rights of the organizers of the parade to decide whom they would include in the parade. The Court in *Boy Scouts of America* was more closely divided. Chief Justice Rehnquist, writing for a five-to-four majority that included himself and Justices O'Connor, Kennedy, Scalia, and Thomas held that the unwanted inclusion in a group unconstitutionally infringes the group's freedom of expressive association if the presence of a person in the group affects in a significant way that group's ability to advocate public or private viewpoints, and found this standard unconstitutionally violated in the application of the state antidiscrimination law to the admission of the gay man in question. In dissent, Justice Stevens, writing for himself and Justices Souter, Ginsburg, and Breyer, denied that the Boy Scouts had proclaimed any antigay philosophy and thus rejected the authority of *Hurley* as governing this case. Unlike GLIB, Dale did not carry a banner or sign, and he expressed no intent to send any message. It was therefore a mistake for the majority to suppose that *Boy Scouts of America*, like *Hurley*, involved the application of a state statute that violated free speech rights.

Both cases illustrate how far the voices of gays and lesbians had come in some thirty years in securing some degree of recognition for their claims of justice — in these cases, state laws that added sexual orientation to already forbidden grounds of discrimination such as religion, race/ethnicity, and gender. There was, of course, reactionary legislation as well, including not only Colorado Amendment Two but state and federal "defense of marriage" legislation and the like. But robust judicial protection of their free speech rights had made gay/lesbian protests possible, including the protection of expressive individuality *Hurley* represented and elaborated. If the Supreme Court protected speech that expressed discriminatory attitudes that are, as a basis for laws, now constitutionally forbidden as suspect classes (like race/ethnicity and gender), it was not surprising that it would protect speech that advocates homophobic discrimination on a ground (sexual orientation) not yet fully recognized as a suspect class. It was much less clear, as Justice Stevens argued in his dissent in *Boy Scouts of America*, that there was any comparable free speech interest involved on the facts of that case.

To summarize, although *Bowers v. Hardwick* was a major setback for gay rights, it energized resistance by many gays and lesbians. Such resistance included successful overturning of President Reagan's nomination to the Supreme Court of Robert Bork, who had criticized the constitutional right to privacy as illegitimate. The person successfully appointed instead was Anthony Kennedy, who was to write for the Court in *Lawrence v. Texas*. Three justices appointed to overrule *Roe v. Wade* declined to do so, and two new justices appointed by President Clinton were clearly favorable to gay rights. The opinion of Justice Kennedy for a six-to-three Court in *Romer v. Evans*, striking down as unconstitutional Colorado Amendment Two (which forbade all laws protecting gays and lesbians from discrimination), indicated to gay/lesbian litigators that the Supreme Court might be willing to reconsider and even overrule *Bowers v. Hardwick*.

CHAPTER 7

Lawrence v. Texas

Background, Briefs, and Oral Arguments

Romer sent a clear message that the Supreme Court might be willing to reexamine *Bowers v. Hardwick*. There were two interpretations of this message. First, the Court would strike down antisodomy statutes that by their terms applied only to gays and lesbians, not to heterosexuals. These laws might be especially problematic because they rested on a prejudice targeting homosexuals that *Romer* found was unconstitutionally irrational. The Court might be willing to strike down such a statute without having to overrule *Bowers*, which involved a state statute directed by its terms against both heterosexual and homosexual sodomy. Second, the Court might be willing to overrule *Bowers* itself.

In the wake of *Romer*, discussions began among two groups of litigators who were to work together closely in fashioning the litigation strategy of *Lawrence v. Texas*. First, Ruth E. Harlow, legal director of the Lambda Legal Defense and Education Fund, worked with her colleagues at Lambda, including Susan L. Sommer and Patricia M. Logue. Second, two openly gay lawyers in the Washington, D.C., law firm of Jenner and Block, Paul M. Smith and William M. Hohengarten, worked closely with the Lambda lawyers. The division of labor was roughly this: Ruth Harlow supervised Susan Sommer in gathering and coordinating the various amici briefs that were, both in their number and their remarkably high quality, so distinguished an aspect of the litigation. Ruth Harlow and William Hohengarten wrote the brief; former clerks of current Supreme Court justices were shown drafts of the brief and gave useful advice. Paul M. Smith, a former clerk for Justice Powell who had made a number of such arguments before the Supreme Court previously, made the oral argument.

The lawyers saw the facts of a Texas sodomy case involving a statute that applied only to gays and lesbians as the most reasonable way to seek review before the Supreme Court in light of *Romer v. Evans*. The facts of *Lawrence v. Texas* were these. In Houston, Texas, officers of the police department were dispatched to a private residence to respond to a reported weapons disturbance, which later turned out to be a false report. They entered an apartment where Lawrence resided. The officers observed Lawrence and another man, Garner, engaged in a sexual act, arrested both, held them in custody overnight, and charged them under a Texas criminal law that forbade sexual relations between parties of the same sex. They were convicted before a justice of the peace. The petitioners exercised their right to a trial *de novo* in Harris County Criminal Court, claiming violations of equal protection guarantees of both the federal and state constitutions. Their claims were rejected, and each was fined and assessed costs. The Court of Appeals for the Texas Fourteenth District considered the petitioners' federal constitutional claims both under the Equal Protection and Due Process Clauses of the Fourteenth Amendment. After hearing the case en banc, the court, in a divided opinion, rejected the constitutional claims and affirmed the conviction, appealing, as the basis for its decision, to the authority of *Bowers v. Hardwick*.

What made this case so appealing to the Lambda and Jenner and Block lawyers was that the sodomy statute, like *Bowers*, targeted sex acts in the home, and, unlike *Bowers*, involved a criminal prosecution that the state had aggressively pursued. It was part of the appeal of its facts that the Texas statute, in contrast to the Georgia statute in *Bowers*, only criminalized gay and lesbian sex acts — in short, it was precisely the kind of discriminatory statute on which *Romer v. Evans* had cast constitutional doubt. The Court, if inclined not to go beyond the facts of *Lawrence v. Texas*, could strike down the Texas statute and leave open the question of whether a statute like that in *Bowers* was unconstitutional. The thinking was that Justice O'Connor, now the swing vote who had been in the majority in *Bowers*, might not be willing to overrule but would join a majority to strike down a discriminatory statute like that of Texas.

The Supreme Court granted certiorari on three questions: whether the Texas statute violated the Equal Protection Clause, whether it violated the Due Process Clause, and whether *Bowers v. Hardwick* should be overruled. Because the Supreme Court granted certiorari to consider whether *Bowers* should be overruled, briefs had to address the issue. In fact, as was to become quite clear in oral argument, the justices were more interested in the due process argument that would call for overruling *Bowers v. Hardwick* than in the equal protection argument limited to the facts of *Lawrence v. Texas.*

The opinion in *Bowers v. Hardwick* was critically vulnerable on a number of fronts. First, the opinion for the Court of Justice White expressed both a general skepticism about the legitimacy of the protection of the constitutional right to privacy as well as a specific skepticism about the application of the right to gay/lesbian sex acts, but this skepticism was in tension with the view of a majority of that Court that privacy applied to abortion. Second, the Court's treatment of history, both in Justice White's and Chief Justice Burger's opinions, problematically failed to note that the history largely pertained to nonprocreational sex acts (a number of which were now constitutionally protected) and was not limited to gay/lesbian sex acts. Third, the Court in *Bowers* was preoccupied with a fairly abstract conception of sex acts without reference to the role of those sex acts in human lives, or the role such laws played in supporting the kinds of irrational prejudice the Court had struck down in *Romer v. Evans.*

Arguments along all these lines would be developed in the brief for the petitioners and find themselves into the opinion for the Court. Some important arguments of the Court's opinion, notably the appeal to comparative constitutional law developments abroad, were not emphasized in the brief, but were prominently made in amici briefs Justice Kennedy used in developing an argument for the majority based on these developments. This aspect of Kennedy's opinion had not been anticipated by the litigators.

The briefs submitted to the Supreme Court included briefs for the petitioners, for the respondent State of Texas, and, in reply, for the petitioners. In addition, there were an unusually large number of amici briefs both in support of the petitioners and respondents, some of which went in depth into arguments that clearly influenced the opinions for the Court (to be discussed in the following chapters). I discuss all of these briefs in this chapter, concluding with the oral arguments before the Supreme Court.

The brief for the petitioner made four basic points: (1) that the Texas criminal statute violated a basic right of privacy (substantively protected by the Due Process Clause) possessed by all Americans that extended to gay/lesbian Americans, as was shown by a number of objective considerations; (2) that Texas had offered no justification that could support abridgment of such a basic right, (3) that, in light of 1 and 2, *Bowers v. Hardwick* should be overruled; and (4) that the Texas statute also unconstitutionally discriminated against gay/lesbian Americans inconsistent with the Equal Protection Clause.

The first point was supported by a close analysis of the Court's elaborations of the constitutional right to privacy as it applied to contraception and abortion, in both cases, to unmarried persons, arguing that the underlying basic right should be understood in terms of what Kenneth Karst has called the right of intimate association. The Court in *Lawrence*, unlike that in *Bowers*, had resolved its doubts about the application of the constitutional right to privacy to abortion. Indeed, the plurality in *Casey* was at pains to argue that one of its reasons for reaffirming the core of *Roe v. Wade* was that, in contrast to Justice White in *Bowers*, its members believed that the inference and elaboration of a free-standing constitutional right to privacy was wholly legitimate.

Since the right itself was wholly legitimate and a basic right belonging to all Americans, there could be no reasonable exception to this basic right for gays and lesbians, because both psychological and demographic evidence showed that "gay Americans have exactly the same vital interests as all others in their bodily integrity and the privacy of their homes." In support of "the reality of these [gay/lesbian] families," the brief cited the 2000 U.S. Census, which identified more than 600,000 households of same-sex partners nationally, "including almost 43,000 in Texas."

Among the objective considerations supporting the extension of this basic right to gays and lesbians was a questioning of the alleged history of criminalization of gay/lesbian sex on which *Bowers v. Hardwick* relied (there had been few actual prosecutions for private sex acts, and the criminal penalties applied to all nonprocreational sex acts, not just to those of gays and lesbians). In any event, the *Lawrence* Court clearly did not accept an originalist approach as decisive, but relied as well on more recent developments to inform how the basic right was reasonably understood in contemporary circumstances. On this latter point, the brief observed that, whereas at the time of *Bowers* twenty-six states had removed consensual sodomy laws from their criminal codes, today "only thirteen states still have such prohibitions. Moreover, of those thirteen states, Texas and the three others that have discriminatory rules have eliminated criminal prohibitions in this area for the vast majority of adult couples." These developments had been limited only to consensual sodomy and fornication, "the *only* criminal laws in American history where the States has acted solely to limit forms of intimacy by consenting adults," and had not extended to other crimes relating to sexuality based on additional elements reflecting state concerns protecting the marriage contract (adultery and bigamy), or protecting vulnerable individuals who might not be capable of true consent (incest and underage sex laws), or commercial or public interactions that had a negative effect on the wider community (prostitution and public sex laws). Such objective considerations were reflected not only in legislative decriminalizations but in the opinions of a number of state supreme courts that had struck down sodomy laws under their state constitutions.

On the second point (compelling state interests), there was "no countervailing interest remotely comparable to those weighted by this Court in other recent cases involving fundamental liberties, such as the State's interests in protecting the potentiality of human life, *Casey*, . . . in protecting the welfare of children, . . . or in protecting and preserving human life." The state claimed no such public interest "other than a pure statement of moral condemnation," a claim of majority moral preferences that had never been enough to justify abridgment of the basic right to privacy or other protected constitutional rights. Yet, such an inadequate rationalization had been used by the State of Texas to justify the arrest and holding in custody of Lawrence and Garner (and used as well to disqualify them from a number of professions) and would be a ground in four states for them to be considered sex offenders who must register with law enforcement. Although the Texas law did not authorize imprisonment as a penalty, "prison terms can be imposed in the twelve other states with sodomy prohibitions, in some cases up to ten years."

Third, *Bowers* was so incoherent with respect to the elaboration of the constitutional right to privacy in other cases that its overruling would render the Court's elaboration of basic constitutional principles more coherent and principled and thus more legitimate. *Bowers* was out of line not only with the constitutional precedents on privacy, but with the steady movement of the nation "rejecting second-class-citizen status for gay and lesbian Americans," including not only *Romer v. Evans* but the states and municipalities that had added sexual orientation to laws barring discrimination.

Fourth, because the Texas statute criminalized only homosexual as opposed to heterosexual sodomy, it violated the Equal Protection Clause. In fact, various nonprocreational sex acts were now conventional among U.S. heterosexual adults, and thus the Texas statute targeted and harmed only gay persons. Using the analysis of *Romer v. Evans*, the petitioner's brief argued that when "broader realities and history are considered," the Texas statute not only lacked a rational basis, but expressed the desire of democratic majorities in Texas to condemn an unpopular group in precisely the mindless way that *Romer* condemned. There was no legitimate purpose that could sustain this law; for example, "the law's discriminatory regulation of 'deviate sexual intercourse' was unrelated to any interest in reproduction, for oral and anal sex are obviously not methods of reproduction for any couple." The statute did what *Romer* said it could not do: brand gay persons as second-class citizens and license wide-ranging discrimination against them, including, as earlier mentioned, disqualification from various professions. The brief ended with a historical analysis of the role of discriminatory statutes like that of Texas in fomenting a modernist prejudice, homophobia, a theme several of the amici briefs amplified as well, as we shall see.

The brief for the respondent addressed both the substantive due process and equal protection claims in the brief for petitioners.

On the due process issue, the brief first questioned whether the record sustained the petitioners' argument that the case was solely one of private consensual sex acts. From lack of prosecution for other offenses, it could not reasonably be inferred that the conduct was noncommercial, or that it did not involve assault, or was indeed private, or whether either Lawrence or Garner was married or exclusively homosexual. On the substantive issue, the brief argued that the Court had adopted a historical approach to the recognition of liberty interests protected by the Due Process Clause, and that *Bowers* correctly argued that homosexual sodomy was not a historically protected liberty interest and therefore was outside the ambit of the constitutional right to privacy. In response to the appeal of the petitioners to the gradual trend to decriminalization of consensual sexual behavior between adults, the respondent argued "Four decades of gradual but incomplete decriminalization does not erase a history of one hundred and fifty years of universal reprobation." This history was interpreted to show "no long-standing tradition of protecting the right to engage in any sort of extramarital sexual conduct," and the *Lawrence* case was distinguishable from the privacy cases: "The conduct at issue in this case has nothing to do with marriage or conception or parenthood and it is not on a par with those sacred choices. Homosexual sodomy cannot occur within or lead to a marital relationship. The decision to engage in homosexual acts is not like the acts and decisions that this Court has previously found worthy of constitutional protection." This claim was supported by Justice Harlan's dissent in *Poe v. Ullman* that, after arguing that constitutional privacy protects the use of contraceptives by married couples, expressly excluded from such protection "adultery, homosexuality, and the like."

On the equal protection issue, the respondent made two points. First, the 1973 reform of the Texas Penal Code (removing criminal sanctions from heterosexual sodomy but retaining such sanctions for homosexual sodomy) "incrementally narrowed the State's neutral proscriptions against sodomy in accordance with contemporaneous developments in due process jurisprudence." What this meant was that the Supreme Court's constitutional protection of both contraception and abortion by both married and unmarried persons extended as well to heterosexual nonprocreational sex acts, and that the Texas statute reflected this constitutional development. Second, there was a rational basis for the limitation of the Texas statute to homosexual sodomy, namely, "the State's moral disapproval in a penal code of conduct for its citizens and . . . creating a disincentive against the conduct." The petitioners suggested only in a footnote that heightened scrutiny was appropriate for sexual orientation–based classifications or gender-based classifications discriminating against homosexuals, but "this assertion is not implicated by the litigation, briefed by the petitioners, or mandated by the law." In fact, the precedents, including *Romer v. Evans*, supported only rational basis scrutiny for classifications using sexual orientation, and the heightened scrutiny for gender applied only to discrimination against women. In any event, the petitioners lacked standing to make an equal protection claim because the record did not show "they possess the same-sex orientation that they contend is singled out for discrimination by the statute." Finally, the statute had a rational basis, namely, "the legitimate governmental interest of promotion of morality," and *Romer v. Evans* was not applicable, because the Texas statute was narrowly directed at immoral conduct, not, like Colorado Amendment Two struck down in *Romer*, a broad program "to disenfranchise individuals because of the mere tendency or predilection to engage in such conduct."

The reply brief of the petitioners addressed not only claims made in the brief for the respondent but claims made in amicus curiae briefs submitted in support of the petitioners and respondent (we shall discuss all these briefs as well shortly).

As an initial matter, the reply brief rejected the plea for dismissal on the respondent's alleged ground that the case might involve other elements besides consensual sex in the home, for example, a commercial element, or that petitioners failed to allege they were exclusively homosexual. The petitioners were charged with one offense that was the subject now of constitutional attack, and speculation that they might have committed some other offense, neither charged nor proved, could not reasonably affect the constitutional analysis of the crime of which they were convicted by the State of Texas.

In reply to the respondent's claim that the Texas law did not burden a fundamental right, the reply brief argued that the opinion in *Casey* clearly showed that a fundamental right was not limited to that defined at the most specific level as originalists believed, and that the cases on which the respondent relied showed, in fact, that a majority of justices rejected the originalist approach taken by some justices. In *Washington v. Glucksberg* (1997), for example, the Court refused to extend the right to constitutional privacy to physician-assisted suicide not solely on the basis of originalist history but on the basis of contemporary legislation and the powerful state interests in protecting life. The brief thus summarized its historical argument:

While the Court examines relevant history in all cases, the personal liberty that is protected by the Due Process Clause is not perpetually frozen in the mold set by the laws of 1868 or any other bygone age. Nor is the Court's job merely to mirror all changes around it. The Court must apply its "reasoned judgment" to determine the deeper question of what is required to protect Americans' ordered liberty today.

The claim of the respondent that the fundamental right to privacy should be limited to the marital bedroom reflected only "the Court's earliest privacy decisions, *Griswold*, and Justice Harlan's dissent in *Poe*," and did not take seriously the later case law that extended the right, protecting both contraception and abortion, to unmarried persons. If the right to privacy extended to a choice by an individual, married or unmarried, whether to bear or beget a child, "the concomitant right to decide whether and with whom to engage in sexual intimacy cannot be for married couples only," and "by the same token, the State may not ban sexual relations by unmarried persons that do *not* lead to procreation." This meant that the "core teaching of the contraception cases is that the state may not force individuals to have only procreative sex." The rejection of Texas's argument that the state might police the sexual choices of all unmarried adults could not, consistent with the principle of constitutional privacy, be accepted. It was for this reason that *Bowers v. Hardwick*, which failed to extend the right enjoyed by unmarried heterosexual couples to homosexual couples, must be overruled, because this "will bring coherence to the Constitution's protection of this deeply personal sphere for *all* Americans."

The reply brief also supported its historical argument by reference to several amicus briefs for the petitioners (those of the Cato Institute, the American Civil Liberties Union [ACLU], and the history professors) that "there is not a single reported nineteenth-century case clearly upholding a sodomy conviction for *private* consensual conduct between two adults." Rather, where the facts are known, "every one of those involves force, minors, animals, or public places." The states historically had laws that technically applied to private consensual conduct, but "the vast majority of the laws proscribed specific conduct whether committed with a person of the same or different sex" and "often applied to married couples." The reply brief then noted, as well, the more recent pattern of decriminalization of sodomy as well as fornication. In this context, the brief limited its argument to sodomy and fornication, arguing that the "laws against bestiality, prostitution, incest, adultery, [and] bigamy" did not impose "such a wholesale and devastating burden on individual liberty" and involved important state interests not present in *Lawrence*.

The reply brief made two observations about the alleged purpose of the Texas law. First, the State of Texas had always claimed that its purpose was public morality, but this purpose came in this case, as in *Romer v. Evans*, to nothing more than "discomfort with and dislike of a particular social group," which *Romer* condemned as an irrational basis for legal discrimination. Texas now claimed that its legislators might have wanted to avoid constitutional litigation over marital behavior when they repealed the prior, more evenhanded sodomy law. But, targeting same-sex couples for criminal penalties did nothing to advance this purpose, and the line drawn by the new statute did not focus on marriage but rather distinguished between same-sex and different-sex couples. The claim in several amicus briefs for the respondent (that the statute protects marriage) failed for the same reason.

Second, several *amicus* briefs for respondent contended that the distinction in the Texas statute was rationally related to public health, particularly HIV and AIDS. But appealing to the authority of an amicus brief for the petitioners, the reply observed that the distinction in the Texas statute antedated HIV and thus was not the basis for the distinction. This explained why the statute overinclusively banned the many forms of same-sex relations that did not involve this risk and underinclusively failed to ban the heterosexual forms of sexuality that did impose this risk. The statute was never concerned with such health risks, which it thus did not rationally prevent.

The reply brief concluded that Texas and its amici acted "as if there were no history of antigay discrimination in this country and as if this law did not function as a badge of inferiority, spreading harms well beyond direct criminal prosecutions." The role of a discriminatory statute like that of Texas in enforcing prejudice could not be ignored when it defended such a rarely enforced law precisely on the ground that it offered official sanction to the condemnation Texas imposed on intimate same-sex life and relationships.

———

One of the most important and remarkable features of the litigation strategy in *Lawrence v. Texas* was that it gathered in its support not only such a large number of amici briefs from diverse sources, but briefs by some of the most distinguished scholars from various disciplines in the United States. Few cases have involved supporting briefs of this number and quality, suggesting that the intellectually threadbare arguments of the *Bowers* majority (in particular, its appeal to history) had so disturbed scholars that they felt an obligation to show how problematic they were.

Amicus briefs for the petitioners came from the alliance of Baptists et al., the American Psychological Association et al., the CATO Institute, the Human Rights Campaign et al., the National Lesbian and Gay Law Association et al., professors of history, Republican Unity Coalition et al., the American Bar Association, the American Public Health Association et al., the Institute for Justice of the NOW Legal Defense and Education Fund, the Log Cabin Republicans et al., Mary Robinson et al., constitutional law professors, and the American Civil Liberties Union (ACLU). Many of these briefs clearly aimed to show the breadth of support along the political spectrum of conservative to liberal for the case of the petitioners, including not only gay political and legal groups such as Human Rights Campaign and the National Lesbian and Gay Law Association, et al., but among many U.S. religions (the alliance of Baptists et al.), libertarian think tanks such as the CATO Institute, Republican groups such as the Republican Unity Coalition et al. and the Log Cabin Republicans et al., as well as a feminist political and legal organization, the NOW Legal Defense and Education Fund.

The opinion of the Court in *Lawrence* made clear that some of these amicus briefs were particularly important to the thinking of the justices and to the opinion for the Court of Justice Kennedy, especially those dealing with history and with the relevance of legal developments abroad, an issue on which the brief for the petitioners did not particularly focus, but that was an important ground for Justice Kennedy's argument.

Finally, the brief of the American Public Health Association et al. apparently entirely undercut the argument about health risks as a reasonable constitutional basis for the Texas statute and apparently placed the issue in light of demographic and psychological facts, including the U.S. history of prejudice, that the Court found appealing. Next I discuss the relevant briefs as they bear on these four issues.

History

Three amicus briefs for the petitioners made historical arguments that clearly compelled the Supreme Court to reconsider the rather crude originalist appeal to history in *Bowers v. Hardwick*. Justice White had argued, in his opinion for the Court in *Bowers*, that the unbroken history of the criminalization of gay/lesbian sodomy put history decisively against the elaboration of the right to constitutional privacy to include gay/lesbian sex. But the historical arguments of Professor William Eskridge of Yale Law School, who cowrote (with Robert Levy) the brief for the CATO Institute, as well as those in the brief for the professors of history and the brief of the ACLU cast doubt on the interpretation of history central to *Bowers*.

The brief for CATO, depending largely on Professor Eskridge's original historical research, divided the legal history of U.S. sodomy laws into three periods: the nineteenth century, the expansion of sodomy laws from 1879 to 1969, and sodomy reform from 1969 to 2002. The CATO brief omitted some relevant historical facts (oral sex was not a crime in most U.S. states before 1791 and remained a crime in Massachusetts until recently). Its overall point — that such statutes applied equally to heterosexual and homosexual nonprocreational sex acts — was, however, quite right.

The first period discussed in the CATO brief condemned a "crime against nature," which involved anal penetration of a man or an animal, a woman or girl, or another man or boy. "Oral sex was not a crime in any American state in 1868, nor did any sodomy law before the twentieth century focus on 'homosexual sodomy' " (rather, such laws applied to both heterosexual and homosexual forms and could be committed within marriage). Moreover, the pattern of prosecutions in this period focused on public indecency or protection of children, women, and weaker men against sexual assault, not on consensual adult sexual relations in the home.

The second period (1879–1969) not only expanded the scope of sodomy laws to include oral sex, but, in 1880, some sixty-three persons were incarcerated for sodomy in the United States, almost all of them people of color and immigrants. "By 1921, hundreds of men were being arrested and imprisoned for the crime each year." The pattern, if anything, worsened during the McCarthy era when "'homosexuals' became the scapegoats for a more brutal campaign of repression," including not only prosecution and incarceration, but deportation or being debarred from entering the country, discharged from public employment, expelled from the armed services, and being exposed by the state as "sex perverts" to their families, employers, and communities. "Although most reported convictions were still for sodomy with minors or forcible sodomy, an alarming number were for sodomy between consenting adults in private places." In response to these excesses, the American Law Institute (ALI) in 1955 recommended decriminalization; New York in 1950 reduced consensual sodomy to a misdemeanor, and Illinois decriminalized it in 1961.

The third period (1969–2002) began with the Stonewall riots of 1969, after which gay people increasingly engaged in political activism to protect their lives against police incursion. Allies included the ABA and the medical profession, which in 1973 resolved that homosexuality is not a mental or psychological defect, and therefore was not a just basis for unequal treatment. Between 1969 and 1976, eighteen states decriminalized consensual sodomy consistent with the ALI's recommendation. But the 1970s saw as well a backlash: one state, Idaho, first decriminalized, and then reinstated its criminal code; whereas Arkansas decriminalized, and then recriminalized only same-sex sodomy. Others, including Kansas, Texas, Montana, Kentucky, Missouri, Nevada, and Tennessee decriminalized consensual sodomy with someone of the opposite sex, leaving same-sex consensual sodomy a misdemeanor. Two other states (Oklahoma and Maryland) reached the same rule through court opinions that construed their sodomy statutes to apply only to gay/lesbian sex. After 1989, state court judges, including the Kentucky Supreme Court in 1992, struck down the state's same-sex sodomy law as inconsistent with principles of equality in the state constitution. Nevada repealed its same-sex sodomy law in 1993, and the courts in other states decriminalized same-sex sodomy. By the time of *Lawrence*, states that openly discriminated were Texas, Kansas, part of Missouri, and Oklahoma.

The brief for CATO undermined the historical appeal in *Bowers* to an unbroken U.S. history of criminal condemnation of same-sex relations, including its claim that what Hardwick did (namely, oral sex) was criminal when the Fourteenth Amendment was ratified. But the Court got its history quite wrong: "no statement in 1868 made oral sex a crime. No state made sex between women a crime. No state code focused only on sex between men. No law and no court decision and no legal treatise invoked the concept of 'homosexual sodomy,' a term that did not exist in 1868. No reported case in the United States between 1787 and 1868 clearly applied sodomy laws to conduct within the bedroom between consenting adults." The Court's understanding of history was "incomplete," for, on closer historical examination, "the fundamental freedoms Americans enjoy have included choices involving the deployment of the body, intimate relationships, and the home. These are freedoms gay Americans enjoyed until the antihomosexual repression of 1945–1969 — an aberration in our history of liberty that this Court should now close forever."

This more complex pattern of history made possible the reasonable normative interpretation the brief for CATO, like other briefs for the petitioners, urged upon the Court, based on the view that the principle of constitutional privacy had long been in the U.S. constitutional and political tradition, albeit sometimes flouted, and that the principle, as already recognized in the earlier cases dealing with contraception and abortion, reasonably applied to gay/lesbian nonprocreational sex as it already clearly did to heterosexual sex. The CATO brief showed, based on the work of myself and others, that a powerful textual, historical, and normative argument would place the protection of unenumerated rights in the Privileges and Immunities Clause of the Fourteenth Amendment, and that the right to intimate life was clearly one of those rights.

The brief of the professors of history (including some of the most distinguished U.S. historians) did not, unlike the brief for CATO, integrate legal history into a constitutional analysis. Rather, it made two historical points that were relevant to legal analysis: "(1) no consistent historical practice singles out same-sex behavior as 'sodomy' subject to proscription, and (2) the governmental policy of classifying and discriminating against certain citizens on the basis of their homosexual status is an unprecedented project of the twentieth century, which is already being dismantled." On the first point, the brief concurred in the CATO brief's critique of the historical analysis in *Bowers:* "The specification of 'homosexual sodomy' as a criminal offense does not carry the pedigree of the ages but is almost exclusively an invention of the recent past." On the second point, the brief of the professors offered a compelling explanation of the relatively recent development of U.S. homophobia, namely, one "motivated by an underlying uneasiness about the dramatic changes underway in gender roles at the turn of the last century," and showed the extent of repression of homosexuals in the twentieth–century United States, culminating in the persecutions "at every level of government after the Second World War" and an executive order of President Eisenhower "requiring the discharge of homosexual employees from federal employment, civilian, or military."

The brief for the ACLU placed great weight on the reasonable interpretation of the principle of constitutional privacy as it was developed and applied to contraception and abortion, and how both "a cramped understanding of the principles of autonomy, of the Court's earlier cases, and of our nation's history, lies at the heart of the error in *Bowers v. Hardwick.*" The privacy cases protected the right to engage in nonprocreative sex, which reasonably extended to gay/lesbian sex. "It would be particularly incoherent – indeed, perverse – to limit the right to engage in *nonprocreative* sex to couples who *could procreate* if they so chose."

Bowers introduced precisely this incoherence into U.S. law on the ground of an unbroken history of criminal condemnation of same-sex relations in the United States. But the ACLU brief argued, appealing to historical arguments by Professor Eskridge and others as well as its own researchers, that there is no such tradition, certainly not one specifically concerned with same-sex relations. Sodomy laws were not historically directed at gays and lesbians, but rather prohibited all sodomy, regardless of the sex of the participants: "sodomy was considered a sin against *procreation*, not an offense against *heterosexuality.*" The *Bowers* Court failed to see that the principle of constitutional privacy (protecting nonprocreational sex in contraception and abortion) extended as well to all sodomy laws. Its alleged historical reason for thus truncating the scope of the right would apply to contraception and abortion as well, and its attempt to distinguish these cases from homosexual sodomy rested on a misunderstanding of that history, which was not concerned only with same-sex sodomy. The ACLU brief added to the CATO brief's three stages yet a fourth stage, prior to the American Revolution, when some of the colonies, such as Massachusetts and others, were "intimately involved in policing private behavior," but otherwise concurred with the three stages: a tolerant early republic throughout much of the nineteenth century, then the expansion of sodomy laws, and the modern period of advancing decriminalization at home and abroad. Nothing in this supported the history to which *Bowers* subscribed; rather, the *Bowers* Court aligned itself with one strand of U.S. history that was inconsistent with the developing principle of constitutional privacy.

<hr>

Legal Developments Abroad

One of the amicus briefs for the petitioners powerfully appealed to legal developments abroad, namely, the brief amici curiae of Mary Robinson et al., written by Professor Robert Wintemute of King's College, London, and others. The brief urged that the issue of *Lawrence* should be assessed in terms of legal developments elsewhere, for "this Court has regularly and traditionally used international and foreign law rulings to aid its constitutional interpretation." The brief on this basis questioned the reasonable authority of *Bowers* because it failed to take seriously dimensions of privacy relating to making decisions, protecting relationships, and preserving zones of privacy, all of which had been grounds accepted abroad for protecting the rights of gays and lesbians. For example, the European Court of Human Rights had decided in *Dudgeon v. United Kingdom* that laws barring male-male sexual contact in the home violated decisional privacy protected by Article 8 of the European Convention on Human Rights; the Constitutional Court of South Africa and the highest appellate court of the United Kingdom had protected relational aspects of gay/lesbian persons; and *Dudgeon* and other cases gave weight to consensual adult gay sex in the home, and showed that such protection in no way reasonably committed a court to protect adultery, incest, or other sex crimes. Finally, the brief discussed as well how these and other cases had invoked as reasons for invalidating sodomy laws that they express irrational prejudice that denied a politically unpopular group equal treatment.

Health Risks

The brief of the American Public Health Association et al., as amici curiae in support of the petitioners, addressed a purpose of the Texas law that had not been offered or defended by the State of Texas, namely, health risks associated, in particular, with the transmission of AIDS. The brief defended Texas's refusal to invoke this purpose because the legislative history of the statute showed health risks were not the rationale of the law, which was passed well before the first known diagnosis of AIDS, and because, on closer examination, the Texas statute was not rationally related to this purpose. The gravamen of the brief's rationality analysis rested on two points. First, the statute was overinclusive because it condemned the many forms of gay/lesbian sex that do not instantiate this risk, and underinclusive because it failed to apply to the many forms of heterosexual sex that did impose this risk. Second, criminalizing homosexual activity did not deter unsafe sexual practices. In fact, decriminalizing sodomy "has coincided with a *decrease* in HIV transmission among gay men," precisely because such decriminalization advanced effective public education and enabled gays and lesbians to speak candidly and think carefully about their sexual lives.

Demographic and Psychological Facts

The brief amici curiae of the American Psychological Association et al. importantly placed before the Supreme Court the views of the leading professional organizations dealing with mental health and human development about the incidence and development of sexual orientation, the recognition that homosexuality is not a "mental disorder," the difficulties in changing sexual orientation, the importance of consensual sexual happiness in the lives of gays and lesbians, and well-attested demographic facts about the numbers of gays and lesbians now living together in the United States. The brief discussed as well the important role sodomy laws played in sustaining forms of irrational prejudice that blight the lives of gays and lesbians.

Amicus briefs for the respondent came from Agudath Israel, the Arizona Policy and Pro-Family Network, the American Center for Law and Justice, the Center for Marriage Law, the Texas Physicians Resource Council et al., the Center for Law and Justice, Concerned Women for America, the Family Research Council, the Liberty Counsel, the Pro-Family Law Center et al., Public Advocates of the United States et al., the Texas Eagle Forum et al., Texas legislators, the Center for the Original Intent of the Constitution, United Families International, and the States of Alabama, South Carolina, and Utah.

On the four points central to the amicus briefs for the petitioners, only one of these briefs even addressed the historical research prominently offered by those for the petitioners, namely, the brief of the Center for the Original Intent of the Constitution, and it did so in precisely the originalist spirit the historical briefs for the petitioners fundamentally questioned in terms of the development of constitutional privacy as a basic constitutional right (which rejected originalism). The question of health risks was raised not by the State of Texas but by the amicus brief of the Texas Physicians Resource Council et al., amici here including the Christian Medical and Dental Associations and the Catholic Medical Association. The religiously sectarian character of these briefs was well illustrated by the brief of the Family Research Council et al., written by Gerard Bradley of Notre Dame Law School and Robert George of Princeton University. George and Bradley were prominent advocates of new natural law, a highly sectarian view that defended the current teachings on sexuality and gender of the hierarchy of the Catholic Church. A view that regarded contraception, masturbation, abortion, and gay/lesbian sex as intrinsically morally wrong was not a view likely to fit the cases to which the Supreme Court has extended the protection of the constitutional right to privacy. The brief barely acknowledged *Roe* and *Casey*, and gave a particularly strained interpretation to *Griswold* (limiting it to marital intercourse), ignoring its later extensions and claiming that the view of Justice Harlan in *Poe v. Ullman* (expressly denying that the right applies to adultery or homosexuality) should be followed. A view of this sort—so unrooted in any respect for the authority of case law—confirmed what seemed to be the intent of many of the other amicus briefs: they stated a fixed sectarian position, one self-consciously external to and critical of existing legal authority.

The comparison between them and the amicus briefs for the petitioners, on so many of the issues that rendered *Bowers v. Hardwick* analytically vulnerable, may have confirmed for many of the justices just how vulnerable *Bowers* was. As the oral arguments clearly showed, many justices—to the pleasant surprise of the lawyers for Lawrence—were clearly ready to move beyond the facts of *Lawrence* and consider overruling *Bowers v. Hardwick*.

Oral arguments before the Supreme Court can be matters of public importance when they touch on issues of human rights central to the lives of large numbers of Americans. If the defeat in *Bowers v. Hardwick* had been experienced by many U.S. gays and lesbians as a dehumanizing insult analogous to the experience of African Americans of *Plessy v. Ferguson,* the Court's willingness to hear a case that might overrule or qualify *Bowers* was a matter that riveted their attention. Lambda, as a matter of public education, had sponsored public fora in which the importance of *Lawrence v. Texas* was made quite clear to gay and lesbian communities in the United States. The interest in attending the oral arguments was, as a consequence, remarkable with numbers of people lining up to get a place long before the oral arguments. The courtroom was crowded with an audience largely of gays and lesbians who followed every turn in the argument with rapt attention and a growing sense of excitement as it became clear, both from the tone and substance of the oral arguments (including a certain levity in jokes coming from the bench, leading to laughter from the audience), the degree to which a majority of this Court, in contrast to the Court in *Bowers,* might indeed be not only open but hospitable to an argument that would overrule *Bowers.*

Paul M. Smith, who argued the case on behalf of the petitioners, reported a sense of an extraordinary moment both in the history of U.S. constitutional law and in the history of gay/lesbian rights in the United States. Even the justices most clearly antagonistic to his argument (Chief Justice Rehnquist and Justice Scalia) were comparatively moderate in their comments, perhaps conscious of the audience they were facing in the Court; Justice Thomas, also antagonistic, was silent, but he was always silent in oral argument (Thomas the Silent, as he is informally known).

Smith's oral argument before the Supreme Court opened with his statement emphasizing the substantive due process right of all adult couples (heterosexual and homosexual) "to be free from unwarranted State intrusion into their personal decisions about their preferred forms of sexual expression" and the equal protection violation of criminalizing nonprocreational sex only of same-sex couples.

Chief Justice Rehnquist immediately engaged Smith on the issue of history, in particular, that the right in question had been banned for a long time and thus was not supported by history. Justice Scalia posed the same question in originalist terms: it sufficed that same-sex conduct was criminal in the nineteenth century to show that its criminalization is not unconstitutional. Smith responded that it was conceded by the State of Georgia in *Bowers* that heterosexual nonprocreational sex could not constitutionally be subject to criminal penalty, and that judgment ran against originalist history as well (such sex was criminal in the nineteenth century). Justice Scalia refused to concede the point, presumably because, on originalist grounds, he opposed the elaboration of the constitutional right to privacy. Smith accepted this was Scalia's view, but said it was not the view of other justices, to whom he addressed his overall argument.

Justice Ginsburg interjected, at this point, the Court's elaboration of the right to use contraceptives to unmarried couples, which suggested a less rigid appeal to history than originalism permitted. Smith took up the point, emphasizing that a close reading of historical tradition showed no record of active enforcement of these laws in much of the nineteenth century except for cases involving coercion, children, or public sexual activity.

Justice Scalia returned the discussion to history: there have been many changes in U.S. public attitudes over time (for example, no longer forbidding flagpole sitting), but certainly not all such changes were constitutionally protected. Smith responded by pointing to the effects of some laws on the real lives of people, which Justice Scalia claimed not to understand. Smith responded that privacy is concerned with procreation or nonprocreation with one's sexual partner, to which Scalia responded that none of the privacy cases involved non-procreation. Smith answered that "it's illogical, fundamentally illogical to say that an unmarried couple has a right [*sic*] free of State intrusion to decide whether or not to have procreative or nonprocreative sex, but it doesn't have the right to be free from State intrusion — free from a law that says you can't have any sexual intimacy at all. There's a — there's a jagged piece missing from the edifice of this Court's substantive fundamental rights jurisprudence."

Smith was then questioned regarding his historical claim that sodomy laws were not enforced against consensual adult sexual activity in the home, a fact that might rest on the difficulties of proof, nothing more. Smith contrasted the aggressive enforcement of drug laws in contrast to sodomy laws, and argued that the different treatment reflected an underlying real difference.

The Court's questioning of Smith then turned to his equal protection argument. Adultery laws and some rape laws applied only to heterosexual sex. Would they therefore violate equal protection? Smith responded he did not claim all such laws were unconstitutional, but only laws that targeted just a minority of people in the state, as Texas's law did. With respect to a rape law, in particular, Smith argued that the exclusion of gays as victims would have to be justified, which it might be, for example, because there was not a real problem here, or victims are more able to protect themselves. Smith's emphasis at this point was on the moral judgments of majorities that allowed freedom for themselves, but imposed coercion for the same conduct on minorities.

The mention of morality led to Scalia's questioning of whether Smith's argument might not apply to bigamy, or, as later suggested, adultery. Smith responded by emphasizing that a law like that of Texas was, in fact, quite recent, criminalizing only same-sex nonprocreational sex. Bigamy, in contrast, reflects legitimate needs to protect the family, and so does, as he later observed, adultery.

Another query from Chief Justice Rehnquist was along these lines: if this law is struck down, does that mean a State could not prefer heterosexuals to homosexuals as kindergarten teachers? Smith responded that such action should not be based on mere dislike.

It was at this point that Justice Ginsburg made quite clear that the Court wanted to hear his argument for overruling *Bowers*. Smith responded that, although it may not have been apparent in 1986 when *Bowers* was decided, it was clear in 2003 "that there are hundreds of thousands of people registered in the 2000 Census who have formed gay families, . . . many of them raising children, and that for those people, the opportunity to engage in sexual expression as they will in the privacy of their homes performs much the same function that it does in the marital context."

Charles Rosenthal then spoke on behalf of Texas. His opening point was that the record did not show that the petitioners were homosexuals, to which justices responded that it sufficed, on the substantive due process issue, that the law criminalized homosexual conduct.

Rosenthal was then questioned about his claim that there has been a change of public opinion about homosexuals, but not homosexual acts, and was directly challenged to address the petitioners' argument that these laws harm real people in a way that understated the constitutional value. Rosenthal did not answer the question, but rather noted that the Texas law made sodomy only a misdemeanor.

Justice Ginsburg followed up this line of questioning by suggesting that the sharp distinction Rosenthal was drawing between gay/lesbian sex acts and the family could not be maintained if in fact gays and lesbians could and do adopt children under Texas law. She asked, accordingly, whether such foster parent arrangements or adoptions by gay/lesbians were legal in Texas. Rosenthal could not answer her question. At this point in Rosenthal's rather lackluster oral argument, Justice Scalia quipped: "You're fairly certain that they can't procreate children, aren't you? [Laughter.]" Rosenthal's apparent difficulties in oral argument continued when he was asked whether Texas criminalized fornication and adultery, to which he responded that neither is criminal; about adultery, in particular, "adultery is not penalized in Texas, but it is certainly not condoned in Texas. [Laughter.]"

It was Justice Breyer who, in the spirit of John Stuart Mill's harm principle, pressed the point that when a statute abridged a constitutionally protected fundamental right, citation of commonly held majoritarian moral views did not suffice. Rather, the state must point to some independently specified secular harm that justified the burden imposed on the fundamental right. Breyer thus asked: "So — so what is the justification for this statute, other than, you know, it's not what they say on the other side, is this is simply, I do not like thee, Doctor Fell, the reason why I cannot tell. [Laughter.]"

Justice Scalia helpfully asked Rosenthal if historical tradition might not be the answer, to which Justice Stevens responded that it was not when the Supreme Court struck down antimiscegenation laws.

After a meandering discussion of when Texas criminalized sodomy and then passed the statute in this case, Justice Breyer pressed the point that mere appeal to majoritarian moral judgments could not be enough in the absence of harm, and that Texas's appeal to moral judgment seemed problematic in precisely this way. Justice Souter supported and underscored Justice Breyer's Millian point: "When the state criminalizes behavior as immoral, customarily what it points to is not simply an isolated moral judgment or the moral judgment alone, but it points to a moral judgment which is backed up by some demonstration of harm to other people." In response to Rosenthal's appeal to drug use, Souter asked: "Well, do you point to a kind of harm here to an individual or to the individual's partner, which is comparable to the harm that results from the harm to the deterioration of the body and mind from drug-taking?"

Rosenthal admitted he could not adduce a harm like that incident to drug taking, but mentioned health risks. When questioned about health risks, Rosenthal did not embrace the argument, noting that an amicus brief had made such an argument, but an opposing amicus brief had answered its claims. From the point of view of the State of Texas, "for each expert there's an equal and opposite expert." To Breyer's pressing for some evidence of harm, Rosenthal appealed to the nonprocreational character of gay/lesbian sex, which, Breyer responded, was a distinction without a difference, since Texas blessed the nonprocreational sex of heterosexuals.

Rosenthal then turned to the equal protection argument: Texas was concerned, he argued, not with orientation, but with conduct, in contrast to *Romer v. Evans.* Justice O'Connor queried whether a violation of criminal law might not make a gay person less appealing in politics, and came back to the point that the Texas law imposed disadvantages on gays and lesbians.

Smith's brief rebuttal made two points. First, the Texas law was applied in *Lawrence* to consensual adult sex in the privacy of the home, and petitioners were not convicted for anything else (commercial sex,

sex with minors, or nonconsensual sex). And second, on the issue of health risks, Texas made no such argument, and the Texas law made no rational distinction between safe and unsafe sex, because it was so overinclusive (forbidding gay/lesbian sex that is safe) and underinclusive (not forbidding heterosexual sex that is unsafe).

To summarize, the facts of *Lawrence v. Texas* involved, like *Bowers v. Hardwick*, an actual criminal prosecution of gay adult men for consensual sex in the home. By the time of *Lawrence*, only thirteen states retained laws against gay/lesbian sex acts, and the Supreme Court had in *Casey* reaffirmed the authority of *Roe v. Wade* and indicated in *Romer v. Evans* that the expression of homophobia in discriminatory state constitutional provisions was unconstitutional. The briefs for *Lawrence* argued that the best interpretive reading of these developments was not only that the Texas sodomy law (applicable only to sex acts of gays and lesbians) unconstitutionally violated the Equal Protection Clause, but that all such laws (including those applicable to heterosexuals as well as homosexuals) were unconstitutional burdens on the basic right of intimate life protected by the Due Process Clause and that *Bowers* accordingly must be overruled. A remarkable number of amici briefs by leading scholars supported these arguments on the basis of history, demographic developments in the U.S. population, health data, and comparative legal developments abroad. The opposing brief argued for the legitimacy of a state criminal statute that expressed majoritarian moral opinions, and was supported by amici briefs defending that position.

CHAPTER 8

Lawrence v. Texas

Opinions of the Court

The Supreme Court, in a six-to-three opinion in *Lawrence v. Texas*, held the Texas sodomy statute unconstitutional. Five justices directly overruled *Bowers v. Hardwick* as well. Justice Kennedy wrote the opinion of the Court for himself and Justices Stevens, Souter, Ginsburg, and Breyer; Justice O'Connor wrote an opinion concurring in the judgment (striking down the Texas statute). Justice Scalia filed a dissenting opinion, joined by Chief Justice Rehnquist and Justice Thomas; and Justice Thomas filed a short dissenting opinion.

Notably, the two justices who wrote opinions holding the Texas statute unconstitutional were among the three justices who had in *Casey* reaffirmed the essential principle of *Roe v. Wade*. Their argument in that earlier case made quite clear their deliberative conviction that constitutional privacy was a legitimate principle of law and that therefore the essential principle of *Roe*, resting on the reasonable interpretation of a valid principle of law, should not be overruled. Presumably, overruling *Bowers* would depend on whether it did justice to this principle of law. Justice Kennedy's opinion for the Court in *Romer v. Evans* had already, as we have seen, cast the continuing authority of *Bowers* in doubt.

It is too early to have access to the papers of the justices who decided *Lawrence v. Texas* in the way we have such access in *Bowers v. Hardwick*; we cannot therefore know how arguments proceeded either in conference or in various drafts of the opinions of the Court, or the role clerks played in this process, all of which we know with *Bowers*. We do know something, and can make reasonable inferences from what we know, including what happened. Because Chief Justice Rehnquist was in the minority after votes were cast in conference, it was the oldest justice, Justice Stevens, who assigned writing the opinion for the Court to Justice Anthony Kennedy. Justice Stevens might have wanted to write the opinion for the Court himself, since he had written a short but cogent dissent in *Bowers*, to which Justice Kennedy paid homage in *Lawrence*. In choosing Justice Kennedy, it is reasonable to believe Justice Stevens would think that, of all the justices then sitting, Justice Kennedy would, in light of his opinion for the Court in *Romer*, put the case for overruling *Bowers v. Hardwick* in the most compelling light, connecting the issue of decriminalization of sodomy to the issue of unconstitutionally discriminatory prejudice central to *Romer*. In fact, the link between the two questions was central to Justice Kennedy's argument for the Court and provided the reasons for five justices to overrule *Bowers*, namely, the role such statutes played in endorsing irrational prejudice that dehumanized gays and lesbians as outside the U.S. community of persons entitled to their constitutionally protected human rights. There may be another reason for the decision of Justice Stevens: his sense that the issue of the case had so fired Justice Kennedy's sense of justice that he would write an opinion for the Court that might stand the test of time, among other opinions of a Court not known for either the analytical powers or eloquence of a Justice Holmes or Justice Brandeis, as in that distinguished tradition. No one was more surprised than the litigators at Lambda and Jenner and Block at the analytical power and moral force of the opinion that their arguments elicited from Justice Anthony Kennedy.

Justice Kennedy's opinion for the Court, in the course of holding the Texas criminal statute unconstitutional, overruled *Bowers v. Hardwick* because, in his view, that case did not do justice to the principle of constitutional privacy as it had been developed and elaborated in case law including *Griswold v. Connecticut*, *Roe v. Wade*, and *Planned Parenthood of Southeastern Pennsylvania v. Casey*. He critically examined *Bowers* on two counts: its understanding of the basic right on which constitutional privacy rests and its treatment of the compelling state purposes that could justify a ban on gay/lesbian sex.

Justice Kennedy questioned the way in which Justice White in *Bowers* described the right in question: "whether the Federal Constitution confers a fundamental right upon homosexuals to engage in sodomy." White's very statement "discloses the Court's own failure to appreciate the extent of the liberty at stake. To say that the issue in *Bowers* was simply the right to engage in certain sexual conduct demeans the claim the individual put forward, just as it would demean a married couple were it to be said marriage is simply about the right to have sexual intercourse."

Kennedy sensitively analyzed the way Justice White's opinion objectified gay/lesbian sexuality in the same way that anti-Semitism imposed a dehumanized conception of their sexuality on Jews or racism reduced black sexuality to the coupling of animals. To be sure, criminal statutes that banned gay/lesbian sexuality applied to sex acts, but consistent with the irrational prejudice that motivated such laws, "their penalties and purposes . . . have more far-reaching consequences, touching upon the most private human conduct, sexual behavior, and in the most private of places, the home. The statutes do seek to control a personal relationship that, whether or not entitled to formal recognition in the law, is within the liberty of persons to choose without being punished as criminals."

Justice Kennedy insisted that a fair-minded understanding of the basic right underlying constitutional privacy would take seriously, both in straight and gay sexual relations, the integrity of sexual affections and lives, the connections between sexual expression and companionate friendship and love:

> It suffices for us to acknowledge that adults may choose to enter upon this relationship in the confines of their homes and their own private lives and still retain their dignity as free persons. When sexuality finds overt expression in intimate conduct with another person, the conduct can be but one element in a personal bond that is more enduring. The liberty protected by the Constitution allows homosexual persons the right to make this choice.

Justice Kennedy's critical observations about Justice White's characterization of the issue in *Bowers* echoed the same concerns in Justice Blackmun's dissenting opinion in the case, in particular, the way in which a right rooted in conviction was erased by homophobic sexualization, turning love into pornography. At the end of his opinion, Justice Kennedy returned to the ugly motives of irrational contempt that motivate such injustice: "The State cannot demean their existence or control their destiny by making their private sexual conduct a crime."

Kennedy connected White's mischaracterization of the basic right to the unreasonable way he treated history in constitutional interpre-

tation. As I earlier observed, Justice White was certainly not an originalist: he believed the interpretation of history mattered in constitutional interpretation not in terms of the situations in the world to
which those who wrote and ratified the Constitution would have
applied its terms but of more abstract connotations or intentions that
could be reasonably ascribed to the text, then recontextualized in a
reasonable understanding of what the text would mean in contemporary circumstances, including the sense of relevant facts and values.
But Justice White's failure to understand or give weight to the basic
right underlying the principle of constitutional privacy led him to a
kind of appeal to history he would in other interpretive areas have
rejected as anachronistic and unreasonable. In fact, Justice Kennedy
showed that history demonstrated, *pace* Justice White, not a specific
concern with gay/lesbian sex but a general concern with all forms of
nonprocreational sex, heterosexual and homosexual. The constitutional privacy cases up to *Bowers* rejected the historical view of the
intrinsic evil of nonprocreational sex as no longer supported by compelling secular arguments in contemporary circumstances. The
Supreme Court found this view of sexual morality an unconstitutional
purpose and thus no longer sufficient to justify the abridgment of so
basic a human right as that of intimate life. *Bowers* unreasonably gave
that anachronistic history controlling weight in the context of homosexuality after having rejected it in the context of heterosexuality.

Moreover, Justice Kennedy argued that specific concern with
homosexuality did not, as the majority in *Bowers* supposed, have
ancient roots. "American laws targeting same-sex couples did not
develop until the last third of the 20th century." Kennedy concluded
that the uses of history in *Bowers* "are not without doubt and, at the
very least, are overstated."

In any event, Kennedy argued that "our laws and traditions in the
past half century are those of most relevance here," which "show an
emerging awareness that liberty gives substantial protection to adult
persons in deciding how to conduct their private lives in matters per-
taining to sex." These developments "should have been apparent when
Bowers was decided." Such developments included the recommendation in 1955 of the American Law Institute that criminal laws not
impose "criminal penalties for consensual sexual relations conducted
in private" and the recommendation in 1957 of the Wolfenden Report

in Great Britain urging the British Parliament to repeal laws punishing homosexual conduct (its recommendations were enacted ten years later). Justice Kennedy put particular weight on the decision of the European Court of Human Rights that, almost five years before *Bowers*, held that laws criminalizing gay sex were invalid under the European Convention on Human Rights, a decision "authoritative in all countries that are members of the Council of Europe" (twenty-one countries then, forty-five nations now), a decision "at odds with the premise in *Bowers* that the claim put forward was insubstantial in our Western civilization."

But, the authorities most decisive on this issue for Justice Kennedy were the Court's own precedents, notably, *Casey* and *Romer*. In *Casey*, Justice Kennedy was one of three justices (Justices O'Connor and Souter were the others) who reaffirmed the legitimacy of the principle of constitutional privacy in general and the essential principle of *Roe v. Wade* in particular. This principle of privacy, thus clarified and reaffirmed, established a basic constitutional right to autonomy in intimate sexual matters, which persons seek in both homosexual and heterosexual relationships. Justice Kennedy also wrote for the Court in *Romer*, holding that Colorado Amendment Two was "born of animosity toward the class of persons affected" and further that it had "no rational relation to a legitimate governmental purpose." Although the plaintiff's attorneys had invited the Court to strike down the Texas statute on equal protection grounds (because it criminalized only homosexual nonprocreational sex acts), Kennedy declined to adopt their suggestion, because that would leave open that the conduct might be criminal, which would invite unjust discrimination against gays and lesbians and not address the constitutional evil of *Bowers* itself, namely, that "its continuance as precedent demeans the lives of homosexual persons."

In overruling *Bowers*, Justice Kennedy adopted as the Court's rationale the dissent of Justice Stevens in *Bowers*:

> Our prior cases make two propositions abundantly clear. First, the fact that the governing majority in a State has traditionally viewed a particular practice as immoral is not a sufficient reason for upholding a law prohibiting the practice; neither history nor tradition could save a law prohibiting miscegenation from constitu-

tional attack. Second, individual decisions by married persons, concerning the intimacies of their physical relationship, even when not intended to produce offspring, are a form of "liberty" protected by the Due Process Clause of the Fourteenth Amendment. Moreover, this protection extends to intimate choices by unmarried as well as married persons.

Because any ban on gay/lesbian sex abridged this basic right of all persons on grounds of principle, rationalized by long-standing moral opinions no longer supported by constitutionally compelling justifications, *Bowers*, which acknowledged neither the right nor the burden of justification, was overruled.

On the issue of the required burden of justification, Justice Kennedy discussed various such burdens not met by a total ban on gay/lesbian sex:

> The present case does not involve minors. It does not involve persons who might be injured or coerced or who are situated in relationships where consent might not easily be refused. It does not involve public conduct or prostitution. It does not involve whether the government must give formal recognition to any relationship that homosexual persons seek to enter. The case does involve two adults who, with full and mutual consent from each other, engaged in sexual practices common to a homosexual lifestyle. The petitioners are entitled to respect for their private lives. The State cannot demean their existence or control their destiny by making their private sexual conduct a crime. . . . The Texas statute furthers no legitimate state interest which can justify its intrusion into the personal and private life of the individual.

Kennedy concluded that the basic principles of U.S. constitutional law were not drafted by the founders in specific terms, a fact suggesting precisely that they did not claim to know "the components of liberty in its manifold possibilities" but were open to new arguments and experience that critically questioned the weight of history on grounds of justice: "They knew times can blind us to certain truths and later generations can see that laws once thought necessary and proper in fact serve only to oppress. As the Constitution endures, persons in every generation can invoke its principles in their own search for greater freedom."

The protesting ethical voices of gays and lesbians, building on earlier protest movements, stand foursquare in this tradition.

Justice O'Connor's opinion, concurring in the judgment of the Court, would not have overruled *Bowers*, in which she was in the majority. O'Connor concurred with the *Lawrence* majority that the Texas criminal statute, which banned only gay/lesbian sex acts, was unconstitutional, but she did not agree that a statute such as the Georgia ban in *Bowers*, equally applicable to heterosexual and homosexual forms of nonprocreational sex (fellatio, cunnilingus, anal intercourse), should be regarded as unconstitutional. Rather than grounding *Lawrence* in what she called "the substantive component of the Fourteenth Amendment's Due Process Clause," O'Connor regarded the Texas statute, precisely because it banned only homosexual as opposed to heterosexual nonprocreational sex acts, as in violation of the Equal Protection Clause of the Fourteenth Amendment.

In assessing the level of equal protection review applicable to the Texas statute, O'Connor argued that a more exacting standard of review is appropriate when "a law exhibits . . . a desire to harm a politically unpopular group" such as gays and lesbians, citing, inter alia, *Romer*. Because the Texas statute condemned sodomy only between homosexuals, it "makes homosexuals unequal in the eyes of the law by making particular conduct — and only that conduct — subject to criminal statute." Although prosecutions were rare and the penalty minor, "the consequences of convictions are not," including disqualification from various professions and the requirement to register as sex offenders in four states if gays/lesbians moved there; and such statutes had collateral effects, rationalizing discrimination in a number of areas. O'Connor regarded *Bowers* as only holding that the government's interest in promoting morality was sufficient to uphold a sodomy statute such as that of Georgia, but did not afford a rational basis for upholding the Texas sodomy statute against equal protection grounds. In fact, she wrote, "moral disapproval of this group, like a bare desire to harm the group, is an interest that is insufficient to satisfy rational basis review under the Equal Protection Clause," again citing *Romer*. The Texas statute was not, according to O'Connor, directed only against acts but "toward homosexuals as a class," and sanctioned discrimination against them on that basis. In effect, the Texas statute created and sustained a stigmatized status for gays and lesbians on a basis it did not and would not extend on fair terms to heterosexuals.

Although O'Connor argued it was not necessary to revisit *Bowers* to decide *Lawrence*, she was "confident, however, that so long as the Equal Protection Clause requires a sodomy law to apply equally to the private consensual conduct of homosexuals and heterosexuals alike, such a law would not stand in our democratic society." O'Connor distinguished the issue of criminalization from same-sex marriage because, unlike in *Lawrence*, where "the moral disapproval of same-sex relations" was the state's asserted interest, "other reasons exist to promote the institution of marriage beyond mere moral disapproval of an excluded group."

Justice O'Connor's unwillingness to overrule *Bowers v. Hardwick* exposed incoherence in her thinking when she earlier joined with two other justices to strike down antiabortion statutes in *Casey* because fetal life was not an adequate basis for criminalization after viability. The weight O'Connor accorded fetal life endorsed a legitimate state moral purpose in criminalization after viability and regulation earlier. If fetal life in this way could be denied constitutional weight for some purposes but not others in the very heartland of substantive due process jurisprudence, it would seem that the moral purposes underlying antisodomy laws, lacking any such basis, must, if anything, be regarded as much more constitutionally problematic, as the majority in *Lawrence* clearly saw when it overruled *Bowers*.

Justice Scalia wrote in dissent for himself, Chief Justice Rehnquist, and Justice Thomas (who also wrote a brief dissent commenting on his own view that such laws were unjustified, indeed "silly," although constitutional).

At work in Scalia's argument, of course, was that, like Justice White in *Bowers*, he was skeptical about the principle of constitutional privacy in general and its application to abortion in particular. Scalia thus began his dissent in *Lawrence* by a parodic citation of the opening line of the opinion for the Court in *Casey:* "Liberty finds no refuge in a jurisprudence of doubt." He continued by observing that all the grounds cited by the three justices writing for the Court in *Casey* when they appealed to stare decisis to justify not overruling *Roe* applied equally to not overruling *Bowers;* and conversely, the reasons for not respecting stare decisis and overruling *Bowers* elaborated by Justice Kennedy in his opinion for the Court in *Lawrence* applied equally to overruling *Roe*. Scalia did not quarrel with Justice Kennedy's claim in his opinion for the Court that *Romer v. Evans* eroded the foundations of *Bowers*, but other opinions (appealing to the nation's traditions) had eroded as well the foundations of *Roe* and yet *Casey* "subjected the restriction of abortion to heightened scrutiny without even attempting to establish that the freedom to abort was rooted in this Nation's tradition." Scalia's preoccupation with *Roe* and *Casey* continued as he explored two books cited by Justice Kennedy for their criticisms of *Bowers*, as each of them also criticized *Roe*.

Justice Kennedy's opinion for the Court had carefully shown the cumulative shift, both abroad and at home, away from the criminalization of gay/lesbian sex acts. Justice Scalia claimed not to be clear "exactly what those nonhistorical criticisms are," because he assumed that the only support for a legitimate opinion of the Supreme Court can be originalist history as opposed to the kind of normative interpretation of our history (appealing to more abstract connotations that can be reasonably recontextualized as circumstances change) that underlay much constitutional interpretation, including the opinion of Justice Kennedy for the Court in *Lawrence*. There was, for Scalia, no such cumulative shift that was constitutionally relevant. Rather, citations of judicial opinions that assumed what Scalia perceived as traditional sexual morality as a rational basis for state action were controlling for him, including a judicial opinion upholding discrimination against gays and lesbians on the authority of *Bowers*. In effect, because *Lawrence* overruled *Bowers*, all state laws dealing with sex were now questionable: "State laws against bigamy, same-sex marriage, adult incest, prostitution, masturbation, adultery, fornication, bestiality, and obscenity are . . . sustainable only in light of *Bowers'* validation of laws based on moral choices." Scalia returned to his real preoccupation with *Roe* and *Casey* when he contrasted "what a massive disruption of the social order . . . the overruling of *Bowers* entails" with how little overruling *Roe* would have changed things.

Scalia's distaste for the constitutional right to privacy took the form of denying that the right to privacy was ever grounded in the Due Process Clause, on which several opinions in *Griswold* clearly based it (including not only Justice Harlan's but the citation with approval of

Harlan's reasoning by, among others, Justices Douglas, Goldberg, and White). The real problem, from Scalia's vantage point, was, again, *Roe*, which he must concede clearly based the right on such a due process argument.

For Scalia, the originalist, nothing in Justice Kennedy's review of relevant history mattered, because the only history that could be relevant was originalist history, which *Bowers*, in his view, properly brought to bear on the question of whether gay/lesbian sex was constitutionally protected. It was, for Scalia, simply not constitutionally relevant that Kennedy pointed out that all forms of nonprocreational sexual activity were proscribed, for if this were relevant, it would raise the question, central to all the cases elaborating the constitutional right to privacy, why this purpose was now constitutionally inadequate when it came to all forms of heterosexual sex, but not to homosexual sex. Since only originalist history had weight for Scalia, any historical shifts since the founding or the Reconstruction amendments had no weight whatsoever, and even less relevant were legal and constitutional developments abroad. Only U.S. history and culture counted, as if that legal culture were hermetically sealed from the constitutional democracies of Great Britain and Europe (commonly known as the Western tradition), let alone elsewhere.

Justice Scalia also sharply questioned Justice O'Connor's equal protection analysis. O'Connor's opinion, as we have seen, rested importantly on *Romer*, and it was not surprising that Scalia, who bitterly dissented in *Romer*, would find her analysis less than compelling. Scalia was, however, particularly concerned to highlight an issue on which Justice O'Connor touched, namely, her claim that although her analysis extended to the Texas statute in *Lawrence*, it would not extend to same-sex marriage. Scalia observed:

> This reasoning leaves on pretty shaky grounds state laws limiting marriage to opposite-sex couples. Justice O'Connor seeks to preserve them by the conclusory statement that "preserving the traditional institution of marriage" is a legitimate state interest . . . But "preserving the traditional institution of marriage" is just a kinder way of describing the State's moral disapproval of same-sex couples. Texas's interest . . . [in its sodomy statute] could be recast in similarly euphemistic terms: "preserving the traditional sexual

mores of our society." In the jurisprudence Justice O'Connor has seemingly created, judges can validate laws by characterizing them as "preserving the traditions of society" (good); or invalidate them by characterizing them as "expressing moral disapproval" (bad).

Scalia's preoccupation with the implications of *Lawrence* for same-sex marriage was the rather politically incendiary appeal that ended his dissenting opinion. In contrast to what he condemned as "the law profession's anti-anti-homosexual culture," Scalia appealed as authority to the "many Americans [who] do not want persons who openly engage in homosexual conduct as partners in their businesses, as scoutmasters for their children, as teachers in their children's schools, or as boarders in their homes." Scalia thus polemically took a stance in the very culture war for which he condemned the Court for engaging in, as he put it, "taking sides." He not only aggressively adopted a posture in this war, but fomented opposition to what he claimed was the writing on the wall, namely, that the United States would follow the European nations who increasingly questioned the justice of legal protections only of heterosexual relationships.

CHAPTER 9

After *Lawrence*

Decriminalization of Other Sexual Offenses and the Case for Same-Sex Marriage

Both Justice Kennedy's opinion for the Court and Justice Scalia's dissent in *Lawrence v. Texas* disagreed over the implications of the Court's decision for other issues of decriminalization. Justice Kennedy emphasized the limited scope of the decriminalization that *Lawrence* required:

> The present case does not involve minors. It does not involve persons who might be injured or coerced or who are situated in relationships where consent might not easily be refused. It does not involve public conduct or prostitution. It does not involve whether the government must give formal recognition to any relationship that homosexual persons seek to enter. The case does involve two adults who, with full and mutual consent from each other, engaged in sexual practices common to a homosexual lifestyle. The petitioners are entitled to respect for their private lives. The State cannot demean their existence or control their destiny by making their private sexual conduct a crime. . . . The Texas statute furthers no legitimate state interest which can justify its intrusion into the personal and private life of the individual.

Justice Scalia, in contrast, argued that *Lawrence*, in overruling *Bowers v. Hardwick*, opened the doors to decriminalization in other areas: "State laws against bigamy, same-sex marriage, adult incest, prostitution, masturbation, adultery, fornication, bestiality, and obscenity are . . . sustainable only in light of *Bowers'* validation of laws based on moral choices." Who was right?

All of the instances Justice Scalia lists involved sexual acts of adults, which are the most clearly protected by the constitutional right to privacy. Scalia did not even raise the question of pedophilia or incest with minors, since Kennedy clearly limited the scope of *Lawrence* to consenting adults, and for the same reason he did not raise the question of rape, which involves force and sometimes fraud (violating the consent requirement). It is thus common ground between the two justices that a claim of privacy cannot be invoked to defend any form of illegal activity taking place behind closed doors; selling narcotics, fixing prices, and planning violent crimes cannot be insulated by a right of privacy. The issue between Justices Kennedy and Scalia was thus twofold. First, did the right protected by constitutional privacy extend to these sexual situations? And second, if it did, was there a legitimate state interest that the criminalization of such acts justified?

A further matter is highly relevant to how we understand and answer both the first and second questions. The constitutional right to privacy arose, as we have seen, in important normative relationship to growing judicial skepticism about the unjust force in our politics of irrational prejudices such as racism and sexism, which rested on a long-standing cultural history that had stripped whole groups of persons of their basic human rights (conscience, speech, intimate life, and workplace equality) and rationalized such dehumanized treatment with stereotypes that rested, in a vicious circularity, on the long-standing abridgment of basic human rights. An irrational religious prejudice, anti-Semitism, shared a comparable history, which explains why religion was comparably suspect. In the cases of people of color, women, and Jews, such stereotypes included dehumanization resting on sexualization, an injustice that arose in turn from abridgment of basic human rights in general and the right to intimate life in particular. Antimiscegenation laws certainly played this role both in racism and anti-Semitism, and laws criminalizing contraception and abortion in sexism, and thus such laws were struck down as unconstitutional abridgments of the right to intimate life.

Justice Kennedy's opinions for the Court both in *Lawrence v. Texas* and *Romer v. Evans* rested on a recognition of comparable normative connections between the irrational prejudice of homophobia and the abridgment of the right to intimate life of homosexuals. It explains Justice Scalia's vigorous dissents in both cases that he did not acknowledge homophobia as an irrational prejudice and thus did not recognize that criminalization of gay/lesbian sex abridged a constitutionally protected right, just as his repudiation of *Roe v. Wade* reflected in the same way Scalia's views on gender. Scalia dissented in the same degree to the case in which his fellow justices found gender classification almost as problematic as racial classifications, *United States v. Virginia* in 1996 (striking down the exclusion of women from the Virginia Military Institute).

Because a majority of the Supreme Court agreed with Justice Kennedy about this normative connection, we can understand why these justices would not think *Lawrence* opened the Pandora's box of decriminalization in the way Justice Scalia proposed. In support of their position, the burden of criminalization affected gays and lesbians in a way arguably much more drastic than any of the other cases of decriminalization about which Justices Kennedy and Scalia disagreed. Criminalization in these cases would forbid one kind of sexual outlet among others a person might want, but not all such forms of sex a person desires. On this ground alone, the line might be drawn at decriminalization of gay/lesbian sex acts. Justice in this instance is of a magnitude that, at least as a matter of the principle of constitutional privacy, the line might be carried here, but no further. The rest could be left to reasonable legislative judgment.

It may, however, be objected that this argument is based not on a difference of kind, but a matter of degree. All of these laws use criminalization against our sexual autonomy, and we may reasonably ask whether they do so in a way that can be justified by compelling secular reasons. In the spirit of this objection, we now investigate more closely whether Justice Kennedy or Scalia was right about these instances.

Arguably, very few of these situations involved such a long history of irrational prejudice, and thus would not raise issues of constitutional privacy. For example, laws criminalizing adult incest or bestiality do not in any obvious way express an irrational prejudice akin to racism, anti-Semitism, sexism, or homophobia, and thus are not in the normative arena from which the constitutional right to privacy arises. Such laws may also be supported (in the case of adult incest) by legitimate state interests against exploitation or genetic harms, and, in the case of bestiality, by state interests that discourage exploitative sexual relationships both intrinsically bad because not fairly consensual or instrumentally because likely to encourage such relationships in general. There may be good reasons of policy why such acts should not be criminalized at all or criminalized very severely, but they do not implicate the constitutional right to privacy.

What about laws against fornication? Fornication, defined as sexual intercourse between two unmarried persons, was illegal in most states until well into the twentieth century. By 2003, however, only eleven states still had criminal laws on their statute books penalizing fornication. Fornication laws are rarely enforced, and they have not occasioned any recent appellate cases involving privacy. It is difficult to see, however, that fornication (in contrast to adultery) involves harms to others or even to self. It is striking that, in the oral argument in *Bowers v. Hardwick* the lawyer arguing for the unconstitutionality of sodomy statutes (Laurence Tribe) in an exchange with Justice Stevens conceded that fornication statutes implicated the right to privacy and probably lacked the tight relationship to a compelling secular justification constitutionally required to legitimate them; and the brief on behalf of Lawrence in *Lawrence v. Texas* made the same point. Because Justice Stevens's dissenting views in *Bowers* are now the law of the land, there is thus reason to think that the Court's invalidation of sodomy laws in *Lawrence* extends or should reasonably extend, as Justice Stevens's exchange with Laurence Tribe in *Bowers* suggests, to fornication laws as well.

Adultery is defined as sexual intercourse involving a man and a woman when at least one of the sexual partners is married to someone else. A substantial minority of U.S. states still makes adultery a crime, although prosecutions are infrequent and convictions are almost unheard of. Adultery, however, remains a leading ground for divorce in many states. Adultery also involves harm not only to the betrayed spouse but to disrupting relationships to children in a marriage. For these reasons, adultery appears to meet the threshold of harm to others that justifies legitimate state concern and intervention in consensual adult sexual relationships.

There is, however, the issue of irrational prejudices that has been so important in the development of the constitutional right to privacy. The issue does not arise in the criminalization of bigamy or polygamy (see discussion later), but it might arise in the criminalization of adultery, which has a long history of being used aggressively against women's legitimate sexual interests in service of a patriarchal conception of arranged marriages, for example, by fathers to advance their dynastic ends through daughters. The extreme sanctions for adultery, both in the Augustan *Lex Julia de adulteries coercendis* and the related provisions of the Christian Emperors Constantius and Constans in 339, express a use of state terror against legitimate sexual desires of women to love freely in resistance to patriarchal marriage. The Christian emperors, for example, imposed on adulterers the traditional Roman penalty for parricide, namely, the "sack," an agonizing death in which the victim was enclosed in a sealed sack with a dog, a cock, a monkey, and a viper and then thrown in a river.

In his masterpiece *The Scarlet Letter*, a U.S. artist of genius, Nathaniel Hawthorne, critically examined the form of this Roman/ Christian condemnation that the American Puritan tradition had inherited. Hawthorne placed at the center of his novel Puritan moralistic fury at adultery by a married woman, Hester Prynne. Hester was portrayed as a woman who had never loved her husband, Chillingworth, whom she not unreasonably believed dead at the time of her adultery with a man she loved, her minister, Dimmesdale. Hester's refusal to name Dimmesdale took the form of a defense of the value of love, including of the offspring of her love, her daughter, Pearl. In contrast, the moralistic rage at her adultery — particularly violent in the case of Puritan women — enforced, for Hawthorne, a false view of both women and sexuality, namely, the sexist double standard that either idealized good women as asexual or denigrated bad women as sexual. In fact, for Hawthorne, Hester, the sexually loving woman (the conventionally bad woman), was the ethical center of the novel, the only truly good woman and person. Indeed, Hawthorne suggested that only a free sexually loving woman such as Hester, whose sexual freedom liberates her ethical intelligence, could "establish the whole relation between man and woman on a surer ground of mutual happiness." Hawthorne certainly knew at close hand antebellum U.S. feminists, including his sister-in-law Elizabeth Peabody. He observed in *The Scarlet Letter* the deep flaw in feminism that could not take seriously the ethical importance of women's free sexual love. Hawthorne's critique reasonably extends to the antisexual feminism of the purity leagues that successfully warred on prostitution in the United States in the late nineteenth and early twentieth centuries (see discussion later). Second-wave feminism, which has taken the sexual autonomy of women and men much more seriously, may well want to rethink and critically repudiate such views.

If the criminalization of adultery remains integrally connected to enforcing the sexist double standard, then it raises the issue of whether such criminalization can be justified any longer in terms of legitimate state interests. U.S. law, including constitutional law, no longer accepts the highly patriarchal conception of marriage (including a man's property right in his wife and a woman's radical economic dependence on her husband) that explains the role antiadultery laws once played in supporting this conception. Nonetheless, sexual betrayal is usually a moral wrong to an unsuspecting spouse, and may harmfully affect dependent children. In the modern world, however, with liberal divorce laws, the harms in question, when they occur, may be more reasonably understood as matters of contractual default or, in appropriate cases of traumatizing betrayal, the infliction of mental distress. Appropriate recoveries for damages should be allowed both under the law of contracts and the law of torts, and the law of spousal and child support might also recognize appropriate recoveries for harms inflicted. If such laws were reasonably in place, there may be no good reason to continue in contemporary circumstances the criminalization of adultery. The legitimate interests of affected parties can be protected in other ways. Because they are thus protected, there is no remaining defensible public moral basis for such criminalization. It is for this reason that we may say that, in contemporary circumstances, laws criminalizing adultery not only do no good, but inflict harm — in particular, harm on women's wholly legitimate sexual interests. The tradition of criminalizing adultery — from Augustus to the Christian emperors to the Puritans to the contemporary United States — is all of a piece, perpetuating a now conspicuously unreasonable view of gender and sexuality.

Laws criminalizing masturbation (sexual pleasure taken by oneself in oneself) and obscenity (the interest in erotic materials) may be more reasonably vulnerable to privacy analysis than is commonly supposed. It may be the case that such laws reflect an unjust cultural history of dehumanizing sexual stereotypes about human sexuality (that of men and women, straight and gay), which arose from the unjust abridgment of basic human rights in general and the right to an intimate life expressive of the legitimate sexual interests of both women and men. U.S. obscenity law, for example, rested on the unreasonable assumption that our erotic interests are of no redeeming value, as if our erotic interests were not valuable both in themselves and for the relationships they make possible. The question remains whether criminalization could today be justified by any legitimate state interest. Certainly, any kind of coercion or exploitation in matters of sex implicates legitimate state interests, including the use of children in sexual depictions. But, independent of such interests, proponents of such laws seem to assume there *must* be such interests rather than show there are such interests, let alone that criminalization reasonably advances such interests. If so, the right of constitutional privacy may require the decriminalization of laws against obscenity and masturbation when no legitimate state interests justify such laws.

It is quite clear that Justice Kennedy did not regard *Lawrence* as implicating the decriminalization of commercial sex, a view most Americans probably intuitively share. Presumably, Justice Kennedy had in mind the long-standing U.S. criminalization of prostitution (except, notably, in Nevada) and the role women played in securing such criminalization (the purity movement, closely allied to the temperance movement). In this view, such criminal laws did not reflect any irrational prejudice such as sexism, but in fact expressed sexual interests unworthy of respect and allegedly protected women from unjust forms of sexual exploitation, including, in contemporary terms, their sexual objectification — a form of dehumanization that supports sexism. These arguments are certainly weighty, and many Americans will reasonably find them sufficient to support Justice Kennedy's assumption that the criminalization of prostitution does not implicate the constitutional right to privacy.

There is, however, some reason to doubt whether Justice Kennedy was right on this point and thus reason to believe Justice Scalia may have been right. Suppose it could reasonably be shown that the U.S. purity leagues were wrong about prostitution because, in fact, criminal laws against prostitution rested on unjust stereotypes that abridged women's basic human rights in general and their rights to an intimate life in particular, including one expressive of their sexual interests (see earlier discussion). In this view, laws criminalizing prostitution normatively supported and legitimated the stereotype of good asexual women and bad sexual women, and thus undermined appropriate respect for the basic human rights of women (including the right to sexual autonomy), who were, by virtue of the double standard, not fairly accorded the same respect for the rights enjoyed by men. Why, on normative grounds, do we condemn consensual adult sexual relations for money as always wrong? We certainly don't think, in general, that all services for money are questionable. Quite the contrary. Why is, other things being equal, sex different? People who believe there is a difference appear to think that sex for pleasure or recreation always must be wrong, particularly wrong when a woman initiates such sex with a man, and irredeemably wrong when for money. But, that may be, on examination, a view of sex as well as a view of gender that supports the unjust double standard (madonnas and whores), a gender binary at the root of sexism. Hawthorne certainly thought it was, and implied that U.S. feminism could not be just unless and until it refused to allow this gender binary to be the basis for laws, especially criminal laws. In this view, laws criminalizing prostitution support, and indeed enforce, the continuing power of sexism in U.S. culture, and for this reason implicate the constitutional right to privacy. The purity leagues in the United States were right to oppose sexism, but wrong to think that the criminalization of prostitution reasonably advanced this end. To the contrary, it entrenched sexism that harmed the reasonable freedom of women as well as men, as if the choice consensually to engage in commercial sex by adults could not secure to both parties real human goods not otherwise available to them. Why must such commercial acts be harmful, as U.S. criminal law now uncritically assumes? Harmful to whom? If there is sometimes pathology in this regard, it hardly seems as though retributive punishment is appropriate as opposed to some fair opportunity of exit and care and cure. Isn't the assumption of pathology at least sometimes a displaced form of now conspicuously unreasonable moral judgment (as in the now discredited view of U.S. psychiatrists about homosexuality)? If retributive arguments in this domain are as bad, indeed as anachronistic, as they appear to be, they enforce not a reasonable ethics in which we believe and by which we can live, but unreasonable burdens on sexual life with which real people cannot reasonably comply and do not. Such unreasonable demands encourage hypocrisy, not democratic ethics.

In one of his most astonishing plays, *Measure for Measure*, William Shakespeare showed us a highly moralistic man, Angelo, who used his newly acquired political powers more aggressively to prosecute commercial sex and indeed any sex outside marriage. We learn about Angelo that he himself could not comply with his moralistic demands, but was willing and able to use his political powers to demand sex from Isabella, a young woman who pleaded for the life of her brother (who was guilty of fornication with a woman he loved, and who was now pregnant). There is reason to believe that today such moralistic demands are, if anything, even more unreasonable in light of the contemporary values of a constitutional democracy. The constitutional right to privacy, the subject of this book, thus condemns the criminalization of many sex acts that traditionally rested on such moralistic demands. If the state cannot constitutionally require that sex between consenting adults must be procreational, that means sex has a range of purposes outside procreation, including pleasure, recreation, and the expression of love. Commercial sex may not be for love, but it affords intimate sexual pleasures that may not be otherwise available. Criminalizing such sex imposes unreasonable demands. We hold ourselves and our leaders to standards with which neither they nor we can reasonably comply. In an age much less moralistic than Shakespeare's, our leaders — claiming to live by the unreasonable values we demand of them — continue mindlessly to play the role of Angelo, a role that destroys them and deprives us of the democratic leadership we need. Isabella in *Measure for Measure* confronted Angelo's overreaching as a failure of self-knowledge because of his political power:

> "Man, proud man,
> Dressed in a little brief authority,
> Most ignorant of what he's most assured,
> His glassy essence, like an angry ape,
> Plays such fantastic tricks before high heaven,
> As makes the angels weep. (II, ii, lines 117–122)

Angelo's form of corruption is a conspicuous problem among U.S. leaders; to name only the most dramatic recent example, Governor Spitzer of my state, New York. Spitzer prided himself on his prosecutorial zealotry, including against prostitution, demanding more aggressive penalties and prosecutions. Yet, we find his vaunted idealism was hypocritically cracked — he availed himself on a number of occasions over time of the services of commercial sex workers. Spitzer ended his career abruptly in disgrace, the victim of an unreasonable moralism he had only encouraged, not resisted.

A democratic people gains nothing from such laws, and loses much because of the role they play in the corruption of democratic politics by perpetuating unreasonably demanding standards of sexual propriety, by which we and our leaders do not and cannot live. In consequence, we measure our leaders not by the way they define and pursue responsible conceptions of justice and the public good (for example, whether they lead us into or away from unjust wars), but by an irresponsible and trivializing interest in their sex lives, as if sexual fidelity, a private virtue, measured democratic leadership, a public virtue. We expect what we should not, and do not demand what we should.

What apparently lies behind U.S. enthusiasm for such laws is a kind of ethical perfectionism that seeks to enforce through the criminal law ideals of the better ways to love sexually. It is not surprising that, under the conditions of nineteenth-century U.S. sexism, women resisting such sexism, believing themselves not implicated in a political and business world resting on slavery as well as racism and sexism (although it certainly supported them economically), should have come to think of themselves as embodying a higher morality. When they were critics of these evils on grounds of human rights, they did. But, when they assumed the dominant Puritan sexual morality was the basis of their higher morality, they abandoned these grounds, and sought to enforce through criminal law ideals of asexuality and abstinence from liquor that were, as ideals, in fact highly controversial, certainly not reasonably appealing to all, as democratic ideals should be. What made their feminism so problematic was that their perfectionism placed them on an idealized pedestal of asexuality, and denigrated all other women who rejected such asexuality as bad women. In dividing women from women on unreasonable grounds, their feminism aligned them, as good patriarchal women, with patriarchal men. If contemporary feminism is really ever to question rather than reinforce patriarchy, it must question as well the role such undemocratic perfectionism plays in rationalizing laws criminalizing commercial sex.

The many European nations that do not criminalize commercial sex are as democratic and civilized as we, perhaps more so as they treat this subject with much less hypocrisy and more humanity. If so, whatever legitimate state interests might justify the regulation of commercial sex (for example, control of disease, protection from exploitative control by pimps, and coercive forms of trafficking) would have to be weighted in the way least restrictive of the right of sexual autonomy women, like men, enjoyed. Regulations of commercial sex (including zoning) might be constitutionally justified along with prohibition in cases of coercion and exploitation of minors. Wholesale criminalization would not be justified.

There remain two cases in Justice Scalia's list: same-sex marriage and bigamy/polygamy. Let us discuss these in reverse order. When Justice Kennedy denied that *Lawrence* extended to "whether the government must give formal recognition to any relationship that homosexual persons seek to enter," he acknowledged the protection of existing marital rights as a legitimate state interest. If so, then nothing in *Lawrence* would require the decriminalization of bigamy or polygamy, because such statutes protect existing institutions and relationships of marital monogamy.

Polygamy, as traditionally understood, reinforced unjust gender roles, and thus cannot be regarded as a constitutionally reasonable form of intimate life consistent with principles of equality under the law. As Nancy Rosenblum recently observed:

Despite rare exceptions, patriarchy has been the dominant form of polygamy. It has never had its basis in reciprocity or friendship, not even ideally. Its justification has never been the expansiveness of affection or cooperation. It has rested on ideological or spiritual accounts of male authority and female subjection, on status associated with numbers of wives, and of course on beliefs about male sexual power (or the need to temper women's sexual power) and male entitlements. It is doubtful that the known doctrinal supports for polygamy could be rehabilitated and made congruent with democratic sex.

Compelling secular arguments of gender equality support the limitation of the right to marriage to monogamous couples. If so, then nothing in the right to constitutional privacy requires, at least in contemporary circumstances, the decriminalization of bigamy or polygamy. Gender equality was certainly not regarded as a compelling state purpose in the nineteenth-century United States (women could not even vote), and thus the criminalization of Mormon polygamy on this ground may be regarded as lacking legitimacy in those circumstances.

Lawrence held that gay/lesbian sex may not be criminalized, not that gay/lesbian relationships must be accorded marriage rights. Justice Scalia may nonetheless be right that grounding the holding of *Lawrence* in the right of constitutional privacy (a right that had its origin in the protection of contraceptive sex in marriage) must have normative implications for the recognition of same-sex marriage.

The question of same-sex marriage, as a constitutional issue, came to the forefront of national attention in light of the decisions under state constitutions of the Hawaii Supreme Court in *Baehr v. Lewin* in 1993 (later overruled by a state constitutional amendment banning same-sex marriage but extending some benefits to gay partnerships) and of the Vermont Supreme Court in *Baker v. State of Vermont* in 1999 (leading to civil union legislation short of same-sex marriage). *Baehr* led to legislation approved by Congress and signed by then-president Clinton to limit the force of the decision, namely, the Defense of Marriage Act (DOMA) of 1996.

The issue of same-sex marriage was again brought to national attention after the Supreme Court's decision in *Lawrence v. Texas* by the 2003 decision of the Supreme Judicial Court of Massachusetts in *Goodridge v. Department of Public Health* (under which gay and lesbian residents of Massachusetts now can marry), and, most recently, the 2006 decision of the New Jersey Supreme Court in *Lewis v. Harris* (requiring the legislature either to pass strong civil partnership laws or to allow gays and lesbians to marry). *Goodridge* led to serious proposals, endorsed by

President George W. Bush, to amend the Constitution of the United States to limit marriage, as an institution, exclusively to one man and one woman; and a number of states have prohibited same-sex marriage, a view state courts have found constitutionally permissible. Until these cases, almost all U.S. courts have held, both under state and federal constitutional law, that failure to recognize same-sex marriage is not unconstitutional, and have failed to accord same-sex couples benefits such as employee insurance coverage or spousal rights under the law of wills or the immigration laws or the law of veteran benefits. These cases suggest, especially in light of *Lawrence v. Texas*, it may be timely to rethink this question fundamentally.

Two important studies, one by William Eskridge and the other by Mark Strasser, have argued that the denial of same-sex marriage was presumptively unconstitutional not only on the ground urged in *Baehr* that such treatment was suspect but also on the independent ground of abridging the basic human right to intimate life, a ground in the decisions in *Baker* and *Goodridge*; an important recent book by Evan Gerstmann has powerfully made a case on the latter ground alone. If such statutes were subject to heightened scrutiny whether on the ground of their suspectness or their abridgment of a fundamental right, these scholars make clear that no compelling justification could constitutionally legitimate such invidious treatment.

There are three crucial features in Justice Kennedy's normative argument for why the basic right to intimate life, already protected by the constitutional right to privacy in a wide range of heterosexual applications, applies to criminal bans on gay/lesbian sex: (1) such bans seriously abridge the right to autonomy in sexual matters, (2) such sexual decisions are the basis for important personal relationships, and (3) such bans demean the very existence of gay/lesbian persons. As I earlier observed, Justice Kennedy importantly started his analysis and critique of Justice White's opinion in *Bowers* by objecting to the way White chose to characterize the claimed right in the case (namely, as a right to sodomy). Bans on gay/lesbian sex certainly bear on sex acts, but Justice Kennedy's point, like the similar point of Justice Blackmun in his dissent in *Bowers*, was that all the earlier constitutional privacy cases do so as well, but the plaintiffs were never characterized in a dehumanizing way that strips them of their personal or relational significance. The Georgia statute in *Bowers* applied its prohibitions equally to heterosexual and homosexual nonprocreational sex acts, but Justice White's opinion homophobically focused only on its homosexual applications, indulging unjust stereotypes of a sexuality without any relational depth or significance that he would never have indulged in the case of the heterosexual applications of the statute. But Justice Kennedy's opinion went a step further when he explained why the majority of the Court did not find acceptable Justice O'Connor's narrower equal protection rationale for the result in *Lawrence* (namely, the statute unconstitutionally discriminated against homosexual sex acts in favor of heterosexual sex acts). Justice Kennedy argued that such statutes did not bear only on acts or the significance of acts, but on the very humanity of gays and lesbians as persons — the "continuance [of *Bowers*] as precedent demeans the lives of homosexual persons." As he remarks at the conclusion of his opinion, "The State cannot demean their existence or control their destiny by making their private sexual conduct a crime." Such statutes were so objectionable because they only have political life when aggressively targeted against gays and lesbians, and it was their agency in such unconstitutional dehumanization that led a majority of the Supreme Court to strike them down.

Thus, in Justice Kennedy's opinion for the Court, as in all constitutional privacy cases, there are two dimensions: identification and protection of the basic human right of intimate life, and questioning traditional reasons for abridging such a right, whether racism or sexism or homophobia. It was, of course, analytically possible that, consistent with these two dimensions, the holding of *Lawrence v. Texas* would be narrowed solely to the criminalization of gay/lesbian sex, as the force of criminal law may be regarded as much more devastating than mere failures to extend legal recognition to gay/lesbian relationships. But it also seems reasonable that, depending in particular on the weight given homophobia as a constitutional evil, constitutional principles would question failures to extend legal recognition to same-sex partnerships. There are two forms such analysis would take, the first suggested by *Baker*, the second by *Goodridge*.

The first such analysis would be that the lack of any legal recognition for same-sex partnerships would be unconstitutional on two grounds: first, it fails to accord to gays and lesbians a respect for their right to intimate life in such grievous ways, in comparison to straight couples, that it unconstitutionally abridges their rights; and second, the grounds for such abridgment are unconstitutionally rooted in irrational prejudice that dehumanizes the interests in companionate love that gays share equally with straights, as if gays could no more love than animals. It is such concerns that led a court like that in *Baker* to strike down the failure to accord any legal recognition of gay/lesbian relationships. But it would be consistent with this view that the same court would regard a legislative response, such as the Vermont civil union bill, as meeting an acceptable constitutional standard.

The second such analysis shares with the first the view that the lack of any legal recognition for same-sex partnerships unconstitutionally burdens a right to intimate life that, on Justice Kennedy's own description of it in *Lawrence*, includes companionate loving relationships over time that must be extended a protection like that already accorded heterosexual couples. But the second analysis would regard, as the court in *Goodridge* did, anything short of equal rights to marry under the law as unacceptable, because such distinctions would lack a compelling secular justification and enforce a homophobic view of gay/lesbian relationships.

There are two dimensions to reasonable discussion of this matter: the nature and force of the constitutional right, and the appropriate constitutional burden of justification for any abridgment or regulation of such a right. On the first point, there can be no doubt at all that precedents of the Supreme Court, including *Loving v. Virginia* (1967), *Zablocki v. Redhail* (1978), and *Turner v. Safley* (1987) now regard the right to marriage, grounded in the right to intimate life, as a basic constitutional right. It is part of the moral logic of the principles protecting such basic rights, for example, the principle of free speech, that it extend to forms of speech that may be highly objectionable, for example, to subversive, racist, or sexist speech, even pornography, or that the principle of religious liberty extend to all forms of conviction, good and bad. The logic of the principle of marriage as a basic right should be similar: it extends to all persons, including, as *Loving* makes clear, to interracial couples, and as *Turner* shows, to criminals. The same logic would extend, as a matter of principle, the right to marriage to same-sex couples, irrespective of the unpopularity of, or distaste for, such relationships.

It seems clear that this basic right underlies the reasoning of Justice Kennedy in *Lawrence v. Texas*, and that the most reasonable understanding of this right is that it is the same right as that protected by the constitutional right to marry. Marriage involves legal recognition, and it seems likely that after the U.S. public comes reasonably to understand what gay/lesbian relationships really are, that understanding will require such recognition. U.S. cultural homophobia means that gays and lesbians are barely *seen* as persons, which explains current understanding of these issues. I speak at this point only of the right itself, leaving to discussion, as the second point, whether there might be a constitutionally reasonable basis for a distinction between heterosexuals and homosexuals. Justice Kennedy's opinion in *Lawrence* is so important, following the dissenting opinions of Justices Blackmun and Stevens in *Bowers*, because of the way he understands the basic right in question, a right abridged equally by laws criminalizing heterosexual and homosexual nonprocreational sex acts. But as Justice Kennedy's opinion makes clear, the right is thus understood to extend to gay/lesbian sex because of the relational significance of sexual intimacy and the way a homophobic tradition has stripped sexually active gays and lesbians of their humanity, as persons who love deeply. It is difficult to see, at the level of discussion of the basic human right involved, how this right could not reasonably extend to gay/lesbian couples who want the benefit of marriage as an institution.

Chief Justice Marshall's opinion in *Goodridge v. Department of Public Health* prominently invoked the analogy on this point of antimiscegenation cases, both the 1948 opinion of the Supreme Court of California in *Perez v. Sharp*, striking down a legislative ban on interracial marriages, and the opinion of the U.S. Supreme Court in *Loving*, nineteen years later, striking down all such laws. The facts of *Goodridge* were, Marshall argues, analogous: "A statute deprives individuals of access to an institution of fundamental legal, personal, and social significance — the institution of marriage — because of a single trait: skin color in *Perez* and *Loving*, sexual orientation here. As it did in *Perez* and *Loving*, history must yield to a more fully developed understanding of the invidious quality of the discrimination." The analogy might reasonably be understood in terms of comparable struggles against unjust dehumanization. The case for such a right for gays and lesbians is connected, as was the similar right for people of color, to the rights-based protests against the moral slavery of homosexuals, that is, appealing to basic human rights (of conscience, speech, intimate life, and workplace equality) to bring to bear on public and private life one's ethical convictions about the good of homosexual love and care and to live a life centered in such convictions and the relationships to which they give rise. At the level of basic human rights, they apply to all persons, including heterosexuals and homosexuals.

On the second point, any basic human right (like the right to intimate life) can only be abridged on compelling grounds of public reason not themselves hostage to a sectarian view that, whatever may once have been the case, can no longer be regarded as justifiable to the public reason of all persons in the community. On this ground, the Supreme Court, as we have seen, correctly struck down both anticontraception and antiabortion laws. Anticontraception laws rested on a view that was, in contemporary circumstances, an unjustly sectarian view of mandatory procreational sexuality that many reasonable people no longer accepted as the measure of sexual love; and antiabortion laws rested on a conception of fetal life in early pregnancy that could not be legitimately enforced to abridge the reproductive autonomy of the many women who did not regard that conception of fetal life as a reasonable conception of moral personality. For the same reason, no compelling argument of public reason exists in contemporary circumstances that could justify the abridgment of the right to love of homosexuals. Neither of the two arguments traditionally regarded as justifying such abridgment (the evil of nonprocreational sex or the conception of homosexual love as lowering one party to the degraded status of a woman), can be regarded as publicly reasonable today. The first argument was justly repudiated by the contraception cases; the second by the many cases repudiating the force of sexist stereotypes in public law. *Lawrence* implicitly repudiated both rationales.

Same-sex marriage is not a threat to heterosexual marriage, but a recognition of the deeper moral values in marriage and the fair extension of those values to all persons; the case for the legitimacy of gay marriage crucially rests on the value (real and symbolic) reasonably placed in our culture on marriage and family life. Richard Epstein has recently put the point cogently:

When President Bush, for example, talks about the need to "protect" the sanctity of marriage, his plea is a giant non sequitur because he does not explain what, precisely, he is protecting marriage against. No proponent of gay marriage wants to ban traditional marriage, or to burden couples who want to marry with endless texts, taxes, and delays. All gay-marriage advocates want to do is to enjoy the same rights of association that are held by other people. Let the state argue that gay marriages are a health risk, and the answer is that anything that encourages monogamy has the opposite effect. Any principled burden of justification is not met.

If the analogy between the use of race in the antimiscegenation case to the use of gender in prohibition of same-sex marriage is as reasonable as many argue it is, there may be a historical parallel as well in the long time the U.S. Supreme Court took between *Brown v. Board of Education* in 1954 and *Loving v. Virginia* in 1967 to acknowledge that the principle of *Brown* extended to anti-miscegenation laws. The nation evidently found it much easier to accept the unconstitutionality of racism in education than in intimate life, and the Supreme Court may have taken this into account in waiting to articulate the full scope of the antiracist principle until the nation was ready for it. We may be in such an early stage of U.S. public understanding of and willingness to address its cultural homophobia, and it may take a similar time period for Americans to come to understand how and why the principle of *Lawrence* extends to same-sex marriage.

Americans have great difficulty, it appears, in thinking about gay and lesbian relationships as having many of the features of contemporary heterosexual relationships. They believe clearly there is a difference, and it is this sense of difference that has made possible a remarkably successful movement, led by religious fundamentalists, to insist that there is a difference, indeed to express such a difference whether by congressional and presidential approval of the Defense of Marriage Act of 1996 or, more recently, by prohibitions on same-sex marriage, including a proposed federal constitutional amendment to that effect. As of 2004, thirty-nine states had passed some form of DOMA (whether statutory or constitutional). Although DOMA laws themselves prohibit same-sex marriage within the state or the recognition of same-sex marriages performed in other jurisdictions, super-DOMAs prohibit any form of recognition of same-sex relationships, including civil union or domestic partnership, and may put into jeopardy private sector arrangements and benefits that recognize same-sex domestic partners. As of 2006, twenty-one states have passed super-DOMA statutes or, more commonly, constitutional amendments. As of 2007, the Marriage Protection Act and the Federal Marriage Amendment have not passed both houses of Congress. When one looks at the arguments for these laws critically, one finds a specious construction of difference — for example, making procreation a requirement for marriage, but only when it comes to homosexuals. Fundamentalists would not have been as successful as they have been with such bad, question-begging arguments if their arguments did not have a resonance in more broadly shared fears and anxieties.

The proposal of a federal constitutional amendment banning same-sex marriage throughout the United States was a particularly remarkable development, reminiscent of the earlier other great U.S. experiment in national morals legislation, the prohibition amendment (the Eighteenth Amendment, repealed by the Twenty-First Amendment). Such constitutional monstrosities are in tension not only with our traditions of federalism but with our deepest normative values of universal human rights and toleration. Such amendments — proposed or enacted — would not have gotten as far as they demonstrably have if they did not express some deep cultural strand of sectarian life that was so threatened as to require constitutional entrenchment of its views. There is a kind of certainty here, but also a fear, an anxiety — both beyond reason and untouchable by reason.

Why is this topic so politically attractive, indeed incendiary in the United States? It is certainly not so in the nations of Western Europe, including Great Britain, that share our traditions and have now broadly adopted not only laws recognizing gay partnerships (Denmark, 1989, Norway, 1996, Sweden, 1996, Iceland, 1996, France, 1999, Germany, 2001, Finland, 2002, Luxembourg, 2004, New Zealand, 2004, Britain, 2005), but gay marriage as well (the Netherlands, 2001, Belgium, 2003, Canada, 2005, Spain, 2005).In the United States, only Massachusetts recognized same-sex marriage (2004) until the recent May 15, 2008, decision of the California Supreme Court, *In re Marriage Cases*, held California statutes limiting marriage to a union between a woman and man unconstitutional under state law. It is symptomatic, however, of the continuing power of reactionary fundamentalist religion in U.S. politics that the California decision may be repealed by a constitutional amendment now pending (California is also an easy state in which to bring such amendments to the ballot). For the time being, gay and lesbian couples are marrying in Massachusetts and California; and several states allow same-sex registered partnerships, including Connecticut (2005), New Jersey (2006), New Hampshire (2008), and Oregon (2008). It is reasonable to connect this difference between U.S. opinion and that in Western Europe to the much longer period of decriminalization of sodomy in these nations than in the United States. Because of the decentralized character of the U.S. federal system, decriminalization has proceeded relatively slowly, only ended quite recently by *Lawrence v. Texas*. It is because Americans, in contrast to Europeans, have long accepted the criminalization of gay/lesbian sex acts that they remain, with the abrupt end of such criminalization in 2003, so culturally unready for the next steps in the just and constitutional recognition of gay rights, in particular, antidiscrimination laws and equal treatment of gay/lesbian partnerships (including same-sex marriage). The problem has been complicated by the forms of patriarchal religion in the United States that have, in contrast to matters of race and gender, not been critically subject to scrutiny for the ways in which they unreasonably read homophobia into religious traditions. Fundamentalists have been politically aggressive for this reason against the legal recognition of gay rights, but they have had such an impact because their patriarchal assumptions have been accepted by other Americans for so long that they confuse culture with nature, a failure of discernment at the root of irrational prejudices in general. Americans for this reason live in contradiction with their deepest and most authoritative constitutional values, the recognition of the universal human rights of all under law.

We must end our history here, for it is here that we now are in the United States. If past is prologue, the long-term consequence of the long overdue decriminalization of gay/lesbian sex in the United States will lead, as European experience shows, to advances in both the areas of antidiscrimination and same-sex marriage. Americans may look back to U.S. attitudes about same-sex marriage in 2008 the same way Americans today look back with revulsion to what was once unquestioned and unquestionable in the United States: the now conspicuously irrational and indeed unconstitutional demands that sexual love must be confined by law to one's own religion or ethnicity or race.

CHAPTER 10

A Concluding Perspective
on Landmark Cases in American
Constitutional Law

Every landmark case in U.S. constitutional law has status and weight because it reveals something about what that law means for Americans, how it can change our lives both personally and politically in terms of justice. U.S. constitutional law was understood differently after *Brown v. Board of Education* and *Reynolds v. Sims*, both landmark opinions of the Warren Court. New constitutional theories such as that of John Hart Ely were forged and had appeal because they grounded such cases in a normative political theory of constitutional democracy that defined an important role for judicial review. For Ely, both racial segregation (struck down in *Brown*) and malapportionment (the subject of *Reynolds*) were the products of a representationally unfair democratic process (which failed to give fair democratic weight either to African Americans or the urban areas not fairly represented under malapportionment). The Supreme Court, under the leadership of Chief Justice Earl Warren (for whom Ely clerked), legitimately exercised its powers of judicial review in *Brown* and *Reynolds* because it was able to accord fair weight both to African Americans and urban voters.

But an obsessional focus on one set of landmark cases may lead even as good a constitutional theorist as Ely not to understand later equally legitimate landmark cases, for example, those that inferred and elaborated the constitutional right to privacy. Ely was a critic of these cases, in particular, of *Roe v. Wade*, because women for him were a political majority and did not, in his view, need the judiciary to help them protect their basic rights. Ely's theory, like the comparable theory of free speech of Cass Sunstein, justifies judicial review in terms of its role in supporting, protecting, and perfecting democracy. These theories explain some things, but they do not even grapple with others, notably, the place of the religion clauses in the First Amendment, which clearly protect substantive human rights of free conscience from unjust political incursions, thus defining spheres of moral independence from politics. The religion clauses do not perfect democracy; they specify areas that precede democracy, that is, the inalienable right to conscience as one of the basic human rights guaranteed to all persons on terms of equal respect. Thus understood, the right of free speech, rooted in the right of conscience, cannot be limited to the political, but includes everything connected to the free exercise of the right of conscience, religion, and antireligion as well as expressive freedoms including the arts and erotica.

Lawrence v. Texas, a landmark case, has also changed forever Americans' sense of constitutional law. I have written this historical study of *Lawrence* to show both its own importance and its place in the larger narrative of the impact of a range of movements for human rights on U.S. constitutional law. The constitutional right to privacy arises at the intersection of a number of these movements — including the role of the protection of intimate life in resisting U.S. anti-Semitism, racism, sexism, and homophobia, all of which dehumanized persons by stripping them of something so personal as the right to an intimate life. My narrative shows that Ely's theory, centered in the legitimacy of *Brown v. Board of Education*, fails to capture the important role that abridgment of the basic human right to intimate life played in U.S. racism, and for this reason does not come to terms with the reality Ely took most seriously, the blight of racism. It is for the same reason, I believe, that Ely, like many other men of his generation, found it so easy to denigrate Blackmun's interpretive achievement in *Roe*, straining, as Blackmun did, justly to define, on terms of principle, what the right to intimate life reasonably meant not just for men but for the other half of the human race, women. The struggles against evils such as anti-Semitism, racism, and sexism dealt with many issues, but at their core was the degree to which irrational, dehumanizing prejudice had stripped people of their basic human rights.

The movement for gay rights came relatively late in the history of these movements in the United States, and certainly built on their constitutional successes, including the inference and protection of the constitutional right to privacy in the areas of contraception and abortion. If *Lawrence* is a landmark case, it is because it is in the tradition of the landmark cases that inferred and protected the constitutional right to privacy first in the domain of contraception (*Griswold v. Connecticut*) and then abortion (*Roe* through *Casey*). It is important to see that the movement for gay rights turned so successfully to U.S. constitutional law because of an important feature of the legitimacy of judicial review in the United States, namely, that it justifies its powers in terms of arguments of principle in a way in which we do not require of other branches of government. The best normative understanding of this requirement is that it ensures that any basic human right protected by constitutional principles be extended on equal terms to all persons. It is because the Supreme Court must justify its powers in this way that it ensures, overall, that U.S. institutions better conform to a respect for human rights that alone renders democratic political power legitimate. The judiciary was the appropriate forum for arguments for gay rights because they aimed to show that a basic human right to intimate life, already robustly extended to the heterosexual majority in the United States, extended to the small homosexual minority as well. Because the normative, historical, and factual arguments bore on that point analogous to comparable arguments successfully made in the struggle against racism and sexism, the judiciary gave them a hearing, ultimately accepting them.

Lawrence unambiguously established, after a period of doubt about the legitimacy of *Roe*, that the right to an intimate life is a basic human right, as basic as conscience or speech, and is thus the basis of a free-standing constitutional right that may, like all such basic rights, only be abridged in service of a compelling secular state purpose. Of course, *Roe v. Wade* remains highly controversial, and the narrowing of its authority may lead one not to be sanguine about future judicial enforcement of the right to privacy. *Lawrence*, however, supports how reasonable the case remains for constitutional privacy as a free-standing constitutional right, as the right was extended in *Lawrence* to a traditionally despised minority. Intimate life is such a basic human right because a loving sexual relationship is, like conscience and speech, at the core of what makes us human. Respecting the free exercise of our choices in these domains treats persons as having the dignity that human rights protect and must protect. Correspondingly, a life without these goods — not lived from conviction or the expression of conviction to others or from loving relationships — is dehumanized. The vehicle of such dehumanization is the widespread acceptance of stereotypes that give expression to such stripping of a group's humanity (the stereotype, for example, that gays in relationship cannot live from or express ethical conviction or love). The Supreme Court clearly recognized this link in *Lawrence*, when it observed that the failure to recognize the loving relationships of homosexuals feeds irrational prejudice that "demeans their existence." Because a loving sexual relationship is a basic human right, it is owed all persons on equal terms — whether male or female, whether straight or gay. *Lawrence* is pathbreaking because it shows that our highest court now recognizes that the right to constitutional privacy — first inferred in *Griswold* and then elaborated and defended in *Roe* through *Casey*, first denied in *Bowers* and then accepted in *Lawrence* — rests on the moral logic of human rights. Protecting such basic rights on equal terms of principle is the normative bedrock of the legitimacy of constitutional democracy. *Lawrence* for this reason, like other great landmark decisions of the Supreme Court, rests on moral bedrock.

We should reflect at this point on the larger question of what the judiciary, endowed with the powers of U.S.-style judicial review, brings to democracy. The most familiar objection to such powers has appealed to democracy itself: how can democracy be consistent with such powers, which withdraw important questions from democratic decision-making. But the popular objection to judicial review rests on a conception of democracy that may itself be democratically flawed. Ely's defense of judicial review rests on this insight: landmark cases such as *Brown* and *Reynolds* show that judicial review sometimes renders a political process more democratic, because it is less exclusionary on racist grounds (*Brown*) or less unrepresentative (*Reynolds*). Ely's mistake was to suppose that all such defects in democracy, legitimately subject to judicial review, are procedural, not substantive. But as I argued earlier, much of the core of the Constitution, such as the values of religious liberty and free speech of the First Amendment, define substantive areas to which democracy cannot legitimately extend. Such substantive areas are defined by a conception of inalienable human rights that the American founders of constitutionalism regarded as the normative benchmarks against which the legitimacy of variant forms of democracy must be critically assessed. Such questions of legitimacy included, in extreme cases of violations of basic human rights not otherwise subject to remedy, the Lockean right to revolution, to which founding leaders had appealed as the justification for the American Revolution against what they perceived as the illegitimate demands placed on the American colonies under the British Constitution.

It was from this perspective as well that moderate and radical abolitionists came to question the legitimacy of the interpretation of U.S. constitutionalism in the antebellum period that would have constitutionally entrenched slavery not only in the states that chose to have it but even in federal territories, to which the Bill of Rights clearly applied. The Civil War was ultimately justified by Lincoln, among others, on Lockean grounds, and the Reconstruction Amendments not only abolished slavery but extended constitutional protection of basic human rights to the states as well as the federal government. Such guarantees of basic human rights included the rights of religious liberty and free speech, which, as I have argued, are substantive protections of domains of personal autonomy from state power, as well as substantive protections from irrational prejudices such as racism that arose from a cultural background of unjust subordination (including abridgment of basic human rights).

We have learned since World War II that the judiciary, with the power of judicial review, not only can but has secured better protection of such basic human rights, and thus rendered our democracy more legitimate precisely because it is more respecting of basic human rights. Neither Ely's theory of perfecting democracy nor originalism can reasonably explain these developments, which are, in their nature, democratizing. These democratizing features are well illustrated by all the landmark cases involving the inference and elaboration of constitutional privacy. *Griswold* and *Roe* came out of social movements in which women such as Margaret Sanger, Emma Goldman, and Sarah Weddington found and expressed their moral voices, consistent with the values of the First Amendment, and demanded that the basic human right of intimate life be extended to women on fair terms (see John W. Johnson on *Griswold v. Connecticut*, 2005; and N. E. H. Hull and Peter Charles Hoffer on *Roe v. Wade*, 2001). Such social movements democratize our politics because, grounding themselves in the values of the First Amendment, they secure more democratic input to and output from our politics. The input is the freer expression of moral and political voices of persons, as democratic equals, and the output is a politics more respectful of such persons as democratic equals. The judiciary performs an invaluable role in U.S. politics because its legitimacy rests on the normative foundation of arguments of principle grounded in universal human rights. Because it is open to and respectful of such interpretive arguments, it lends its legitimacy both to the democratizing input and output such social movements bring to U.S. politics.

Nothing about this democratizing process can reasonably be understood in terms of Learned Hand's worry in *The Bill of Rights* (1968) about the Supreme Court justices as "Platonic Guardians." Members of the judiciary, when they perform their role legitimately, are not, as Plato's Guardians were, antidemocratic elitists to whom alone truth was accessible. The judiciary draws its legitimacy, rather, from its invaluable openness to hearing on just terms the voices of often marginalized, subordinated minorities, appealing to the basic human rights that democratic majorities have always enjoyed but never extended to such minorities. The impact of a range of social movements on U.S. constitutionalism in the twentieth and now twenty-first century marks the degree to which the judiciary has been open and responsive to just moral voices traditionally ignored, marginalized, and sometimes brutally suppressed and silenced. Our moral growth as a people has thus not been passed down from on high but driven by the resisting voices of minorities with claims to basic justice who have found in the judicial process the indispensable acoustic that has recognized and rendered more audible their voices challenging our most entrenched injustices, and made possible our deeper public understanding of the meaning of the universal human rights at the center of the best in U.S. constitutional culture. This process moves many of us in that it has sometimes been the nonviolent resistance of people of good will, unjustly stigmatized and brutally silenced, that has found in U.S. constitutional law a voice that pierced the arrogance and complacency of the powerful and the prejudiced, who confused their being in the majority politically with their being what the nation is and should and can be.

Gays and lesbians, like Jews, African Americans, and straight women before them, have come a long way through finding their voices and a resonance for their voices in the larger narrative of the recognition of basic human rights under U.S. constitutional law. It is important to keep these successes firmly in mind, some of which could not have been reasonably predicted even ten or twenty years ago. Resistance must continue, and constitutional arguments must be made. If the arguments are just, then there is reason to hope, based on U.S. history, that even constitutional arguments that discrimination based on sexual orientation should be fully suspect or that the right to marriage belongs to gays and lesbians may in time be accepted, because they may be as well grounded in compelling arguments of principle as the other arguments the Supreme Court has now recognized.

The distance U.S. gays and lesbians have traveled since World War II is from unspeakability to a moral and constitutional voice now recognized as at the cutting edge of the recognition of universal human rights under U.S. constitutional law. The movement for gay rights began as a social movement of gay men and lesbians struggling to find each other in a world that gave them no place or voice, and, under the impact of the model of other human rights movements, became a political and constitutional movement. It is unlike any other such movement, as is shown by the impact of the closet not only on gay voices, but on a public tolerance that regards the closet as the measure of acceptability. The closet, once a refuge from unjust state violence and stigma, retains understandable appeal for gays and lesbians in a culture still quite homophobic. We have investigated its continuing impact not only on U.S. culture generally but even on the story I have been telling — as the first important argument for gay rights before the Supreme Court was affected by the distortions and lies the closet imposed on the moral voices of gay men and lesbians (see chapter 6 on the way the oral argument in *Bowers* was made and on the background of Justice Powell's change of mind, later repudiated as a mistake in judgment).

It is not only a matter of interest to gays and lesbians that still-popular stereotypes of homosexuality are critically contested and, we hope in time, constitutionally rejected as a basis for laws and policies, including the now politically popular rejection of same-sex marriage. Such stereotypes, as the basis for laws and policies, impose a falsifying script on our national discourse about and understanding of the personal relationships at the heart of a life worth living, portraying the personal relationships of gay and straight Americans in terms that have no rational basis. The imposition of such irrationality bespeaks, as I have suggested, not only hatred, but also fear, as if marriage would be less attractive to heterosexuals were it fairly available to homosexuals. What makes personal relationships happy or fulfilling or enduring has nothing to do with the gender of the partners but is rooted in the love of persons as individuals, which will be as complex or as simple as the individuals it unites. U.S. cultural homophobia, as the basis for laws and policies, falsifies our collective sense of what is at the heart of our loving relationships; this untruth, in turn, undermines our sense of the ethical responsibilities of free and equal persons living and sharing their lives in loving relationship. No one can live in a responsible sense of our moral freedom under the rule of law when the essential values of such freedom are thus denied to any person.

More than any other such movement, the struggle for gay rights centers on intimately personal matters, loving and being loved, because traditionally denied gays and lesbians was the love that centers a human life. It shows the psychological depth in our human natures of love that, despite the odds against them, gays and lesbians have made and continue to make claims rooted in the place of loving relationships in human life. Love's gravity, its weight in our human natures, pulls and pushes their resistance. The struggle against their unspeakability rests on this human need for love and recognition as an individual, a value most Americans assume and passionately pursue without facing what gays and lesbians have had to face, the denial and denigration of their loving relationships. *Lawrence v. Texas* is the most important legal landmark of gay rights because it acknowledges this wrong and does so in the name and on the ground of a constitutional principle, the right to intimate sexual love, that is a universal human right at the very heart of the passions, relationships, and free moral choices that make us human.

538/544   Justinian, Christian emperor of the Roman Empire, condemns homosexual acts on the grounds that they are responsible for "famines, earthquakes, and pestilences" (Nov. 77) on the biblical authority of "those who lived in Sodom" (Nov. 141).

1533/1562   First British statute forbidding homosexual acts, 25 Hen., c. 6 (1533), when Henry VIII transferred powers of the ecclesiastical courts to the king's courts. When Henry's statute was revived under Elizabeth I, the new statute, confirming the religious grounds of its alleged legitimacy, recited that the law was made necessary to combat the prevalence of the "horrible and detestable vice of buggery, aforesaid, to the high pleasure of Almighty God," 5 Eliz. 1, c. 17 (1562).

1641/1697/   Massachusetts: (1641–1642) Capitall Lawes of New
1785/1887   England (Mass. Bay) sec. 8 ("man lyeth with mankind"); 1697 Mass. Acts No. 74 ("buggery"); 1785 Act against Sodomy; 1887 Mass. Acts ch. 436 (new crime: "unnatural and lascivious acts").

1665/1787/   Duke of York's Law, March 1, 1665 ("sodomy"); 1787 N.Y. Laws
1886   ch. 21 ("buggery"); 1886 N.Y. Laws ch. 31, sec. 303.

1848   First rights-based feminist conference held at Seneca Falls, New York.

1850/1915/   Cal. Stat. ch. 99 ("crime against nature"); 1915 Cal. Stat. ch. 586
1921   (invalidated); 1921 Cal. Stat. ch. 848 (new crime: "oral copulation").

1855   Walt Whitman publishes *Leaves of Grass*.

1898   Oscar Wilde criminally prosecuted, convicted, and imprisoned in Great Britain for having gay sex.

1912   Edward Carpenter publishes *The Intermediate Sex: A Study of Some Transitional Types of Men and Women.*

1923   *Meyer v. Nebraska*: U.S. Supreme Court holds that a state law, under which a parent was prosecuted for hiring a teacher to educate his child in the German language, is an unconstitutional intrusion into rights of parents.

1925   *Pierce v. Society of Sisters*: U.S. Supreme Court holds that it is unconstitutional to forbid parents to a send child to religious school.

1936	U.S. Court of Appeals for the Second Circuit rules in *U.S. v. One Package* that the sending of contraceptives through the mails by licensed medical personnel does not violate the Comstock Act.
1948	Alfred Kinsey publishes *Sexual Behavior in the Human Male*, documenting homosexual activity among U.S. men.
1950	New York reduces criminalization of gay/lesbian sex from a felony to a misdemeanor.
1950	Harry Hay founds the Mattachine Society, the first organization in the United States for gay civil rights.
1951	Donald Webster Cory (pseudonym for Edward Sagarin) publishes *The Homosexual in America: A Subjective Approach*.
1955	American Law Institute (ALI) recommends decriminalization of gay/lesbian sex acts.
1955	Phyllis Lyon and Del Martin found Daughters of Bilitis to advance lesbian civil rights.
1957	Wolfenden Committee in Great Britain recommends that consensual homosexuality be decriminalized (Parliament enacted the substance of their recommendations ten years later in 1967).
1957	*Roth v. United States:* U.S. Supreme Court limits the legal definition of obscene, as unprotected speech, to erotic material, later further narrowed to hard-core pornographic material.
1961	**Stage 1 of sodomy reform (1960–1970):** Illinois decriminalizes sodomy.
1961	*Poe v. Ullman:* U.S. Supreme Court decides that the appeal from Connecticut does not present a "case or controversy" under the U.S. Constitution. Strong dissenting opinions by John Marshall Harlan and William O. Douglas rely on an emerging right of privacy, which the criminalization of the sale and use of contraceptives violates.
1963	Betty Friedan publishes *The Feminine Mystique*.
1965	*Griswold v. Connecticut:* U.S. Supreme Court, by a vote of seven to two, strikes down an 1879 Connecticut statute criminalizing the sale or use of contraceptives as a violation of a constitutionally guaranteed right to privacy.
1969	Gay men and lesbians resist police action against Stonewall, a gay bar in New York City's Greenwich Village, followed by the first gay rights parade in 1970.

1971	**Stage 2 of U.S. sodomy reform (1971–1983):** Connecticut decriminalizes sodomy consistent with 1955 recommendation of the American Law Institute followed by other states. By 1983, only twenty-four states retained operational sodomy laws.
1971	*Reed v. Reed:* U.S. Supreme Court for the first time strikes down as unconstitutional the use of a gender classification (in this case, one that forbids women from administering estates).
1971	Dennis Altman publishes *Homosexual Oppression and Liberation.*
1972	*Eisenstadt v. Baird:* U.S. Supreme Court extends the right of privacy in the use of contraceptives to unmarried persons. William Brennan, for the Court, bases his ruling on the Equal Protection Clause of the Fourteenth Amendment.
1973	*Roe v. Wade:* U.S. Supreme Court upholds a woman's right to abortion in the first trimester of her pregnancy but permits the state regulation of abortion during the last six months of pregnancy. Majority opinion written by Harry Blackmun declares that the right of abortion is guaranteed by the Due Process Clause of the Fourteenth Amendment.
1973	Board of Trustees of the American Psychiatric Association decides to remove homosexuality from the *Diagnostic and Statistical Manual of Psychiatric Disorders (DSM-I).*
1976	*Doe v. Commonwealth's Attorney:* U.S. Supreme Court summarily affirms two-to-one federal court opinion rejecting the unconstitutionality of a law criminalizing gay/lesbian sex.
1976	Adrienne Rich publishes *Of Woman Born: Motherhood as Experience and Institution.*
1977	*Carey v. Population Services International:* U.S. Supreme Court rules unconstitutional a New York statute placing various restrictions on the dissemination of contraceptives, including to minors under age sixteen.
1981	*Dudgeon v. United Kingdom:* European Court of Human Rights holds that laws proscribing gay/lesbian sex acts are invalid under the European Convention on Human Rights.
1981	*People v. Onofre:* New York Court of Appeals finds the criminalization of gay/lesbian sex unconstitutional under New York Constitution.
1984–1991	**Stage 3 of U.S. sodomy reform:** no additional states decriminalize.
1986	*Bowers v. Hardwick:* U.S. Supreme Court upholds the constitutionality of a Georgia sodomy law five to four.

1987   Robert Bork's nomination to the U.S. Supreme Court is rejected by the U.S. Senate, largely because the nominee refuses to accept the existence of a constitutional right of privacy.

1992   *Planned Parenthood of Southeastern Pennsylvania v. Casey:* U.S. Supreme Court reaffirms the central principle of *Roe v. Wade,* upholding a woman's right to abortion in the first trimester of her pregnancy, but permits more regulation than *Roe* allowed. Majority follows the "undue burden" test in determining the constitutionality of state regulations of abortion.

1993   President Clinton and Congress endorse Don't Ask, Don't Tell as the condition for service of gays and lesbians in the military.

1992   **Stage 4 of U.S. sodomy reform (1992–2003):** Twelve states decriminalize, starting in 1992 with Kentucky's invalidation of its sodomy law (in eight states, decriminalization by legal challenge; in four states, by legislative reform).

1993   *Baehr v. Lewin:* Hawaii Supreme Court holds that limitation of marriage to heterosexual couples violates the Hawaii State Constitution.

1996   Congress passes Defense of Marriage Act, limiting the legal effect under federal law of same-sex marriages under state law.

1996   *Romer v. Evans:* U.S. Supreme Court holds unconstitutional a 1992 Colorado constitutional amendment that outlawed any legal protections of gays and lesbians.

1999   *Baker v. State of Vermont:* Vermont Supreme Court holds limitation of marriage to heterosexual couples violates state constitution, and that either civil partnerships or marriage rights must be extended by state legislation to gays and lesbians (legislature opted for civil partnerships).

2003   *Lawrence v. Texas:* U.S. Supreme Court explicitly overrules *Bowers v. Hardwick* and holds that a state law prohibiting sodomy involving consenting same-sex adults violates the right of privacy protected by the Due Process Clause of the Fourteenth Amendment. *Goodridge v. Department of Public Health:* Supreme Judicial Court of Massachusetts rules that "barring an individual from the protections, benefits, and obligations of civil marriage solely because the person would marry a person of the same sex violates the Massachusetts Constitution." The Massachusetts court bases its decision on the equal protection and due process protections of the state constitutions, but cites as authorities numerous Supreme Court privacy decisions, including *Lawrence v. Texas*. Federal constitutional amendment prohibiting same-sex marriage proposed in Congress.

2004 Massachusetts Supreme Judicial Court issues advisory opinion that a proposed civil union status for same-sex couples discriminates against gays on equal protection and due process grounds. Massachusetts begins issuing marriage certificates to same-sex couples. Same-sex marriage becomes an issue in the 2004 presidential election campaign.

2008 California Supreme Court holds unconstitutional under California law statutes limiting marriage to a union between a man and a woman. Gay men and lesbians are now marrying under the decision. An amendment to the state constitution is now pending that, if adopted by the voters, would repeal this decision.

Able v. United States, 880 F. Supp. 968 (E.D.N.Y. 1995), at 974-5, *rev'd Able v. United States*, 1996 WL 391210 (2d Cir. 1996)

Baehr v. Lewin, 74 Haw. 645, 852 P.2d 44 (1993)

Baker v. State of Vermont, 170 Vt. 194, 744 A.2d 864 (Vt. 1999)

Boutelier v. Immigration and Naturalization Service, 387 U.S. 118 (1967)

Bowers v. Hardwick, 478 U.S. 186 (1986)

Boy Scouts of America v. Dale, 530 U.S. 640 (2000)

Brown v. Board of Education, 347 U.S. 483 (1954)

Carey v. Population Services International, 431 U.S. 678 (1977)

Cruzan v. Director, Missouri Dept. of Health, 497 U.S. 261 (1990)

Davis v. Beason, 133 U.S. 333 (1890)

Doe v. Commonwealth's Attorney, 425 U.S. 901 (1976), *aff'g mem.* 403 F. Supp. 1100 (E.D. Va. 1975)

Dred Scott v. Sanford, 60 U.S. (19 How.) 393 (1857)

Dudgeon v. United Kingdom, 45 Eur. Ct. H.R. (1981) P 52

Eisenstadt v. Baird, 405 U.S. 438 (1972)

Engel v. Vitale, 370 U.S. 421 (1962)

Goesaert v. Cleary, 335 U.S. 464 (1948)

Gonzales v. Carhart, 550 U.S. 1 (2007)

Goodridge v. Department of Public Health, 440 Mass. 309, 798 N.E.2d 941 (Mass. 2003)

Griswold v. Connecticut, 381 U.S. 479 (1965)

Hoyt v. Florida, 368 U.S. 57 (1961)

Hurley v. Irish-American Gay, Lesbian, and Bisexual Group of Boston, 515 U.S. 557 (1995)

In re Marriage Cases, 43 Cal.4th 757, 183 P.3d 384, 76 Cal. Rptr.3d 683 (2008)

Lawrence v. Texas, 539 U.S. 558 (2003)

Lemon v. Kurtzman, 403 U.S. 602 (1971)

Lewis v. Harris, 188 N.J. 415 (2006)

Lochner v. New York, 198 U.S. 45 (1905)

Loving v. Virginia, 388 U.S. 1 (1967)

Meyer v. Nebraska, 262 U.S. 390 (1923)

Moore v. City of East Cleveland, 431 U.S. 494 (1977)

Nebbia v. New York, 291 U.S. 502 (1934)

People v. Onofre, 51 N.Y.2d 476 (1980), *cert.den.*, 451 U.S. 987 (1981)

Perez v. Sharp, 32 Cal.2d 711, 198 P.2d 17 (1948)

Pierce v. Society of Sisters, 268 U.S. 510 (1925)

Planned Parenthood of Southeastern Pennsylvania v. Casey, 505 U.S. 833 (1992)

Plessy v. Ferguson, 163 U.S. 537 (1896)

Poe v. Ullman, 367 U.S. 497 (1961)

Reed v. Reed, 404 U.S. 71 (1971)

Reynolds v. Sims, 377 U.S. 533 (1964)

Reynolds v. United States, 98 U.S. 145 (1878)

Roe v. Wade, 410 U.S. 113 (1973)

Romer v. Evans, 517 U.S. 620 (1996)

Roth v. United States, 354 U.S. 476 (1957)

Sherbert v. Verner, 374 U.S. 398 (1963)

Skinner v. Oklahoma, 316 U.S. 535 (1942)

Stanley v. Georgia, 394 U.S. 557 (1969)

Stenberg v. Carhart, 530 U.S. 914 (2000)

Turner v. Safley, 482 U.S. 78 (1987)

United States v. Ballard, 322 U.S. 78, 86 (1944)

United States v. One Package, 86 F.2d 737 (2d Cir. 1936)

United States v. Virginia, 518 U.S. 515 (1996)

Washington v. Glucksberg, 521 U.S. 702 (1997)

Webster v. Reproductive Health Services, 492 U.S. 490 (1989)

Williams v. Florida, 399 U.S. 78 (1970)

Zablocki v. Redhail, 434 U.S. 374 (1978)

BIBLIOGRAPHIC ESSAY

Notes from the Series Editors: The following bibliographic essay contains the primary and secondary sources the author consulted for this volume. We have asked all authors in the series to omit formal citations in order to make our volume more readable, inexpensive, and appealing for students and general readers. In adopting this format, Landmark Law Cases and American Society follows the precedent of a number of highly regarded and widely consulted series.

Primary Materials

The oral argument in *Bowers v. Hardwick* may be heard online at http://www.oyez.org/cases/1980-1989/1985/1985_85_140/argument.
The oral argument in *Lawrence v. Texas* may be heard online at http://www.oyez.org/cases/2000-2009/2002/200202102/argument.
The papers of justices serving on the Supreme Court at the time of *Bowers v. Hardwick*, including Justices Blackmun and Marshall, are available for examination by scholars in the Manuscript Division of the Library of Congress in Washington, D.C., and were read for this book. No such papers are yet available for *Lawrence v. Texas*.
Interviews were conducted with Ruth E. Harlow, legal director of Lambda at the time of *Lawrence v. Texas*, and with Paul M. Smith, who gave the oral argument for the petitioners before the Supreme Court in *Lawrence*.

Secondary Materials

Important historical studies of homosexuality in the ancient world include William Armstrong Percy III, *Pederasty and Pedagogy in Archaic Greece* (Urbana: University of Illinois Press, 1996); Kenneth J. Dover, *Greek Popular Morality in the Time of Plato and Aristotle* (Oxford, U.K.: Blackwell, 1974); Dover, *Greek Homosexuality* (London: Duckworth, 1978); James Davidson, *The Greeks and Greek Love: A Radical Reappraisal of Homosexuality in Ancient Greece* (London: Weidenfeld and Nicolson, 2007); Eva Cantarella, *Bisexuality in the Ancient World*, trans. Cormac O. Cuilleanain (New Haven, Conn.: Yale University Press, 1992); David M. Halperin, *One Hundred Years of Homosexuality and Other Essays on Greek Love* (New York: Routledge, 1990); and David M. Halperin, John J. Winkler, and Froma I. Zeitlin, eds., *Before Sexuality: The Construction of Erotic Experience in the Ancient Greek World* (Princeton, N.J.: Princeton University Press, 1990). Leading historical studies of Christian attitudes are Peter Brown, *The Body and Society: Men, Women, and Sexual Renunciation in Early Christianity* (New York: Columbia University Press, 1988); Derrick Sherwin Bailey, *Homosexuality and the Western Christian Tradition*

(Hamden, Conn.: Archon Books, 1975, originally published 1955); John Boswell, *Christianity, Social Tolerance, and Homosexuality* (Chicago: University of Chicago Press, 1980); Bernadette J. Brooten, *Love between Women: Early Christian Responses to Female Homoeroticism* (Chicago: University of Chicago Press, 1996); and Mark D. Jordan, *The Invention of Sodomy in Christian Theology* (Chicago: University of Chicago Press, 1997). On homosexuality in the Renaissance (Venice and Florence), see Guido Ruggiero, *The Boundaries of Eros: Sex Crime and Sexuality in Renaissance Venice* (New York: Oxford University Press, 1985); and Michael Rocke, *Forbidden Friendship: Homosexuality and Male Culture in Renaissance Florence* (New York: Oxford University Press, 1996). On the treatment of homosexuality by the Amerindians, see Walter L. Williams, *The Spirit and the Flesh: Sexual Diversity in American Indian Culture* (Boston: Beacon, 1986); Richard C. Trexler, *Sex and Conquest: Gendered Violence, Political Order, and the European Conquest of the Americas* (Ithaca, N.Y.: Cornell University Press, 1995); and Rudi C. Bleys, *The Geography of Perversion: Male-to-Male Sexual Behavior outside the West and the Ethnographic Imagination, 1750–1918* (New York: New York University Press, 1995). On the European interpretation of these practices, see Anthony Pagden, *The Fall of Natural Man: The American Indian and the Origins of Comparative Ethnology* (Cambridge: Cambridge University Press, 1982); and Alden T. Vaughan, *Roots of American Racism: Essays on the Colonial Experience* (New York: Oxford University Press, 1995).

On the early modern British interpretation of homosexuality as a degradation of the male gender role, see the following studies by Randolph Trumbach: "Gender and the Homosexual Role in Modern Western Culture: The Eighteenth and Nineteenth Centuries Compared," in Dennis Altman, et al., *Homosexuality, Which Homosexuality? Essays from the International Scientific Conference on Lesbian and Gay Studies* (London: DMP Publishers, 1989); "Sex, Gender, and Sexual Identity in Modern Culture: Male Sodomy and Female Prostitution in Enlightenment London," in John C. Fout, ed., *Forbidden History: The State, Society, and the Regulation of Sexuality in Modern Europe* (Chicago: University of Chicago Press, 1992); "The Birth of the Queen: Sodomy and the Emergence of Gender Equality in Modern Culture, 1660–1750," in Martin Duberman, Martha Vicinus, and George Chauncey, Jr., eds., *Hidden from History: Reclaiming the Gay and Lesbian Past* (1989); and "The Origin and Development of the Modern Lesbian Role in the Western Gender System: Northwestern Europe and the United States, 1750–1990," *Historical Reflections* 20, no. 2 (1994): 288–320.

On the British treatment of homosexuality, see William Blackstone, *Commentaries on the Laws of England* (Chicago: University of Chicago Press, 1979, originally published 1765–1769); Alan Bray, *Homosexuality in Renaissance England* (London: Gay Men's Press, 1982); Stephen Jeffery-Poulter, *Peers, Queers,* and Commons: The Struggle for Gay Law Reform from 1950 to the Present (London: Routledge, 1991); Jeffrey Weeks, Coming Out: Homosexual Politics in Britain from the Nineteenth Century to the Present (London: Quartet Books, 1990); Jeffrey Weeks, Against Nature: Essays on History, Sexuality, and Identity (London: Rivers Oram, 1991); Graham Robb, Strangers: Homosexual Love in the Nineteenth Century (New York: Norton, 2003); Nicholas Bamforth, Sexuality, Morals, and Justice: A Theory of Lesbian and Gay Rights Law (London: Cassell, 1997); and Tony Honore, Sex Law (London: Duckworth, 1978). For the report of the Wolfenden Committee, see The Wolfenden Report (New York: Stein and Day, 1963).

For a historical study of the German treatment of homosexuality, see James D. Steakley, The Homosexual Emancipation Movement in Germany (New York: Arno, 1975); and Richard Plant, The Pink Triangle: The Nazi War against Homosexuals (New York: Henry Holt, 1986).

For a general historical study of the development of U.S. feminism from the antebellum period until the late twentieth century (including studies of Mary Wollstonecraft, Sarah and Angelina Grimke, Sojourner Truth, Lydia Maria Child, Harriet Jacobs, Stephen Andrews, Victoria Woodhull, Lucretia Mott, Elizabeth Stanton, Emma Goldman, and Margaret Sanger) and its connections to arguments for gay rights both in the antebellum period (including Walt Whitman and his impact on Oscar Wilde, Edward Carpenter, and John Addington Symonds) and later, on which the argument of this book draws, including the conception of moral slavery, see David A. J. Richards, Women, Gays, and the Constitution: The Grounds for Feminism and Gay Rights in Culture and Law (Chicago: University of Chicago Press, 1998). On gay life in New York City before World War II, see George Chauncey, Gay New York: Gender, Urban Culture, and the Making of the Gay Male World, 1890–1940 (New York: Basic Books, 1994); and Timothy J. Gilfoyle, City of Eros: New York City, Prostitution, and the Commercialization of Sex, 1790–1920 (New York: Norton, 1992). On the Harlem Renaissance, see George Hutchinson, The Harlem Renaissance in Black and White (Cambridge, Mass.: Harvard University Press, 1995). On gay life and politics in the United States during and after World War II, see Allan Berube, Coming Out under Fire: The History of Gay Men and Women in World War II (New York: Free Press, 1990); Randy Shilts, Conduct Unbecoming: Gays and Lesbians in the U.S. Military (New York: St. Martin's, 1993); John D'Emilio, Sexual Politics, Sexual Communities: The Making of a Homosexual Minority in the United States, 1940–1970 (Chicago: University of Chicago Press, 1983); John D'Emilio and Estelle B. Freedman, Intimate Matters: A History of Sexuality in America (New York: Norton, 1988); Martin Duberman, Stonewall (New York: Plume, 1993); Elizabeth Lapovsky Kennedy and Madeline D. Davis, Boots of Leather, Slippers of Gold: The History of a Lesbian Community (New York: Routledge, 1993); Urvashi Vaid, Virtual

Equality: The Mainstreaming of Gay and Lesbian Liberation (New York: Anchor, 1995); and David Mixner, *Stranger among Friends* (New York: Bantam, 1996). On the representation of homosexuals in U.S. movies, see Vito Russo, *The Celluloid Closet: Homosexuality in the Movies* (New York: Harper , 1987); and Lisa Ades and Lesli Klainberg, *Fabulous! The Story of Queer Cinema* (DVD, 2006). Historically important statements by Americans of the case for gay rights after World War II include Donald Webster Cory (pseud.), *The Homosexual in America: A Subjective Approach* (New York: Castle, 1951); Harry Hay, *Radically Gay*, ed. Will Roscoe (Boston: Beacon, 1996); Dennis Altman, *Homosexual Oppression and Liberation* (New York; Avon, 1971); Dennis Altman, *The Homosexualization of America, The Americanization of the Homosexual* (New York: St. Martin's, 1982), Audre Lorde, *Sister Outsider: Essays and Speeches* (Freedom, Calif.: Crossing Press, 1983); Adrienne Rich, *Of Woman Born: Motherhood as Experience and Institution* (New York: Norton, 1976); Adrienne Rich, *On Lies, Secrets, and Silence: Selected Prose 1966–1978* (New York: Norton, 1979); Adrienne Rich, "Compulsory Heterosexuality and Lesbian Existence," in Catharine R. Stimpson and Ethel Spector Person, eds., *Women: Sex and Sexuality* (Chicago: University of Chicago Press, 1980); and Leo Bersani, "Is the Rectus as a Grave?" in Douglas Crimp, *Cultural Analysis/Cultural Activism* (Cambridge: Massachusetts Institute of Technology Press, 1988). On the impact of AIDS on gay life, see Gabriel Rotello, *Sexual Ecology: AIDS and the Destiny of Gay Men* (New York: Dutton, 1997). On the impact of gay rights on the personal lives and loves of gay men and lesbians, see David A. J. Richards, *The Case for Gay Rights: From* Bowers *to* Lawrence *and Beyond* (Lawrence: University Press of Kansas, 2005). On lesbian couples raising sons, see Peggy Drexler, *Raising Boys without Men: How Maverick Moms Are Creating the Next Generation of Exceptional Men* (New York: Rodale, 2005). For a defense of homosexuality as consistent with Christianity, see Gareth Moore, *A Question of Truth: Christianity and Homosexuality* (London: Continuum, 2003). On the scientific literature on the etiology of sexual orientation, see Edward Stein, *The Mismeasure of Desire: The Science, Theory, and Ethics of Sexual Orientation* (New York: Oxford University Press, 1999). Arguments for the recognition of gay rights as judicially enforceable under U.S. constitutional law include a number of works by David A. J. Richards, including "Unnatural Acts and the Constitutional Right to Privacy: A Moral Theory," *Fordham Law Review* 45 (1977): 1282; "Sexual Autonomy and the Constitutional Right to Privacy: A Case Study in Human Rights and the Unwritten Constitution," *Hastings Constitutional Law Quarterly* 30 (1979): 957; *The Moral Criticism of Law* (Encino, Calif: Dickenson- Wadsworth, 1977); *Sex, Drugs, Death, and the Law: An Essay on Human Rights and Overcriminalization* (Totowa, N.J.: Rowman and Littlefield, 1982); *Toleration and the Constitution* (New York: Oxford University Press, 1986); *Foundations of American Constitutionalism* (New York: Oxford University

Press, 1989); and *Conscience and the Constitution: History, Theory, and Law of the Reconstruction Amendments* (Princeton, N.J.: Princeton University Press, 1993). Other such arguments can be found in the works of Richard D. Mohr, including *Gays/Justice: A Study of Ethics, Society, and Law* (New York: Columbia University Press, 1988); *Gay Ideas: Outing and Other Controversies* (Boston: Beacon, 1992); and *A More Perfect Union: Why Straight America Must Stand Up for Gay Rights* (Boston: Beacon, 1994). See also Michael Nava and Robert Dawidoff, *Created Equal: Why Gay Rights Matter to America* (New York: St. Martin's, 1994); Lisa Duggan and Nan D. Hunter, *Sex Wars: Sexual Dissent and Political Culture* (New York: Routledge, 1995); Robert Wintemute, *Sexual Orientation and Human Rights: The United States Constitution, the European Convention, and the Canadian Charter* (Oxford: Oxford University Press, 1995); William N. Eskridge, *Gay Law: Challenging the Apartheid of the Closet* (Cambridge, Mass.: Harvard University Press, 1999); and Kenneth L. Karst, "The Freedom of Intimate Association," *Yale Law Journal* 89 (1980): 624. On the recognition of same-sex partnership rights as a matter of comparative constitutional law, see Yuval Merin, *Equality for Same-Sex Couples: The Legal recognition of Gay Partnerships in Europe and the United States* (Chicago: University of Chicago Press, 2002). Important arguments for same-sex marriage are William N. Eskridge Jr., *The Case for Same-Sex Marriage: From Sexual Liberty to Civilized Commitment* (New York: Free Press, 1996); William N. Eskridge, Jr., and Darren R. Spedale, *Gay Marriage: For Better or for Worse? What We've Learned from the Evidence* (New York: Oxford University Press, 2006); Mark Strasser, *Legally Wed: Same-Sex Marriage and the Constitution* (Ithaca, N.Y.: Cornell University Press, 1997); Evan Gerstmann, *Same-Sex Marriage and the Constitution* (Cambridge, U.K.: Cambridge University Press, 2004); and Andrew Koppelman, "The Miscegenation Analogy: Sodomy Laws as Sex Discrimination," *Yale Law Journal* 98 (1988): 145. On the unusual character of Justice Kennedy's appeal to constitutional developments abroad in *Lawrence v. Texas*, see William N. Eskridge, Jr., "United States: *Lawrence v. Texas* and the Imperative of Comparative Constitutionalism," *International Journal of Constitutional Law* 2, no. 3 (July 2004): 555–560. For a more extensive critique of the military exclusion policy, see David A. J. Richards, *Women, Gays, and the Constitution: The Grounds for Feminism and Gay Rights in Culture and Law* (Chicago: University of Chicago Press, 1998). For an illuminating comparative study of how and why the social movement for gay rights has been more successful in Canada (where gay marriage is now legal) than in the United States (where it is legal only in Massachusetts and, very recently, California, if not repealed), see Miriam Smith, *Political Institutions and Lesbian and Gay Rights in the United States and Canada* (New York: Routledge, 2008).

On the use of adultery laws to support patriarchal marriage and on patriarchy in general and its inconsistency with the values of constitutional democracy, see Carol Gilligan and David A. J. Richards, *The Deepening Darkness: Patriarchy, Resistance, and Democracy's Future* (Cambridge, U.K.: Cambridge University Press, 2009).

For arguments for a more expansive interpretation of the constitutional right to privacy than that accorded by the U.S. Supreme Court, see David A. J. Richards, "Commercial Sex and the Rights of the Person: A Moral Argument for the Decriminalization of Prostitution," *University of Pennsylvania Law Review* 127 (1979): 1195; "Drug Use and the Rights of the Person: A Moral Argument for the Decriminalization of Certain Forms of Drug Use," *Rutgers Law Review* 33 (1981): 607; "Constitutional Privacy, the Right to Die, and the Meaning of Life: A Moral Analysis," *William and Mary Law Review* 22 (1981): 327; and *Sex, Drugs, Death, and the Law: An Essay on Human Rights and Overcriminalization* (Totowa, N.J.: Rowman and Littlefield, 1982).

On the continuities among heterosexual and homosexual forms of intimacy in the modern world in general, see Anthony Giddens, *The Transformation of Intimacy: Sexuality, Love, and Eroticism in Modern Societies* (Cambridge, U.K.: Polity, 1992); Philip Blumstein and Pepper Schwartz, *American Couples* (New York: William Morrow, 1983); Claudia Goldin, *Understanding the Gender Gap: An Economic History of American Women* (New York: Oxford University Press, 1990); Barbara Ehrenreich, Elizabeth Hess, and Gloria Jacobs, *Remaking Love: The Feminization of Sex* (New York: Anchor, 1986); Ann Snitow, Christine Stansell, and Sharon Thompson, eds., *Powers of Desire* (New York: Monthly Review Press, 1983); Carol S. Vance, ed., *Pleasure and Danger: Exploring Female Sexuality* (Boston: Routledge and Kegan Paul, 1984); Nancy L. Rosenblum, "Democratic Sex: *Reynolds v. U.S.*, Sexual Relations, and Community," in David M. Estlund and Martha C. Nussbaum, eds., *Sex, Preference, and Family: Essays on Law and Nature* (New York: Oxford University Press, 1997); and Edward O. Laumann, John H. Gagnon, Robert T. Michael, and Stuart Michaels, *The Organization of Sexuality: Sexual Practices in the United States* (Chicago: University of Chicago Press, 1994).

On the abuse of science, including psychiatry, against people of color, women, and homosexuals, see Stephen Jay Gould, *The Mismeasure of Man* (New York: Norton, 1981); Bram Dijkstra, *Idols of Perversity: Fantasies of Feminine Evil in Fin-de-Siecle Culture* (New York: Oxford University Press, 1986); Sander L. Gilman, *Difference and Pathology: Stereotypes of Sexuality, Race, and Madness* (Ithaca, N.Y.: Cornell University Press, 1985); Sander L. Gilman, *Freud, Race, and Gender* (Princeton, N.J.: Princeton University Press, 1993); Kenneth Lewes, *The Psychoanalytic Theory of Male Homosexuality* (New York: Simon and Schuster, 1988); and Ronald Bayer, *Homosexuality and American Psychiatry: The Politics of Diagnosis* (New York: Basic Books, 1981). For a penetrating analysis of prejudice (including the roots of homophobia in sexism), including its dehumanizing sexualization of stigmatized groups, see Elisabeth

Young-Bruehl, *The Anatomy of Prejudices* (Cambridge, Mass.: Harvard University Press, 1996). See also Suzanne Pharr, *Homophobia: A Weapon of Sexism* (Inverness, Calif.: Chardon Press, 1988); and Sylvia A. Law, "Homosexuality and the Social Meaning of Gender," *Wisconsin Law Review* 1988 (1988): 187.

On political anti-Semitism, see Hannah Arendt, *The Origins of Totalitarianism* (New York: Harcourt, Brace, Jovanovich, 1973). On Arendt's early life, education (including her affair with the philosopher Heidegger), and fleeing from Germany to the United States, see Elisabeth Young-Bruehl, *Hannah Arendt: For Love of the World* (New Haven, Conn.: Yale University Press, 1982). On Hitler, see Ian Kershaw, *Hitler: 1889–1936—Hubris* (New York: Norton, 1998); and Ian Kershaw, *Hitler: 1936–1945—Nemesis* (New York: Norton, 2000).

On the impact of Martin Luther King Jr.'s movement on U.S. constitutional law, including the law of free speech, see David A. J. Richards, *Free Speech and the Politics of Identity* (Oxford: Oxford University Press, 1999). On the roots and appeal of King's nonviolence, see David A. J. Richards, *Disarming Manhood: Roots of Ethical Resistance* (Athens, Ohio: Swallow Press/Ohio University Press, 2005). Important studies of U.S. slavery and racism bearing on abridgment of the right to intimate family life include Kenneth M. Stampp, *The Peculiar Institution* (New York: Vintage, 1956); Eugene D. Genovese, *Roll, Jordan, Roll: The World the Slaves Made* (New York: Vintage, 1974); Herbert G. Gutman, *The Black Family in Slavery and Freedom, 1750–1925* (New York: Vintage, 1976); Peggy Cooper Davis, *Neglected Stories: The Constitution and Family Values* (New York: Hill and Wang, 1997); and Kenneth S. Greenberg, *Masters and Statesmen: The Political Culture of American Slavery* (Baltimore: Johns Hopkins University Press, 1985). For an important abolitionist analysis of the immorality of U.S. slavery, see Theodore Dwight Weld, *American Slavery as It Is* (New York: Arno/New York Times, 1968; originally published 1839). For examples of proslavery racism bearing on denials of the right to intimate life of persons of color, see Thomas R. R. Cobb, *An Inquiry into the Law of Negro Slavery in the United States of America* (New York: Negro Universities Press, 1968; originally published 1858); and Drew Gilpin Faust, ed., *The Ideology of Slavery: Proslavery Thought in the Antebellum South, 1830–1860* (Baton Rouge: Louisiana State University Press, 1981). On *Brown v. Board of Education* as a landmark case, see Robert J. Cottrol, Raymond T. Diamond, and Leland B. Ware, Brown v. Board of Education: *Caste, Culture, and the Constitution* (Lawrence: University Press of Kansas, 2003).

Historical studies of the role of Margaret Sanger on the development of the right to constitutional privacy include Ellen Chesler, *Woman of Valor: Margaret Sanger and the Birth Control Movement in America* (New York: Anchor, 1992); John W. Johnson, Griswold v. Connecticut: *Birth Control and the Constitutional Right to Privacy* (Lawrence: University Press of Kansas, 2005); and

David A. J. Richards, *Women, Gays, and the Constitution* (1998). Sanger's major writings are *The Pivot of Civilization* (Elmsford, N.Y.: Maxwell Reprint Company, 1969; originally published 1922) and *Woman and the New Race* (Elmsford, N.Y.: Maxwell Reprint Company, 1969; originally published 1920).

On the historical background of the right to intimate life as a basic human right, see Francis Hutcheson, *A System of Moral Philosophy* (New York: Augustus M. Kelley, 1968, originally published 1755); John Witherspoon, *Lectures of Moral Philosophy*, ed. Jack Scott (East Brunswick, N.J.: Associated University Presses, 1982); and David A. J. Richards, *Toleration and the Constitution* (New York: Oxford University Press, 1986). On the right to intimate life as one of the basic rights protected against the states by the Privileges and Immunities Clause of the Fourteenth Amendment, see David A. J. Richards, *Conscience and the Constitution: History, Theory, and the Law of the Reconstruction Amendments* (Princeton, N.J.: Princeton University Press, 1993).

For a historical and critical study of the view that sexuality must be procreational (taken by Augustine and Thomas Aquinas, among others), see Nicholas Bamforth and David A. J. Richards, *Patriarchal Religion, Sexuality, and Gender: A Critique of New Natural Law* (Cambridge, U.K.: Cambridge University Press, 2008).

On the elaboration of the constitutional right to privacy as applied to abortion and the resulting controversies on and off the Supreme Court, see N. E. H. Hull and Peter Charles Hoffer, Roe v. Wade: *The Abortion Rights Controversy in American History* (Lawrence: University Press of Kansas, 2001); the volume also contains a valuable review of the secondary literature. For an important study of the impact of *Roe v. Wade* on women's voices, see Carol Gilligan, *In a Different Voice: Psychological Theory and Women's Development* (Cambridge, Mass.: Harvard University Press, 1982). For Learned Hand's criticism of judicial review, see Learned Hand, *The Bill of Rights* (New York: Atheneum, 1968). John Hart Ely's theory of judicial review is stated in *Democracy and Distrust: A Theory of Judicial Review* (Cambridge, U.K.: Cambridge University Press, 1983); his critique of *Roe v. Wade*, on the basis of his theory, appears in "The Wages of Crying Wolf: A Comment on *Roe v. Wade*," *Yale Law Journal* 82 (1974): 920. For a view similar to Ely's in the domain of free speech, see Cass R. Sunstein, *Democracy and the Problem of Free Speech* (New York: Free Press, 1993). For other critiques of *Roe* by legal scholars, see Charles Fried, *Order and Law: Arguing the Reagan Revolution — A Firsthand Account* (New York: Simon and Schuster, 1991); and Kent Greenawalt, *Religious Convictions and Political Choice* (New York: Oxford University Press, 1988). For defenses of *Roe v. Wade*, see Ronald Dworkin, *Life's Dominion: An Argument about Abortion, Euthanasia, and Individual Freedom* (New York: Knopf, 1993); and David A. J. Richards, *Toleration and the Constitution* (1986).

For a review and justification of the judicial interpretation of the religion clauses (the Free Exercise and Establishment Clauses of the First Amendment), including their roots in the argument for toleration of John Locke and Pierre Bayle, see David A. J. Richards, *Toleration and the Constitution* (1986).

On U.S. religious fundamentalism, see George M. Marsden, *Fundamentalism and American Culture* (New York: Oxford University Press, 2006); and Didi Herman, *The Antigay Agenda: Orthodox Vision and the Christian Right* (Chicago: University of Chicago Press, 1997). See, for critique, David A. J. Richards, *Fundamentalism in American Religion and Law: Constitutional Democracy under Siege* (forthcoming). On the psychological and cultural roots of fundamentalism, drawing on the culture and psychology of ancient Roman patriarchy and its role in Christian thought and practice, see Carol Gilligan and David A. J. Richards, *The Deepening Darkness: Patriarchy, Resistance, and Democracy's Future* (Cambridge, U.K.: Cambridge University Press, 2009). See also Nicholas Bamforth and David A. J. Richards, *Patriarchal Religion, Sexuality, and Gender: A Critique of New Natural Law* (Cambridge, U.K.: Cambridge University Press, 2008).

On Justice Lewis Powell, see John C. Jeffries, Jr., *Justice Lewis F. Powell, Jr.: A Biography* (New York: Fordham University Press, 2001). A firsthand account of Justice Blackmun's way of thinking is Pamela S. Karlan, "Bringing Compassion into the Province of Judging: Justice Blackmun and the Outsiders," *North Dakota Law Review* 71 (1996): 173. An invaluable study of the arguments among the justices at the time of *Bowers v. Hardwick*, including the role of clerks in the process, is Joyce Murdoch and Deb Price, *Courting Justice: Gay Men and Lesbians v. the Supreme Court* (New York: BasicBooks, 2001). On the role of lawyers in gay rights litigation, two studies are outstanding, namely Ellen Ann Andersen, *Out of the Closets and into the Courts: Legal Opportunity Structure and Gay Rights Litigation* (Ann Arbor: University of Michigan Press, 2006); and Patricia A. Cain, *Rainbow Rights: The Role of Lawyers and Courts in the Lesbian and Gay Civil Rights Movement* (Boulder, Colo.: Westview Press, 2000). See also Jason Pierceson, *Courts, Liberalism, and Rights: Gay Law and Politics in the United States and Canada* (Philadelphia, Penn.: Temple University Press, 2005). Other illuminating sources include Dennis J. Hutchinson, *The Man Who Once Was Whizzer White: A Portrait of Justice Byron R. White* (New York: Free Press, 1998); Linda Greenhouse, *Becoming Justice Blackmun: Harry Blackmun's Supreme Court Journey* (New York: Times Books, 2005); Edward Lazarus, *Closed Chambers: The Rise, Fall, and Future of the Modern Supreme Court* (New York: Penguin, 1999); and James F. Simon, *The Center Holds: The Power Struggle inside the Rehnquist Court* (New York: Simon and Schuster, 1995). Helpful sources on *Lawrence v. Texas* include Jeffrey Toobin, *The Nine: Inside the Secret World of the Supreme Court* (New York: Doubleday, 2007); and Jeffrey Rosen, *The Most Democratic Branch: How the Courts Serve America* (New York: Oxford University Press, 2006).

For the Bork hearings, see *Nomination of Robert H. Bork to Be Associate Jus-*

tice of the Supreme Court of the United States: Hearings before the Senate Committee on the Judiciary, 100th Cong., 1st Sess. (1987). See also Ethan Bronner, *Battle for Justice: How the Bork Nomination Shook America* (New York: Norton, 1989). On the hearings of Clarence Thomas, see Jane Mayer and Jill Abramson, *Strange Justice: The Selling of Clarence Thomas* (Boston: Houghton Mifflin, 1994).

On the seriousness of Scalia's rather conservative Roman Catholicism and the relationship of his religious convictions to his work as a constitutional judge, see Antonin Scalia, "God's Justice and Ours," *First Things* 123 (2002): 17. For the view of another conservative Catholic thinker who would decriminalize gay/lesbian sex acts but not extend antidiscrimination protections or partnership rights, see John Finnis, "Law, Morality, and 'Sexual Orientation,'" *Notre Dame Journal of Law, Ethics, and Public Policy* 9 (1995): 11. See also Hadley Arkes, "Testimony on the Defense of Marriage Act, 1996," Judiciary Committee, House of Representatives, 1996 WL 246693 (F.D.C.H.), 11; Germain Grisez, *The Way of the Lord Jesus: Volume Two: Living a Christian Life* (Quincy, Ill.: Franciscan Press, 1993); George Will, "Discussing Homosexual Marriage," *Washington Post*, Sunday, May 19, 1996; William Bennett, "Leave Marriage Alone (Legalizing Same-Sex Marriage Would Tamper with Centuries of Tradition and Demean the Institution of Marriage)," *Newsweek* (June 3, 1996). For a response from the right to the right, see Richard A. Epstein, "Live and Let Live," *Wall Street Journal*, Tuesday, July 13, 2004, A14.

On originalism, see Raoul Berger, *Government by Judiciary* (Cambridge, Mass.: Harvard University Press, 1977) and *Death Penalties* (Cambridge, Mass.: Harvard University Press, 1982); Robert H. Bork, *Tradition and Morality in Constitutional Law* (Washington, D.C.: American Enterprise Institute, 1984); "Neutral Principles and Some First Amendment Problems," *Indiana Law Journal* 47 (1971): 9; Antonin Scalia, *A Matter of Interpretation: Federal Courts and the Law* (Princeton, N.J.: Princeton University Press, 1997); Richard A. Brisbin, Jr., *Justice Antonin Scalia and the Conservative Revival* (Baltimore: Johns Hopkins University Press, 1997); Scott Douglas Gerber, *First Principles: The Jurisprudence of Clarence Thomas* (New York: New York University Press, 1999); and Hadley Arkes, *Natural Rights and the Right to Choose* (Cambridge, U.K.: Cambridge University Press, 2002). For a critique based on the views of the founders of U.S. constitutionalism, see David A. J. Richards, *Foundations of American Constitutionalism* (New York: Oxford University Press, 1989). See also David A. J. Richards, *Fundamentalism in American Religion and Law: Constitutional Democracy under Siege* (forthcoming).

Scholarly criticisms of *Bowers v. Hardwick* include David A. J. Richards, "Constitutional Legitimacy and Constitutional Privacy," *New York University Law Review* 61 (1986): 800; Anne B. Goldstein, "History, Homosexuality, and Political Values: Searching for the Hidden Determinants of *Bowers v. Hard-*

wick," *Yale Law Journal* 97 (1988): 1073; Janet E. Halley, "Reasoning about Sodomy: Act and Identity in *Bowers v. Hardwick*," *Virginia Law Review* 79 (1993): 1721; Nan D. Hunter, "Life after *Hardwick*," *Harvard Civil Rights–Civil Liberties Law Review* 27 (1992): 531; and Kendall Thomas, "The Eclipse of Reason: A Rhetorical Reading of *Bowers v. Hardwick*," *Virginia Law Review* 79 (1993): 1805.

Two literary works are discussed in the text: Nathaniel Hawthorne, *The Scarlet Letter* (New York: Penguin, 1986; originally published 1850); and William Shakespeare, *Measure for Measure* (New York: Signet, 1964).

INDEX

abortion
  criminalization of, 64, 67
  free speech and, 17
  history of treatment of, 58
  regulation of, 70–71, 77
  state, secular interest, and, 63–64
  viability and, 61, 62–64
  women and, 56, 64
  See also *Roe v. Wade*
abridgment of rights
  compelling reason for, 173
  to intimate (sexual) life, 44–45
  irrational prejudice and, 171
  justification for, 103
  to privacy, 51–52, 60–61
  See also compelling state interest
abroad, legal developments, 137,
  149–150. See also *Dudgeon v.*
  United Kingdom
abstractly connotative approach,
  96–97
ACLU. *See* American Civil
  Liberties Union
adultery
  concerns about decriminalization
    of, 87, 97, 102, 142
  criminalization of, 160–162
African cultures, 7
AIDS health crisis, 24–25, 112, 131,
  138
Altman, Dennis, 22
American Civil Liberties Union
  (ACLU)
  Bowers and, 78
  gay rights and, 21
  Lawrence brief by, 136–137
  sodomy laws and, 26
American Law Institute, 149
American Psychological
  Association, 81–82, 138
American Public Health
  Association, 81–82, 132, 138

Amerindians of New World, 7
amicus briefs in *Lawrence v. Texas*
  demographic and psychological
    facts, 138
  health risks, 138
  historical arguments, 133–137
  legal developments abroad, 137
  number of, 124
  reply brief and, 130
  for respondent, 139–140
  sources of, 131–132
Andrews, Stephen, 40
Angels in America (Kushner), 26–27
Anthony, Susan B., 36
antiabortion laws, history of,
  64–65, 173
anticontraception laws, 173
antimiscegenation laws, 16, 38, 97,
  172
antiwar movement, 15
asexuality, Christian moral thought
  and, 6, 166–167
associations, protection of privacy
  of, 47

Baehr v. Lewin, 168
Baker v. State of Vermont, 168
Baldwin, James, 13, 17, 21
bestiality, criminalization of, 159
bigamy, concerns about
  decriminalization of, 87, 142,
  167
Bill of Rights, 41, 48, 49, 50, 94
Black, Hugo L., 45, 48, 49, 53
Blackmun, Harry
  Bowers opinion, 99–102, 103–104
  Casey and, 63
  retirement of, 109
  Roe and, 57, 58–61
  Webster and, 67, 68
Blackstone, William, 3, 6, 99
Bork, Robert, 66, 109–110

Halley, Janet, 113
Hamilton, Alexander, 40–41
Hand, Learned, 182
Hardwick, Michael, 78, 112
Harlan, John Marshall
    dissent of, 38
    Griswold and, 45, 49–53
    Poe and, 68, 94–95
    privacy rights and, 32, 80–81
Harlow, Ruth E., 122
harm principle, 2, 103, 143
Hawthorne, Nathaniel, 161–162, 164
Hay, Harry, 20
health risk, 138, 139. *See also* AIDS
    health crisis
Henry, Patrick, 41
Hirschfeld, Magnus, 12, 13
history professors, brief by, 135–136
Hobbs, Michael E., 82, 84, 87–88
Hohengarten, William M., 122
homophobia
    Bowers and, 113
    cultural, 184
    religion and, 176
    resistance to, 30
    silencing of ethical voice and,
        104–106
    in U.S., 75
    White opinion and, 100
    Whitman and, 11
    before World War II, 18
The Homosexual in America (Cory),
    19–20
homosexuality
    cultural history of, 3
    definition of, 5
    in European cultures, 8–9, 12–13,
        14, 75, 175, 176
    as mental illness, 14, 22
    stereotypes of, 183–184
    in U.S., 9–10, 11–12, 13–14
    in Western culture, 5–10
    See also gay rights; homophobia;
        sexuality
Hoyt v. Florida, 35
Hughes, Langston, 12

human rights
    judicial review and, 181–182
    moral logic of, 180
    at time of American Revolution,
        40–41
    See also intimate (sexual) life;
        privacy rights
Hunter, Nan, 113
*Hurley v. Irish-American Gay,
    Lesbian, and Bisexual Group of
    Boston*, 119–120
Hutcheson, Francis, 40
Hutchinson, Denis J., 93

illegal activity, claim of privacy and,
    97, 102, 157–158
Illinois, 74
incest
    concerns about decriminalization
        of, 87, 90, 97, 102
    criminalization of, 159
intimate (sexual) life
    Africans and, 7
    Amerindians and, 7
    Constitution and, 40–41
    Harlan and, 51, 95
    justification for abridgment of,
        44–45
    Lawrence and, 179
    Reconstruction amendments and,
        94–95
    resistance movements and, 16
    right to, and racism, 38, 178
    right to, argument for, 40
    same-sex marriage and, 169–170,
        171
    Sanger and, 35
    slavery and, 41–42, 43–44
    tradition of respect for, 95
    White opinion and, 95–96
    women and, 181–182
    See also contraception, privacy
        claims to

judicial review
    democracy and, 180–182

{ *Index* }